Borderless Press is a publisher of works primarily written by Majority World scholars and knowledge activists. Like all academic publishers, we are committed to rigorous peer-review processes, celebrating scholarship that makes important contributions to academic discourse. Beyond this tradition, we seek to decolonize knowledge production and distribution through equality, creativity and justice. This focus guides us not only in manuscript selection, but also in the ways we approach our work and organizational structures.

Our authors:

- Are from around the world, and especially from the Majority World
- Choose the language in which they seek to write and publish their book
- Collaborate with us on all publishing decisions, including retail book price

The books we publish:

- Include a range of authorial voices, from scholarly to experiential
- Are focused on justice concerns from around the world

Thank you for supporting our work and the work of our authors.
All inquiries should be addressed to Dr. Joseph F. Duggan,
editor@borderless.press.com.

INDECENT THEOLOGIANS

INDECENT THEOLOGIANS

Marcella Althaus-Reid
& The Next Generation of Postcolonial Activism

Nicolas Panotto, ed.

© 2016 Nicolas Panotto

Published by Borderless Press
Alameda, California
www.borderlesspress.com
info@borderlesspress.com

Cover artwork by Patricio Madera
Design by Melody Stanford

Library of Congress Control Number: 2016906357

ISBN-13: 978-0-9962017-3-5
ISBN-10: 0-9962017-3-4

First edition

Printed in the United States of America

*A la nueva generación de teólogos indecentes que
con valentía se atreven a cuestionar las fronteras
del sentido en pos de un mundo otro.*

*To the new generation of indecent theologians
who courageously dare to question the boundaries
of social, political and religious ideas and practices
towards a vision for a different world.*

CONTENTS

PART I MARCELLA ALTHAUS REID'S INDECENT THEOLOGY

FOREWORD

From the Publisher of Borderless Press

Every book Borderless Press publishes is an embodiment of our mission of "knowledge activism." Knowledge activism disrupts colonial systems of knowledge production that sanitize narrative according to a universalized set of values and standards, set by a few, for all.

Our knowledge activism goes well beyond the locations and contexts of our Majority World authors — though Majority World context is a critical aspect that differentiates us from most other academic publishers. We seek to redefine power centers through collaboration and radical sharing of resources. By changing the way knowledge is cultivated, produced, and distributed, we actively challenge hegemonic norms that cause injustices for authors and readers by extension.

Our readers participate in our knowledge activism in two ways:

1) Readers choose to support our authors by reading Borderless Press books, assigning our books to students, offering book recommendations through social networks, and citing our authors in books and articles.

2) Readers choose to adapt their reading lens, allowing them to encounter texts that might employ unfamiliar style, tone, grammar, syntax, and even spelling. This requires reading with flexibility and value of vocative multiplicity.

WHAT DOES IT MEAN FOR READERS TO "ADAPT THEIR READING LENS?"

Due to the remnants of colonial systems of knowledge production, scholarly readers have been trained to expect a specific style of English in the written form. Copy editors at many academic presses routinely correct authors when their use of a word or phrase appears to the editor as an "awkward" construction. These routine corrections, to which authors are compelled to submit, or of which they may not be informed, often result in the erasure of the author's indigenous voice and their contextually-informed usage of words and meanings. In this way, the publisher, through their copy editors and even peer reviewers, can dominate and subordinate the author's editorial choices. When this happens, it is not the authors' scholarship being judged, rather their particular expression of scholarship.

Efforts to conform manuscripts to a "universal" standard are sometimes not about understandability. Sometimes this plays into a larger system which forces Majority World authors into unnatural angles in order to appease the publisher's perception of the desires of North American and European academic readers. Commonly, readers in North America and Europe have a great deal of tolerance for fellow scholars who write lengthy sentences. Complex rhetorical constructions are the gold standard of "scholarly" discourse, lauded as excellent and erudite. Much less tolerance, if any, is granted to Majority World authors, both native and non-native speakers of English, who are writing with understandability as used in their home context but stylistically "other." Nor are localized sources of knowledge, such as oral traditions and narrative, typically revered with the same gravitas as "high" colonial sources of knowledge.

Natural multiplicity of scholarly expression ought to reflect our global diversity of thoughts and arguments, but this variety is regularly smoothed by notions of "professional" uniformity. Difficult questions, such as who determines these standards, and why those individuals get to choose, often remain unasked.

Typical academic publishers serve the interests of their scholarly readers, institutions of higher education, and academic authors, most of whom are North American and European. Borderless Press focuses primarily on serving Majority World authors who seek to make a contribution to scholarship, and we serve the readers who take interest in this valuable work. Like other publishers, we are committed to the highest standards of double blind peer review processes. However, we seek to upend the current system where Majority World authors who seek to publish must not only standardize their use of English, but moreover, in order to participate in the system at all, are typically asked to pay thousands of dollars to have their manuscripts "fixed."

At Borderless Press, we make a point to struggle with decisions such as when to spell check in USA, UK or other forms, when to "correct" punctuation or word usage — when to consult the author, and when to proceed without question in juggling time constraints. Peer reviewers and editors face significant decolonial challenges as they strive to fairly judge the quality of writing and the degree necessary for revision. The most challenging choice is when we choose to proceed without question in the act of accepting what we might read as an "unusual" construction because, while the meaning has clarity to us, the narrative comes through in an unfamiliar style.

We have chosen err on the side of flexibility. In the midst of our learning curve in reviewing Majority World scholarship, as the

Borderless Press executive editorial team working principally in the context of in the USA, we are not the experts. There are few examples to follow. Borderless Press completes all the rigorous double blind peer review processes. Full stop.

The alternative to our efforts at Borderless Press is to outright reject manuscripts as falling below the line of "acceptable" academic scholarship. Many Majority World authors have faced systematic discrimination over the course of centuries. In our first year, we were compelled to reject several manuscripts because the author lacked preparation to make a significant contribution to scholarship. This was determined not by whim or market analysis, but by the peer review process, input from multiple trusted advisors throughout the Majority World, and our own experiences in published scholarship and research.

In other cases, where the work was deemed both promising and forward-leaning, we have made every effort to provide resources that make it possible for authors to complete their valuable projects with fluidity and excellence. These resources range from offering authors the benefit of our pre-peer review processes, connecting them with scholar mentors, assisting in the planning and hosting of writing workshops, and identifying other points of support such as library access, editorial feedback and flexible deadlines. These are efforts we hope to grow over time, so that we may transform the publisher-scholar relationship from the mechanics of antagonism to reconciliation and mutual growth.

ABOUT THIS BOOK

Indecent Theologians: Marcella Althaus-Reid and the Next Generation of Postcolonial Activism is a knowledge activism project in that we hear from the next generation of indecent theologians. Some of these theologians are located in Marcella Althaus-Reid's homeland city, nation and continent. Likely some of these indecent theologians without Borderless Press would not otherwise have had the opportunity to publish outside of Latin America due to lack of access to translators and other publishing resources.

This project was exceedingly complex as chapters had to be translated and peer reviewed in two languages. The cost to translate a one hundred thousand words book is exorbitant for most scholars, not the least Majority World scholars. This project benefitted from the generous, voluntary gift of The Rev. Rosa Lindahl — an Episcopal priest and Episcopal Church Foundation Fellow — who translated the entire project post peer review. Dr. Hugo Cordova Quero also translated the pre-peer review manuscripts at a dramatically reduced cost.

The *Indecent Theologians* project has been in progress since the 2009 American Academy of Religion (AAR) meeting in Montreal, Quebec. Marcella Althaus-Reid passed away on February 20, 2009 and the next AAR meeting included several conversations to recognize her scholarly activist legacy. At that meeting I was inspired through the shared memories of some of her closest friends — including Dr. Mario Aguilar Benitez and Dr. Lisa Isherwood — to press on with Marcella's work, especially at postcolonial and queer intersections.

After several false starts and innumerable complications associated with deciding on a location and meeting framework, Postcolonial Networks was able to organize the July 2013 meeting through the collaborative leadership of Dr. Nestor Miquez, formerly Professor of Theology at ISEDET in Buenos Aires, Argentina, and Nicolas Panotto, the editor of this book and a Postcolonial Networks board member.

The Buenos Aires meeting was not the first meeting that Postcolonial Networks initiated in the Majority World (Africa, Asia and South America). Our meetings in the Majority World tend to attract very few North American and European scholars for a variety of reasons, including limited travel budgets through their institution's departments. Typically these scholars choose the annual AAR meeting for professional networking over meetings outside their country. Over the last decade Postcolonial Networks has exclusively held meetings in the Majority World in locations such as Buenos Aires. It often seems to be the only way to prioritize the voices of Latin American scholars who, due to their own financial limitations, are precluded from participating in North American and European professional theology meetings.

Our meeting was historic because until that point all of Marcella's works were celebrated and promoted by first generation indecent theologians, for the most part North American and European scholars in the United States and the United Kingdom.

At the Buenos Aires meeting there were scholars who had regular email communications with Professor Althaus-Reid about their Masters' Thesis projects. Latin American graduate students wrote to Professor Althaus-Reid and she graciously wrote back, but not with the customary, abbreviated response of many senior scholars. It is to be underscored that these are students for whom Professor Althaus-Reid had no professional responsibility through an institutional affiliation. She generously maintained ongoing conversations with these students, expressed interest in their work and supported their desire to apply and expand her theology in their projects. Without any recognition during her life Professor Althaus-Reid was breathing life into the next generation of indecent theologians so that they could press on with the urgent work she initiated.

At the outset of the project (and before Borderless Press was established) I searched for a publisher for this forthcoming book and found none. I have no need to list by name the publishers that rejected the project, but they might surprise you. The publication of this book demonstrates to me, and I trust to our readers, the absolute need for Borderless Press.

— Joseph F. Duggan

AGRADECIMIENTOS

Al Instituto Universitario ISEDET, que amablemente abrió sus puertas para poder convocar a académicos de distintos países para desarrollar la consulta en honor a Marcella — en particular, la persona de Néstor Míguez, quien facilitó la organización — y al Grupo de Estudios Multidisciplinarios sobre Religión e Incidencia Pública (GEMRIP) por su colaboración en la organización del encuentro.

A Joseph Duggan, fundador de Postcolonial Network y Borderless Press, por permitir que este libro sea publicado y tener la visión e insistencia para que el proyecto se haga realidad. También al equipo de Borderless Press: Caroline Brennan, editora general, y Melody Stanfor, quien realizó el diseño del manuscrito. Por último, a RS Wafula, gerente editor, por su persistencia para que el libro sea concretado.

ACKNOWLEDGMENTS

To ISEDET, who kindly opened its doors to gather scholars from different countries to develop the conference in honor of Marcella Althaus-Reid — in particular, to the person of Néstor Míguez, who facilitated the organization — and the Group of Multidisciplinary Studies on Religion and Public Advocacy (GEMRIP) for their assistance in organizing the meeting.

My gratitude to Joseph Duggan, Founder of Postcolonial Networks and Borderless Press, for allowing us to publish this book with Borderless Press and many his encouragements towards this goal. I would like to thank the staff of Borderless Press; Caroline Brennan, the copy editor, Melody Stanford the production editor, and RS Wafula, the managing editor, for having the persistence to make this project a reality.

CONTRIBUTORS

Jorge A. Aquino, Ph.D. is associate professor of Theology & Religious Studies at the University of San Francisco, in San Francisco, California, where he teaches Latin American and U.S. Latino/a theologies and religious history. He is a former president of the Academy of Catholic Hispanic Theologians of the United States, and former Co-Chair of the Religion in Latin America and the Caribbean Group of the American Academy of Religion. Aquino is a member of the working group on "Theology, Ethics, and Politics" of the Consejo Latinoamericano de Ciencias Sociales (CLACSO). He is completing a book on the role of religious discourse in the formation of racism in Latin American history.

Oscar Cabrera is from Guatemala and obtained a Masters in Sacred Scripture at the University Institute ISEDET, Buenos Aires, Argentina. He also holds a Masters in Bioethics from the Latin American Social Sciences Institute (FLACSO), Buenos Aires, Argentina. Currently he is an assistant at Globalethics.net South America and the Bioethics Program at FLACSO Argentina, while working as an independent researcher.

Cláudio Carvalhaes, Originally from São Paulo Brazil, Cláudio Carvalhaes is a former shoe-shining boy. He received his Ph.D. from Union Theological Seminary in NYC and is currently an activist, liturgist, theologian, artist, and the Associate Professor of Worship at Union

Theological Seminary in New York City, USA. He has three books published in Brazil, and his first book in English is *Eucharist and Globalization. Redrawing the Borders of Eucharistic Hospitality* (Wipf and Stock, Pickwick Publications, 2013). He edited *Only One is Holy: Liturgy in Postcolonial Lenses* (Palgrave, 2015). Personal Website: www.claudio-carvalhaes.com.

Leopoldo Cervantes-Ortiz is an author and Professor of Theology, Theological Community of Mexico, Mexico City and former member of the Committee for Ecumenical Formation of the World Council of Churches.

Susannah Cornwall is an Advanced Research Fellow in Theology and Religion at the University of Exeter, UK, and Director of EXCEPT (Exeter Centre for Ethics and Practical Theology). Her books include *Sex and Uncertainty in the Body of Christ* (Routledge, 2010); *Controversies in Queer Theology* (SCM, 2011); and *Theology and Sexuality* (SCM, 2013). She is the editor of *Intersex, Theology, and the Bible: Troubling Bodies in Church, Text, and Society* (Palgrave Macmillan, 2015); and, with John Bradbury, *Thinking Again About Marriage: Key Theological Questions* (SCM, 2016).

Emilce Cuda, Research Professor of Theology at the Faculty of Theology, Pontifical Catholic University of Argentina (UCA) and at Faculty of Philosophy, University of Buenos Aires (UBA); Associate Professor at National University Arturo Jauretche, Buenos Aires, Argentina (UNAJ), and Director at the research center in that university: Program of Culture Studies. Permanent member of International Regional Committees at Catholic Theological Ethics in the World Church (CTEWC), and the International Political Science Association (IPSA). Active member at Argentine Theological Society (SAT). Dr. Cuda obtained her Bachelour in Theology at the Pontifical Catholic University of Argentina (UCA); her Magister in Moral Theology; and her Doctorate in Moral Theology at the Pontifical Catholic University of Argentina (UCA). She has been visiting scholar at North Western University in 2011, and visiting professor at Boston College in 2016. Her publications include *Catolicismo y democracia en Estados Unidos* (Buenos Aires: Agape, 2010), *La democracia en el magisterio pontificio* (Buenos Aires: Agape, 2011) and *Para leer a Francisco. Teología, ética y política* (Buenos Aires: Manantial, in edition). Dr. Cuda has published many chapters of books about theology and politics, and over 30 articles about democracy, migration, populism, labor, poverty, and Liberation Theology. She is currently coordinating an international research team about "Theology, Ethics and Politics" at Consejo Latinoamericano de Ciencias Sociales (CLACSO).

Gabriela González Ortuño, BA in Political Science, Master in Latin American Studies, and Ph.D. Candidate in Latin American Studies at the National Autonomous University of Mexico (UNAM). She has published in journals such as OXÍMORA of the University of Barcelona and Raíz Diversa, specializing in Latin American Studies magazine on issues related to sexual dissidence and gender construction. Her current research is on the liberators subjects in African-American feminist theologies and queer theology in Latin America. She is founder and director of the collective "Muñeca Fea". The group develops projects of popular education with urban indigenous children.

Robyn Henderson-Espinoza, PhD, visiting professor of ethics at the Pacific School of Religion, Berkeley, CA, earned a Ph.D. in the Joint Doctoral program at the University of Denver-Iliff School of Theology, Denver, CO in Constructive Philosophical Theology, with a primary interest in the ethics of interrelatedness stemming from a New Materialist account. Robyn's work exists in the in between spaces of ontology, epistemology, and ethics, working to establish a speculatively queer material realism. Robyn uses the thought and theory of Gloria Anzaldúa, queer theories, the New Materialisms movement, along with queer epistemologies to consider a queer materialist philosophy. Robyn's interests, while wildly philosophical, are also at the intersection of addressing issues of race, class, gender, and sexuality. Using imagination in queer ways, Robyn hopes to destabilize traditional theopoetic discourse into a queer theopoetics that takes both race and sexuality seriously. Robyn's scholarly work starts at the point of departure of 'what is reality?' to address existing disparities and pays careful attention to element of desire, imagination, possibility, potentiality, difference, and becoming to help an affirmative reality emerge.

Adrián Emmanuel Hernández-Acosta is a doctoral student in Religion at Harvard University. He focuses on theology and Caribbean literatures, with an emphasis on cultural studies, transnational feminisms, and queer studies. He is currently interested in tropes of "the religious" in twentieth century Caribbean novels, the racialization of religious sexualities, and the writing of theology in relation to the writing of Caribbean anthropology.

Nicolás Panotto received his Master in Theology from ISEDET Buenos Aires, his Master in Social and Political Anthropology from FLACSO Argentina, as currently working towards a PhD in Social Sciences from FLACSO Argentina. Panotto serves as the Director of the Multidisciplinary Study Group on Religion and Public Advocacy (GEMRIP) and is member of the board of Postcolonial Networks. He is the author of *Religión, Política y Poscolonialidad en América Latina* (2016), *Hacia una Teología del Sujeto Político* (2013), and *Sendas Nómades* (2012).

INTRODUCTION

NICOLÁS PANOTTO

The theological work is an event. It represents a meeting place where many elements converge, with the aim of re-imagining everything that is at stake in this call. Bodies, gestures, speeches, dogmas, ideologies, stories, demands, hopes, complaints, among many more elements, are combined as an *agape* that questions, deepens and — in the words of Marcella Althaus-Reid — *perverts* what is presented sutured and normalized, to get out from there what is relegated, strange and forbidden as an act of liberation.

This work is a mirror reflex of that exercise. From 9th to 11th of July 2013 we convened as a group of theologians of different traditions and countries in Buenos Aires, Argentina, in an act of memory of one of the most important theologians of the last decades, that unfortunately we lost too early: Marcella Althaus-Reid. During the meeting, this "emerging generation" of thinkers –compromised with the challenges that homophobia, lack of pluralism at all levels, increasing racial discrimination, problems with migration processes and the oppression of the global financial system faces actual society — retook the unique legacy of this theologian from a space of dialogue, exchange and inspiration from various desires and experiences.

The so-called *queer theology* developed by Althaus-Reid represents a *disruptive* way of thinking, feeling and doing, that dares to radicalize the normalized principles of theology — including those that consider themselves progressive — to bring to light what is understood as nonexistent, evil, improper and indecent. As Marcella says, it means *to get under the skirt*, to what the prudish politically correct theology does not want to publicize, but still part of the divine economy in history. This exercise involves a daring and creative play, involving all fields and disciplines. But above all, this disruption represents a radical practice of liberation, where everything and everyone is exposed in front of divine grace, without any shame (actually, as result of our own repressions!)

This meeting was also significant for two reasons. First, although Marcella was Argentinean, her proposal was never well rooted in the theological spaces in Latin America. Therefore, the fact of having developed this event in his homeland, became an act of vindication and raising her voice, often silenced by her strong objections to liberation theology, or simply because her proposal — as many affirm — is not "properly" considered "theology." We know that face our repressed desires gives fear; and fear brings silencing. Therefore, this meeting represented a release of Marcella's own voice in many circles in the region.

The second reason was that the meeting represented an extremely rich approchement between Latin American and Hipano/Latino theologians in the US. This bridge is virtually nonexistent, both in Latin America and North America. Those who participated in the meeting, realized the great need to create a common space of theological development and existential dialogue between these groups. Again, Marcella made it!

Finally, as a close friend of Marcella said: "This was her dream." And so the power of that dream was present and felt among those who participated in the conference. Her spirit became real, in body and soul, while questions, dialogues, contributions, silences, looks and laughs filled the classroom that welcomed us.

It is impossible to contain in a book the richness of the dialogues and exchanges during this event. Anyway, we have tried to be faithful to what happened and try to create a general picture of that experience. Therefore, we have divided the papers presented in three parts. The first one -*Marcella Althaus Reid's Indecent Theology* — introduces us to the core elements of the proposal of this theologian. The work of Susannah Cornwall is a central chapter because it synthesizes very well documented and in a deepened way the main elements of Marcella's work: from her hermeneutics to the different stages of her work, going through postcolonial theology, Latin American theologies, feminists theologies and finally queer theology. Leopoldo Cervantes-Ortiz complements this introduction entering to a central element of Marcella's legacy: her relationship, tension and critical rereading of the Latin American theologies, in dialogue with the main spaces and renames production in the region.

Following these presentations, there are two works that explore some of the most important approaches of Marcella. Adrian Emmanuel Hernandez-Acosta develops the concept of "Queer Holiness" made in Marcella's famous work entitled *The Queer God*, making a link with different perspectives and postcolonial approaches. From his part, Jorge Aquino makes an interesting and original theological rereading of the perfomance of the famous Russian group *Pussy Riot*, analyzing their socio-political impact from of Althaus-Reid perspective, in collaboration with the work of Judith Butler.

The second section — *Epistemological Frameworks* — allows us to expand the work of Marcella towards methodological questions and from the contribution of her legacy to other traditions and theological approaches. Gabriela González Ortuño does an excellent linking between Indecent Theology with Latin American liberation theology (and its critical reception) and the various approaches from Latin American de/postcolonial theories. Nicolas Panotto follows the same line, developing specifically Marcella's questioning of liberation theology methodology, using certain postfoundational philosophical approaches and finally developing the example of Juan Luis Segundo, one of the most heterodox characters of Latin American theology. Finally, the theologian and philosopher Emilce Cuda makes an interesting reinterpretation of the concept of *people* — very present in Latin American theology and episcopal documents, in this case Aparecida-, linking the proposal of Marcella with various approaches in political philosophy.

The last section — *Indecent Theologies Pressing On* — introduces us to some specific cases of application of the Athaus-Reid theological proposal, from theological ethical and biblical reinterpretations. Claudio Carvalhaes develops a comprehensive and rich work on the elementary aspects within liberation theology that help us understand how this stream understand and define processes of subjectivation. From, Carvalhaes links to various Latin American authors — especially Rubem Alves and Jaci Maraschin — in what refers specifically to the discourses on sexuality and embodiment. From here, the author makes an original proposal to rethink the concepts of identity/corporeality from liberation theology in dialogue with the Indecent Theology of Althaus-Reid.

Robyn Henderson-Espinoza address from a theological and philosophical perspective the concept of "perversion" in the legacy of Marcella, to propose what she calls *Perversion ethics* from *creative disregard method*. From here, she makes a very interesting theological link between desire, corporeality and ethics. This paper articulates deep and original perspectives on new materialism, continental theory and (post)delleuzian approaches. Finally, Oscar Cabrera proposes a postcolonial exegesis on Bartimaeu's story that opens the way for a critical analysis of the socio-political, colonial and religious situation un Guatemala, from a biblical and theological approach, departing from the most important bible studies work in Latin America.

As you have seen, the path is vast but extremely rich. As stated by the dedication of this book, we hope that this work inspire the same desires that gathered the participants of the meeting in Buenos Aires: the sense of community and the need for dialogue reflected in the strength and experience in the Other's closeness, constant action of perverting bequests, stories and dogmas to release the bodies from the hetero-normative and colonialist oppression in all levels, and the commitment to create new spaces, new gestures, new speeches and new corporalities that enrich theological work in the current world.

PART I

MARCELLA ALTHAUS REID'S INDECENT THEOLOGY

✣

STRANGE ENCOUNTERS

Postcolonial and Queer Intersections

SUSANNAH CORNWALL

*"Theologizing in a 'post-colonial' context ...
involves 'strange encounters.'"* [1]

Marcella Althaus-Reid, whose work and legacy is examined in this volume, believed that there was a hidden heteronormativity at the heart of the Christian story, such that specific core doctrines and traditions were responsible for reinscribing norms of legitimate and good sexual behaviour and embodiment onto the devout. Since Althaus-Reid's death, many theologians, activists, educators and people of faith have continued on their journey of seeking to imagine a world otherwise. Inspired by her daring to conceive theology indecently, and tantalized by those aspects of her thought left frustratingly underworked, they have sought to continue in a tradition of questioning power and speaking up for the hearts at the bottom of the heap. Postcolonial and queer concerns occasionally clash but more often find connection and accord. In this chapter, I discuss

---

1. Sharon A. Bong, "Postcolonialism," in *The Blackwell Companion to the Bible and Culture (ed.* John Sawyer; Oxford: Blackwell, 2006), 498-514.

some affinities and tensions between postcolonial and queer theologies and suggest that both theologies pave the way for newly strange encounters: recognitions of our own interactions with God and the world, and endorsements of the spirituality of the quotidian. I show that there is potential for queer accounts to be reparative as well as deconstructive, and that postcolonial strategies may be an effective counterpoint to some of the Westernism and Eurocentrism of which queer theologies and theories have been accused. I point to one example, that of Patrick S. Cheng's "rainbow theology," and suggest that it provides an important perspective on sitting with apparent disparity and rendering formerly mutually repellent associations generative. I show that Althaus-Reid's work wove together queer and postcolonial perspectives in a way that set up an acknowledgement of intersectional experience and diverse forms of power, and made abundantly clear that the Church had often failed to recognize its various sites of privilege.

It was not insignificant, believed Althaus-Reid, that the center of Christianity contains tropes such as an apparently all-male Holy Trinity, or an ostensibly heterosexual nuclear Holy Family. The Church, particularly the Roman Catholic Church in Latin America had, she believed, used images such as these to reinforce and police the behaviour of those on whom its narrative had been imposed.[2]

Althaus-Reid recognized that this dynamic was always already simultaneously sexual, religious, political, and economic, with European colonizers bringing heteronormativity to the Americas alongside their particular patterns of Christianity and political governance. Indeed, in *The Queer God* she wrote that the Christian theology taken to Latin America by European colonizers allowed only certain approved

---

2. Marcella Althaus-Reid and Lisa Isherwood, "Thinking Theology and Queer Theory," *Feminist Theology* 15:3 (2007): 305.

conceptual "paths" or routes to be taken. It is necessary to travel outside these and to form alliances beyond those sanctioned by the colonizers, thereby seeking God in unfamiliar places, in order not to take on all the colonial assumptions of theological imperialism.[3] Just as colonized peoples have sometimes avoided using the literal roads built and controlled by the governing powers in favor of their own alternative ways (which have deliberately circumvented involvement in imperial economies), so postcolonial theologies have sought ways around the straight road of Western-sanctioned hermeneutics, biblical interpretation, and doctrinal emphasis.

For Althaus-Reid, postcolonial reconfigurations were also queer or "indecent" ones. It was significant, she held, that people whose sexual behaviour or gender play were considered beyond the pale by "respectable" society were also likely to be those who were economically vulnerable. Such vulnerability was sometimes an unsought and undesired consequence of failing to play the decency game and resulted in being cast out from jobs, institutions, families, and other support structures. But those living at the margins without access to secure shelter, food, money, healthcare, or other goods had nonetheless won themselves a kind of freedom from the structures (and strictures) of heterosexual nuclear family life, and could thereby live, and model, other kinds of kinship and community. She held:

> The best and most compassionate efforts in theology should not try to adapt and reformulate institutions such as the family, when the economic agreements surrounding the family no longer exist. New economic and affective ways develop and therefore new ways of loving people and understanding God are unveiled. [4]

---

3. Althaus-Reid, *The Queer God* (London: Routledge, 2003), 31–32.

4. Althaus-Reid, *From Feminist Theology to Indecent Theology: Readings on Poverty, Sexual Identity and God* (London: SCM Press, 2004), 8.

Althaus-Reid's apparent appeal to libertinism may not adequately take into account the ways in which women, children, and non-heterosexual men are disproportionately vulnerable to rape and sexual abuse in contexts where sexual activity is unregulated, even if "traditional" monogamous marriage has also not always promoted safety and vitality for them. However, her broader point is that Christian theology and Christian sexual ethics cannot be separated, and that each of these carries with it a legacy of Christianity's close association with the upper hand of empire. Indeed, she asserted:

> The fact is that Christianity more than a theology has a sexual programme. The story of colonization shows this quite distinctively. For instance, Christianity came to Latin America with a sexual intention behind the catechisms in order to produce a conversion not to Christ but to the then revalent European ... patterns of relationships .... The preaching was done on sex, not on God [5]

Interrogating naturalized empire in Christianity therefore meant, for Althaus-Reid, re-examining norms of sexuality, gender, family, and governance as preached by those whose privilege rendered them immune from interference. Naturalized heteronormativities in Christianity were, she believed, as damaging to those who never sought to question them as to those forced to comply with them or face the consequences — for when such sexual-theological norms were no longer challenged, they had become hegemonic, and their insidious influence crushed the creative capacity to imagine otherwise.

---

5. Althaus-Reid, "Queer I Stand: Lifting the Skirts of God," in *The Sexual Theologian: Essays on Sex, God and Politics* (ed. Marcella Althaus-Reid and Lisa Isherwood; London: T&T Clark, 2004), 101.

POWER, HEGEMONY, AND
SUSPICIOUS HERMENEUTICS

Queer and postcolonial theologies share with queer and postcolonial critical theories of other kinds a commitment not to let norms of power and hegemony pass unremarked. This critical, suspicious bent often chimes with those of the liberationist theologies of the 1960s and 70s that were queer and postcolonial theologies' forerunners, and which aimed to interrogate too-close allegiances between the Church and the secular authorities. As Jeremy Punt notes, queer and postcolonial theories alike destabilize "the self-evidence of power and marginality, center and periphery"[6] They both seek to privilege subjectivity –and especially that of marginalized people-groups– over "the object(s) of religious faith."[7] Nonetheless, they do not usually seek a return to either strong essentialism or strong constructivism, but rather they explore the interactions and tensions within the production of discourses and subjectivities.[8]

Queer theologies, particularly those that followed closely in the footsteps of lesbian and gay theologies, have often been particularly aware of the ways in which the Bible is used to reinforce norms of legitimacy in identity and behavior among people of faith. An important aspect of the queer theological project has, then, been resisting readings of sacred texts, aiming to unmask the heteronormative ideology of the Bible's writers, disseminators and interpreters. In this way, queer theologians and biblical scholars have often appealed to a "greater good" of love and justice that exceeds any specific passage's

---

6. Jeremy Punt, "Queer Theory, Postcolonial Theory, and Biblical Interpretation: A Preliminary Exploration of some Intersections," in *Bible Trouble: Queer Reading at the Boundaries of Biblical Scholarship* (ed. Teresa J. Hornsby and Ken Stone; Atlanta, GA: Society of Biblical Literature, 2011), 322.

7. Ibid., 324.

8. Ibid., 328.

apparent condemnation of same-sex activity. Likewise, postcolonial theologians and interpreters have sought to show that many commentators', preachers', and teachers' exegeses of Scripture betray a distinctively Western and imperial bias. Interrogating and showing up this bias has been understood as part of these contextual theologies' mission to find a more authentic and less compromised Christianity.

Queer and postcolonial theologies also therefore share a checkered and uncertain relationship with "mainstream" (often understood as heteronormative, imperially allied) Christian traditions. Drawing on suspicious reading and interpretative strategies, queer and postcolonial hermeneutics have, for example, often explicitly sought out marginalized people's and outsider interpretations, and have resisted readings of texts and traditions which seem to repeat excluding patterns. Postcolonial biblical critics, in particular, have sometimes rejected the liberation-theological emphasis on the Bible's preferential option for poor and excluded people, suggesting instead that the Bible is, at best, an ambiguous and ambivalent collection, carrying with it the legacy of its own imperial history as well as sometimes (more or less explicitly) challenging it. For instance, R.S. Sugirtharajah holds that Jesus' injunction to render to Caesar what is Caesar's and to God what is God's *may* be understood as a subversive refusal to accept that the emperor's authority extends over anything but a very limited area. As scholars including Ched Myers [9] and Richard Horsley [10] believe, it is significant that imperial authorities throughout the ages have successfully managed to use this text as a basis for exhorting quietism and capitulation in the face of empire. If this *is* an anti-

---

9. Ched Myers, *Binding the Strong Man: A Political Reading of Mark's Story of Jesus* (Maryknoll, NY: Orbis Books, 1988).

10. Richard A. Horsley, "Submerged Biblical Histories and Imperial Biblical Studies," in *The Postcolonial Bible* (ed. R.S. Sugirtharajah; Sheffield: Sheffield Academic Press, 1998), 152–173.

imperial text, suggests Sugirtharajah, it is a staggeringly ineffective one, and people have managed quite well to ignore or reinterpret it when it was more convenient to read the New Testament as endorsing imperial powers.[11] Similarly, notes Stephen D. Moore, anti-colonial readings of New Testament texts such as Myers' "fail to account for ... a single inconvenient but colossal fact –namely, that ... the vast majority of Christian interpreters through the ages have managed to read these same texts as supportive of empire, when not as actual divine warrants for inexorable imperial expansion."[12] In short, if the New Testament texts are so clearly anti-imperial, it is odd that they have so often been read otherwise.

So queer and postcolonial scholars have found themselves in an uncertain position: is the Christian tradition irredeemably bound-up with heteronormativity and empire, such that the healthiest thing to be done now is to sever ties and begin again? Or are Christianity's sexual and imperial alliances distortions of its true core, to be gouged out and thrown away much as the lion peels the skin from Eustace, a boy trapped in the body of a dragon in C.S. Lewis' novel of Narnia, *The Voyage of the Dawn Treader*? "The very first tear he made was so deep that I thought it had gone right into my heart", says Eustace. "And when he began pulling the skin off, it hurt worse than anything I've ever felt. The only thing that made me able to bear it was just the pleasure of feeling the stuff peel off. You know –if you've ever picked the scab of a sore place. It hurts like billy-oh but it *is* such fun to see it coming away".[13] Eustace is left pink, vulnerable, sore and tender, but also free of the artifice and greed that had become his prison.

---

11. R.S. Sugirtharajah, *Postcolonial Criticism and Biblical Interpretation* (Oxford: Oxford University Press, 2002), 88–89.

12. Stephen D. Moore, *Empire and Apocalypse: Postcolonialism and the New Testament* (Sheffield: Sheffield Phoenix Press, 2006), 122.

13. Clive S. Lewis, *The Voyage of the Dawn Treader* (London: Fontana Lions, 1980), 86.

In the same way, postcolonial scholars have affirmed that the layers of imperial alliance and dubious affiliation which have accumulated within Christianity may be a distortion of its true identity, and that there may, underneath the dragon-skin, still be a heart of the Christian story unsullied by allegiance with empires of various kinds. Joerg Rieger describes this capacity to exceed the distortions of empire as a theological or Christological surplus, refusing to be drawn into imperial power struggles and always transcending the systems and norms that humans construct for themselves [14] Although it would be anachronistic to describe Karl Barth as a postcolonial thinker, Rieger's analysis nonetheless chimes with Barth's insistence in his 1922 commentary *The Epistle to the Romans* that no human ideology may be the last word, for God stands beyond all human ideology and cannot be colonized by any particular group.

Nonetheless, queer and postcolonial theologians cannot but be aware that neither colonialism nor heteronormativity is unproblematically "over," outside the Church or within it. The legacy of Christianity's historical alliances with heteronormativity and empire means that, even where it has consciously renounced them, both former colonizers, formerly colonized people, and those who simply live in a world with empire as part of its history must continue to deal with the consequences.

REPARATIVE READINGS

However, for both queer and postcolonial theologians, while critique and resistance continue to be important, and since an awareness of the ways in which the Christian tradition has been damaging is significant because it holds the tradition accountable for those it

---

14. Joerg Rieger, *Christ and Empire: From Paul to Postcolonial Times* (Minneapolis, MN: Augsburg Fortress, 2007), 9.

has wounded and harmed, there is also a redemptive or reparative stream in evidence. Althaus-Reid claimed that queer theologians "find tradition through discontinuation,"[15] but many of those who have come after her have felt that there must be continuity with as well as rupture from the mainstream Christian tradition in order for queer theologies to be life-giving. In this context, reparation does not mean denying the damaging legacy of Christianity's imperial dalliances, but rather investing and believing in hope for things to be different. In this way, both queer and postcolonial agents might find themselves in a position of straddling worlds, inhabiting a zone (exemplified in Gloria Anzaldúa's concept of *la frontera*, the borderlands[16]) in which they pass between identities and allegiances and find themselves semi-strangers wherever they are.

Many who claim this hybrid, in-between identity understand it positively. Inhabiting liminal space allows one to be critical of the worst excesses of a given group, since one has a different and potentially fuller perspective which may not be evident from the inside. For Anzaldúa, the challenge to dualism which *mestiza* identity brings by inhabiting multiple and perhaps apparently contradictory spaces actually creates a new consciousness; it may have the power to "heal the split" caused by dualistic thinking which, she believes, cultivates rape, violence, war, ethnic and gender struggle.[17] Embracing multiplicity, la mestiza rejects the "doubleness" of identity imposed by others.

Such hybridity of identity is not an unambiguous good, for it may lead to the continued elision of "undesirable" facets of the self. Anzaldúa herself is well aware of the vulnerability that comes

---

15. Althaus-Reid, "Queer I Stand," 101.

16. Gloria Anzaldúa, *Borderlands/La Frontera: The New Mestiza* (San Francisco, CA: Aunt Lute Books, 1987).

17. Ibid., 80.

from different ways of thinking and seeing.[18] Nonetheless, the "space between" might be understood as having its own integrity. Rita Nakashima Brock's concept of "interstitial integrity"[19] speaks of a fruitful space between difference and assimilation. For Tracy Sayuki Tiemeyer, such interstitial integrity allows for "complex, multifaceted identities and communities of struggle and salvation ... The interstitial self ... is the self of the strong and connective spaces between worlds. Interstitial integrity is not mere survival: it is a flourishing within these dis/junctures of worlds."[20] This concern for flourishing underlies queer and postcolonial scholars' advocations of maintaining some kind of relationship with traditions that have been damaging. The existence of multiple alliances, as Anzaldúa and others insist, means that one is not merely a sum of the identities inscribed onto one by others, but may also claim a consciousness characteristic of itself, which transcends all these.

Reparative reading is an affirmation of community formation: a conscious decision to reject incessant critique, not because there is nothing which bears criticism, but rather as an affirmation that critique may not be healthy as a long-term or sole strategy for survival. Both queer and postcolonial theologies have often been characteristically critical, resisting and (in Eve Kosofsky Sedgwick's term) "paranoid", that is, hyper-aware of all that is wrong and must be subverted. But Sedgwick also acknowledges the sense among some card-carrying queer theorists that one simply cannot be paranoid and deconstructive forever. Critique matters, but can becoming grinding

---

18. Ibid., 82.

19. Rita Nakashima Brock, "Interstitial Integrity: Reflections Toward an Asian American Woman's Theology," in *Introduction to Christian Theology: Contemporary North American Perspectives* (ed. Roger A. Badham; Louisville, KY: Westminster John Knox Press, 1997), 183–196.

20. Tracy Sayuki Tiemeyer, "Retrieving 'Asian Spirituality' in North American Contexts: An Interfaith Proposal," *Spiritus* 6:2 (2006): 230.

and destructive. It must be tempered by practices of hope and affirmations of the good.[21]

A key piece of the reparative account is the insistence that queerness and resistance to empire are not late add-ons to the Christian tradition, but have been there at its heart all the time. So it is not necessarily a question of highlighting how queer and postcolonial strategies are different and resistant to the Christian tradition, but rather of embracing the ways in which they are in continuity with it. As Gerard Loughlin holds, theology has always been queer or strange, "because it sought the strange ... the mystery it was called to seek through following Jesus."[22] This is what Anzaldúa means when she appeals to "the queer of me in all races,"[23] which means she can find streaks of solidarity and affinity among all peoples and groups, even those which have overtly rejected her as belonging to them. Reparative accounts that engage with aspects of Christian theology are among those that appear in this volume.

TENSIONS BETWEEN POSTCOLONIAL AND QUEER THEOLOGIES

Despite their affinities, there are also significant instances in which queer and postcolonial theologies have been in tension with one another. For example, postcolonial theologians who consider themselves the heirs of a liberation-theological tradition have to consider some of the charges levelled at classic liberation theologies — namely, that they characterize some types of oppression, such as poverty, as particularly significant or prior, and take too little account of how

---

21. Eve Kosofsky Sedgwick, *Touching Feeling: Affect, Pedagogy, Performativity* (Durham, NC: Duke University Press, 2003), 128.

22. Gerard Loughlin, "What is Queer? Theology After Identity", *Theology and Sexuality* 14:2 (2008): 144.

23. Anzaldúa, *Borderlands/La Frontera,* 80.

sex, sexuality, and gender come into play (for example, where LGBT people and women find themselves doubly- or triply-marginalized, or rendered particularly vulnerable via masculine alliances with imperial powers). While nationhood may be an important locus of identity for some postcolonial scholars (especially those reclaiming or reasserting a national identity quashed or erased under empire), it may be a more ambiguous good for queer people disavowed or disowned by their compatriots on the grounds that non-heterosexuality is a kind of voluntary deracination. In short, holds William Spurlin, "Postcolonial studies have seriously neglected the ways in which heterosexism and homophobia have also shaped the world of hegemonic power."[24]

Conversely, some scholars based in formerly-colonized countries, or living in diaspora in metropolitan contexts, have believed that queer theology is predominantly a white, middle-class preoccupation taking into account too little of the pressing imperatives of food, shelter, and survival in favor of "luxury goods" such as the time necessary to reflect on sexuality,[25] or by simply failing to realize that not all non-heterosexual sexualities resemble those of the West.[26] The term "queer" has been criticized for lumping together a range of identities, positionalities, and sexual, gender, and other experiences within an amorphous whole. Although queer ostensibly challenges normativity, it may thereby be responsible for reinscribing a new

---

24. William J. Spurlin, "Broadening Postcolonial Studies/Decolonizing Queer Studies: Emerging 'Queer' Identities and Cultures in Southern Africa," in *Post-Colonial, Queer: Theoretical Intersections* (ed. John C. Hawley; Albany, NY: State University of New York Press, 2001), 185.

25. Lisa Isherwood and Marcella Althaus-Reid, "Queering Theology," in *The Sexual Theologian: Essays on Sex, God and Politics* (ed. Marcella Althaus-Reid and Lisa Isherwood; London, UK: T&T Clark, 2004), 1; Marcella Althaus-Reid, "The Bi/girl Writings: From Feminist Theology to Queer Theologies," in *Post-Christian Feminisms: A Critical Approach* (ed. Lisa Isherwood and Kathleen McPhillips; Aldershot, UK: Ashgate, 2008), 106.

26. Spurlin, "Broadening Postcolonial Studies/Decolonizing Queer Studies," 185.

normativity of its own. Postcolonial critics have asserted that "queer" is not always as subversive as it could be, but colludes with normative structures of authority, agency, and power. An especial area of tension surrounds the question of LGBT rights in formerly-colonized contexts: while many Western (and formerly-colonizing) nations have legalized homosexual activity and currently sanction same-sex civil partnerships and/or marriages, there are many former colonies, particularly in Africa, where same-sex activity is criminalized. While queer theologians and their allies may deem LGBT rights an irreducible aspect of justice and civilization, postcolonial scholars have pointed out that some people from outside the West consider them a characteristically Western preoccupation and reject their imposition on postcolonial grounds.[27] For this reason, the term "queer" may be unhelpful in some postcolonial contexts even where there seem to be close affinities between postcolonial scholars' concerns and those of queer theorists.

Where queer theology is closely bound up with queer critical theory, the former may face the accusation that it is too high-flown to be of any use "on the ground". Even where queer theologies and biblical readings have successfully challenged hegemonies of maleness and heteronormativity, they have been less successful at intersectional acknowledgements of the ways in which exclusions and oppressions overlap. For instance, Tat-siong Benny Liew has argued that queer theory as it pertains to biblical studies "should develop a multifocal reading that attends simultaneously to sexuality, gender, class as well as race and ethnicity."[28] In this way, suspects Liew, queer interpreta-

---

27. Spurlin, "Broadening Postcolonial Studies/Decolonizing Queer Studies," 196–197.

28. Tat-siong Benny Liew, "(Cor)Responding: A Letter to the Editor," in *Queer Commentary and the Hebrew Bible* (ed. Ken Stone; Sheffield, UK: Sheffield Academic Press, 2001), 188.

tion will more adequately interrogate its own allegiances, which may unwittingly have been white, Western, economically privileged, and abstractly intellectualist ones.

In light of this kind of critique, the last decade has seen an increase in work by scholars and practitioners who consciously aim to promote this intersectional approach, insisting that the cluster of concerns around ethnicity-race-empire and those around sexuality-gender-sex cannot and must not be thought about in isolation from one another, nor from the economics-class-subalternity cluster. Examples of scholars inhabiting this intersectional context and exploring the overlaps and affinities between queer and postcolonial contexts include Patrick S. Cheng, Joseph N. Goh, and Sharon A. Bong, as well as several of the scholars whose work, informed by a specifically Latin American context, appears in this volume.

RAINBOW THEOLOGY: AN INTERSECTING QUEER-POSTCOLONIAL THEOLOGY

Cheng has been at the forefront of developing what he calls "rainbow theology," that is, theology that celebrates the contexts and specificities of experience of queer people of colour, who may be first- or second-generation immigrants to the West from formerly-colonized nations.[29] Such persons may face particular tensions as they navigate life between their communities, especially if their cultures of heritage have traditionally been hostile toward non-heterosexual and non-cisgender identities[30] Similarly, as Bong comments, queer people whose heritage is from beyond the West may not be able to happily frame the narrative of their journey as one of overcoming an

---

29. Patrick S. Cheng, *Rainbow Theology: Bridging Race, Sexuality, and Spirit* (New York, NY: Seabury Books, 2013).

30. Ibid., 253.

oppressive past, since this may mean disrespect for or severing links with their ancestral cultures:

> Coming into one's own – the discipline, repression even renunciation of desire to its deregulation, realisation and celebration –is ritualised by a coming out to self and others that characteristically demarcates the past from the present and future. The seeming linearity of this process is countered by the cycle of affirmation and disapprobation received from familial spaces, both secular (home) and sacred (church). Within the spiritual-sexual nexus of these postcolonial narratives, the Western discourse of constructing 'being-closeted-to-being-out as a one-dimensional trajectory' is problematised as it often discounts mitigating factors such as respect for parents and the need to maintain family name and honour.[31]

However, suggests Cheng, people who simultaneously inhabit queer/LGBT identities and non-white or non-Western identities may have particular gifts of multiplicity and mediation which can be gifts to the broader Church as it navigates its relationship with worldly powers and authorities.

Patrick S. Cheng calls upon "monochromatic" liberationist theologies (which are from the same stable as what Althaus-Reid called "theological mono-loving." simultaneously monotheistic and monarchical in theological, economic and political terms[32] — to be accountable for how they may have reinforced the idea that power is a simple, one-way affair, and that in the battle of oppressor and oppressed, all that matters is cheering for the underdog. In fact, he holds, clearly influenced by Foucault, power is rarely straightforward:

31. Sharon A. Bong, "Sexualising Faith and Spiritualising Sexuality in Postcolonial Narratives of Same-Sex Intimacy," in *Persons and Sexuality* (ed. Allison Moore and Carlo Zuccarini; Oxford, UK: Inter-Disciplinary Press, 2009), 41.

32. Althaus-Reid, "Queer I Stand," 100.

people hold more or less power in different contexts and may exercise it more or less generatively.[33]

Cheng's account is not unproblematic. His advocating of a move from the margins to the centre of Christian theology for queer people of color may do too little to problematize the ontology of margins and center, or the idea that the center remains the locus of conceptual and semiological significance. Becoming "central" rather than "marginal" might simply rob queerness of its oppositional energy and render it ineffectual: for Althaus-Reid and Isherwood, "Queer Theology takes its place not at the centre of the theological discourses conversing with power, but at the margins ... Terrible is the fate of theologies from the margin when they want to be accepted by the centre!"[34]

Furthermore, Cheng's picture of multiplicity and the inhabitation of middle spaces shares many of the risks of other postcolonial accounts of hybridity. For example, people who develop hybrid identities under imperial rule (and who may take on facets of colonial subjectivity even as they retain an irreducible otherness and difference from the mouthpieces of empire) may find such hybridity so unsettling and discomfiting as to be psychologically destructive. People who advocate hybridity, mixedness, or multiplicity as goods, or who endorse intersectionality as an inevitable good, may themselves fail to recognize that hybridity can appear more positive from the perspective of someone who is comfortably sheltered and buffered from the world than from that of someone just clinging on to survival. Hybridity and mixedness might themselves be too costly as goods for those who might be expected to endorse them.

Even so, rainbow theology provides an attractive schema. For Cheng, human rainbow multivalence echoes the multiplicity of the

33. Cheng, *Rainbow Theology*.
34. Althaus-Reid and Isherwood, "Thinking Theology," 304.

Trinity and does not force him to choose some aspects of his identity to the exclusion of others. Stereotypical identities and allegiances, such as heterosexuality in Asian Americans, are shown to be inadequate.[35] Jesus, too, is figured as hybrid:

> Jesus Christ is the ultimate tertium quid, or a 'third thing,' between the divine and the human. The Chalcedonian formula that rejects confusion or change on the one hand, and division or separation on the other, is a marvelous way of thinking about hybridity and holding open that interstitial space between the two binaries of humanity and divinity.[36]

In this respect, rainbow theology stands in the indecent theological (anti-)tradition, bringing together what could not be brought together and making formerly mutually-repellent associations generative.

CONCLUSION

The overlaps and intersections between queer and postcolonial theories have been multiple and significant. Punt summarizes them as falling into six main areas: epistemology and hermeneutics; difference; marginality and exclusion; agency; colonial mimicry; and "prophetic vision for inclusivity or a new world."[37] This last point is, I suggest, most important as a site of overlap in a specifically theological account of these theories.

Queer and postcolonial theologies are *theologies,* informed by prayer, contemplation, and liturgical practice; they are the festivals and everyday life of a worshipping community. They are the activities of a group inherently bound together by a shared commitment

---

35. Patrick S. Cheng, "The Rainbow Connection: Bridging Asian American and Queer Theologies," *Theology and Sexuality* 17:3 (2011): 247.

36. Ibid., 253.

37. Punt, "Queer Theory, Postcolonial Theory, and Biblical Interpretation," 329.

to the life of faith. In this way, they will inevitably differ from their secular theoretical parallels. This is not unproblematic: the lure of the Church may be, and has been, likened to the emotional hold that an abusive partner has over one. But it means that, however much or little queer and postcolonial theologians find that they are able to continue in relation to the structures and doctrines of the Church, they cannot but continue to theologize in relation to God, the same God to whom mainstream theologians also relate.

Despite their differences and tensions, there is potential for fruitful, ongoing collaboration between queer and postcolonial scholars of religion. Increasingly, the emphasis is on solidarity with multiply-marginalized people and an interrogation of inequalities of various kinds in light of the theological imperative of justice. As Spurlin notes, "The sexual is not separate from regimes of power."[38] As Christian theology becomes increasingly decentralized and continues to emerge and develop traditions in contexts beyond the West — which may, in some respects, mean a ceding of its sometime privilege as culturally dominant and established — it must resist any tendency to sanction new imperialisms, including sexual imperialisms. This is a difficult process, especially given Christianity's laudable tradition of vocally outlawing abuse and exploitation in sexual relationships (even if its practice has not always lived up to its own ideals). Christian ethicists are unlikely to willingly cease to contribute to broader conversations on what modes of sexual activity are and are not likely to be life-giving in the broadest sense. What I mean by sexual imperialism in this context is, rather, the assertion that only church-sanctioned models of sexual praxis may be considered legitimate.

In one of Althaus-Reid's most well-known images, she muses about being a theologian who puts one's hands under the skirts of God. As

---

38. Spurlin, "Broadening Postcolonial Studies/Decolonizing Queer Studies," 199.

she insists, this is not simply about disrupting the heterosexual idols that she believes to have been naturalized in mainstream Christianity. It is also about relating to God Godself differently. In a move that chimes with the process-theology-informed relational theologies of writers like Carter Heyward and Catherine Keller, Althaus-Reid asserts that reaching under God's skirts is "establishing a different pattern of dialogue with God," oneself, and one's "community of resistance."[39] This new kind of sexual intimacy with God allows us to encounter God as the stranger that God always was, and thereby recognize anew God's closeness to us.

If theologians have grown unused to strange encounters, they may find it difficult to see what queer and postcolonial discourses share, or indeed what either of these has in common with their own traditions. But theologians are not the only ones who like to impose boundaries, disciplinary demarcations, and thought-walls that keep modes of writing and acting firmly in their places. If a secular commentator finds it laughable that Christian theology might be understood as queer, subversive, or a challenge to power and empire (in light of its own deeply dubious legacy of alliances with the strong), what is that but a lack of creative vision to hope otherwise? Althaus-Reid's legacy has ensured that scholars and others from beyond the Christian tradition have come to see Christianity as more than a religion fatally embroiled in dalliances with empire. Although, as Thelathia Young notes, it does not hold a monopoly on ethical practice or justice-making,[40] Christianity does have the capacity to be a self-critical and socially-critical voice which may continue to challenge injustices and exclusions.

---

39. Althaus-Reid, "Queer I Stand," 102.

40. Thelathia Young, "De-Centering Religion as Queer Pedagogical Practice," *Bulletin for the Study of Religion* 39:4 (2010): 13–18.

Althaus-Reid's work began to show that queer and postcolonial theologies worked best when they went hand-in-hand, highlighting one another's trouble spots and thereby honing one another's capacity to be effectively critical of a mainstream Western theological tradition which, according to Althaus-Reid, had failed to adequately interrogate its privileges or name its biases, including the sometime alliance with capitalist norms. In this way, Althaus-Reid and those who have followed her have reclaimed and reframed the potential of what may look like unpromising events and interactions to show forth the activity of God in and alongside the world. The intersectionality of Althaus-Reid's approach is likely to become ever more important for those scholars seeking to demonstrate that ethnicity, gender, sex, sexuality, class, ability, and other innate and perceived specificities of the bodily context can dramatically influence which narratives of embodied life will be taken seriously — particularly beyond universities, seminaries, and other recognized and publicly legitimated institutions of theological knowledge.

References

Althaus-Reid, Marcella. *The Queer God.* London: Routledge, 2003.

Althaus-Reid, Marcella. "Queer I Stand: Lifting the Skirts of God," Pages 99-109 in *The Sexual Theologian: Essays on Sex, God and Politics.* Edited by Marcella Althaus-Reid and Lisa Isherwood. London: T&T Clark, 2004.

Althaus-Reid, Marcella. *From Feminist Theology to Indecent Theology: Readings on Poverty, Sexual Identity and God.* London: SCM Press, 2004.

Althaus-Reid, Marcella and Isherwood, Lisa. "Thinking Theology and Queer Theory." *Feminist Theology* 15:3 (2007): 302-314.

Althaus-Reid, Marcella. "The Bi/girl Writings: From Feminist Theology to Queer Theologies." Pages in *Post-Christian Feminisms: A Critical Approach.* Edited by Lisa Isherwood and Kathleen McPhillips. Aldershot, UK: Ashgate, 2008.

Anzaldúa, Gloria. *Borderlands/La Frontera: The New Mestiza.* San Francisco, CA: Aunt Lute Books, 1987.

Bong, Sharon A. "Postcolonialism." Pages 498-514 in *The Blackwell Companion to the Bible and Culture. Edited by* John Sawyer. Oxford: Blackwell, 2006.

Bong, Sharon A. "Sexualising Faith and Spiritualising Sexuality in Postcolonial Narratives of Same-Sex Intimacy." Pages 33-44 in *Persons and Sexuality.* Edited by Allison Moore and Carlo Zuccarini. Oxford, UK: Inter-Disciplinary Press, 2009.

Brock, Rita Nakashima. "Interstitial Integrity: Reflections Toward an Asian American Woman's Theology." Pages 183–196 in *Introduction to Christian Theology: Contemporary North American Perspectives.* Edited by Roger A. Badham. Louisville, KY: Westminster John Knox Press, 1997.

Cheng, Patrick S. "The Rainbow Connection: Bridging Asian American and Queer Theologies." *Theology and Sexuality* 17:3 (2011): 235-264.

Cheng, Patrick S. *Rainbow Theology: Bridging Race, Sexuality, and Spirit.* New York, NY: Seabury Books, 2013.

Horsley, Richard A. "Submerged Biblical Histories and Imperial Biblical Studies." Pages 152–173 in *The Postcolonial Bible.* Edited by R.S. Sugirtharajah. Sheffield: Sheffield Academic Press, 1998.

Isherwood, Lisa and Althaus-Reid, Marcella. "Queering Theology," Pages 1-15 in *The Sexual Theologian: Essays on Sex, God and Politics.* Edited by Marcella Althaus-Reid and Lisa Isherwood. London, UK: T&T Clark, 2004.

Lewis, C.S. *The Voyage of the Dawn Treader.* London: Fontana Lions, 1980.

Liew, Tat-siong Benny. "(Cor)Responding: A Letter to the Editor." Pages 182-192 in *Queer Commentary and the Hebrew Bibl*e. Edited by Ken Stone. Sheffield, UK: Sheffield Academic Press, 2001

Loughlin, Gerard. "What is Queer? Theology After Identity." *Theology and Sexuality* 14:2 (2008): 143-152.

Myers, Ched. *Binding the Strong Man: A Political Reading of Mark's Story of Jesus.* Maryknoll, NY: Orbis Books, 1988.

Moore, Stephen D. *Empire and Apocalypse: Postcolonialism and the New Testament.* Sheffield: Sheffield Phoenix Press, 2006.

Punt, Jeremy. "Queer Theory, Postcolonial Theory, and Biblical Interpretation: A Preliminary Exploration of some Intersections," Pages 321-341 in *Bible Trouble: Queer Reading at the Boundaries of Biblical Scholarship.* Edited by Teresa J.

Hornsby and Ken Stone. Atlanta, GA: Society of Biblical Literature, 2011.

Rieger, Joerg. *Christ and Empire: From Paul to Postcolonial Times.* Minneapolis, MN: Augsburg Fortress, 2007.

Sedgwick, Eve Kosofsky. *Touching Feeling: Affect, Pedagogy, Performativity.* Durham, NC: Duke University Press, 2003.

Spurlin, William J. "Broadening Postcolonial Studies/Decolonizing Queer Studies: Emerging 'Queer' Identities and Cultures in Southern Africa," Pages 185-206 in *Post-Colonial, Queer: Theoretical Intersections.* Edited by John C. Hawley. Albany, NY: State University of New York Press, 2001.

Sugirtharajah, R.S. *Postcolonial Criticism and Biblical Interpretation.* Oxford: Oxford University Press, 2002.

Tiemeyer, Tracy Sayuki. "Retrieving 'Asian Spirituality' in North American Contexts: An Interfaith Proposal." *Spiritus* 6:2 (2006): 228-233.

Young, Thelathia. "De-Centering Religion as Queer Pedagogical Practice." *Bulletin for the Study of Religion* 39:4 (2010): 13–18.

"LIFTING UP GOD'S SKIRT"

The Postmodern, Post-Liberationist and Postcolonial Theology of Marcella Althaus-Reid: A Latin American Approach

LEOPOLDO CERVANTES-ORTIZ

Indecent sexual theologies need neither teleology nor systems, but can be effective in representing the resurrection of both the excessive in our contexts and a passion for organizing lustful transgressions of theological and political thought. The excessive of our famished lives: our hunger for food, of contact with other bodies, of love, and of God; a multitude of famines never met that grow and spread, and put us at risk and challenge us, a carnival of the poor, the textbooks for standards of living.

— Althaus-Reid[1]

Reading the theological work of Marcella Althaus-Reid (1952–2009) from Latin America has been a unique experience marked by a certain distance mixed with an air of familiar origin. Her stark language,

---

1. Marcella Althaus-Reid, *La teología indecente. Perversiones teológicas en sexo, género y política* (Barcelona, Spain:Bellaterra Edicions, 2005), 15. Originally published in University General Series, 43 (New York and London: Routledge, 2000).

highly unusual for Protestant and Evangelical contexts, became recognizable even when reading a few lines. Her commitment to take on sexuality, gender, and politics in an explosive package made her overcome the barriers of the politically and religiously correct. Unclassifiable at superficial glance, her work manifests a hyper-realistic freshness which could unbalance even the most experienced in the novel theological territories due to the resounding critical intensity that developed since she became known.[2]

From her striking essay in *Ministerial Formation* — a publication of the World Council of Churches — it became very clear that her theological subversion was aimed at questioning the ideas and behaviors of those who held "theological power" and distributed work. In that sense, the false opposition between academy and church is part of a dualistic mechanism to which one had to make a false choice, because this dilemma is in itself false. Such text — real personal manifesto to which it was easy to adhere, given the premises we shared with her background — went to the bottom of pressing issues in our environment: Is it possible to make a serious, critical and pastoral theology at the same time? Or do we have to give up any of these elements in order to save some dignity with certain components of the equation? She expressed this in the following way:

> The alleged crisis of the church is a theological crisis. Or, conversely, the theological crisis exists because the church has been clinging to outdated structures of thought, and a thought that is not welcome in the modern believer. This, of course, comes from the dualistic thinking, the church-theology divide, common in the Western mind.

2. Cf. Leopoldo Cervantes-Ortiz, "*La teología indecente*, de Marcella Althaus-Reid: un libro explosivo, antisolemne, (de)constructivo", en *Lupa Protestante,* 10 de julio de 2006, www.lupaprotestante.com/blog/articulo-la-teologia-indecente-de-marcella-althaus-reid-por-lepoldo-cervantes-ortiz.

But although the church is not a theater, it is an industry, this said with no offense. It is an economic space of human relationship, governed by ways of thinking that are metaphors for models of known production.[3]

Her conclusion was exemplary, as she bridged the false questions with indisputable statements:

> Theology cannot focus on a discourse of self-preservation. What matters is the people. People who try to elucidate the true needs imposed by the free market. It is the future of women that matters. It is the future of males that matters. Let there be future, while we deal in perpetuating dualisms, death proceeds on the planet. And what if the people who is organizing and fighting gets out of an alleged discourse or church organization structured? The kenosis of Christianity is the act of greatness that is expected from us, to talk about God and sexuality, God and culture, God and economic policy, not about theology-church. Let us work for the second coming of new forms of organization and thinking that are neither excluded nor praise themselves. Let it be living spaces, in this life, for people and not for old monuments of knowledge and ecclesial mental architecture that we inherit, not God, but a Western model of thinking and feeling, already overcome.[4]

Something similar happened with her article published in *Revista de Interpretación Bíblica Latinoamericana* [Latin American Bible Interpretation Journal], from another side of the same source. There

---

3. Althaus-Reid, "Who needs whom? Does The Church Need Theology Or Theology Need The Church? A Materialist Analysis of The Theological Industry And The Church Market." *Ministerial Formation* (July 1998): 4; reproduced in the *Newsletter*, Basel Research and Support Center, 21 (January–March 2006), www.issuu.com/centrobasilea/docs/bol21-ene-mar2006.

4. Ibid., 13

she pondered about "the illegal loves of God" and rediscovered that face denied to the Creator, allegedly opposed to eroticism and passion in all its manifestations:

> No only the abortion of God in Christ re-symbolizes this horizon removed from a God who is not a Machiavellian prince, calculating and cunning, who neither created the world and human beings because of loneliness nor abandoned his child because he is angry with his neighbors who owe him something, but of the erotic God, spontaneous and de-regulated that creates and loves 'just because.' This unauthorized divine thought subverts commodifications of biological life and feelings unauthorized, that is, crazy crushes of God and of women. Let's remember life while we remember loves for no profit, without expectations as the messianic love in the New Testament. Interestingly, the only forms of love that scape from those tributaries love systems of the Scriptures are non-heterosexual loves. I do not refer only to Jonathan and David or Judith and her maid but to loving systems built by Jesus: his passionate love for his fellow fishermen is an example of homo-eroticism non-productive but subversively creative.[5]

Any feminist theology pales before the depth of the intentions defined in this way, because in essence it seeks not only the claim of one sex but goes to the root of the problem: the patriarchal theology has "contaminated" the core of the faith of the majority with its repressive, absolutist view that is disrespectful of the nuances of human life. Watching indigenous lemon vendors in Buenos Aires and taking them as a starting point for her postmodern, postcolonial and

---

5. Althaus-Reid, "Living la vida loca: reflexiones sobre los amores ilegales de Dios y la defensa de la vida," *Revista de Interpretación Bíblica Latinoamericana* 57, n.p. [cited September 10 2016]. Online: www.claiweb.org/index.php/miembros-2/revistas-2#52-63.

post-liberationist vision, she gave us a lesson of contextualization in order to outline her work without mitigations:

> Indecent Theology is one that questions and undresses the mythical layers of multiple oppressions in Latin America, a theology which, taking the starting point at the crossroads of the theology of liberation and queer thought, wreaks havoc with economic and theological oppression with passion and recklessness. An indecent theology questions the Latin American traditional field of decency and order that permeates and sustains multiple structures (ecclesiological, theological, political and lovemaking) of life in my country, Argentina, and in my continent.[6]

The final words of Indecent Theology were terse:

> It is an encounter with indecency, and the indecency of God and Christianity. The path of the per-versions and the path to in-righteous Messiahs, of hermeneutic options re-twisted in the way of thinking theology, politics and gender from our own sexual experiences and our identities. Of thinking theology without underwear.[7]

Though she walked the path traveled many times by other Latin American theologians who studied in Europe, her theology was not merely an academic exercise, cold, calculated, and remote-controlled to a particular audience. To understand this, we must remember her work in Argentina and Scotland among underserved communities. She came out as she testified — from the guts of Argentine Protestantism, in her studies she learned firsthand from scholars who many only read from afar: José Miguez Bonino, Severino Croatto, Beatriz Melano, her first teachers and her first interlocutors. Attesting the

---

6. Althaus-Reid, *La teología indecente,* 12.

7. Ibid., 281.

beginning of her path and the way in which her thought became radicalized, she positions herself — in the introduction of her most renowned work — in continuity with the work of Liberation Theology,[8] although marking clear differences and qualifications:

> My purpose in this book is not to demolish the European-like theology of liberation but to thoroughly explore this contextual hermeneutic circle of suspicion and questioning how to make traditional liberationist theology in context. Thus the project of Indecent Theology represents both a continuation of liberation theology as well as a disruption of it. And I made this my primary theological reference because in it I have been professionally educated. Here I am. And it has been the basis from which I have worked in miserable communities both in Buenos Aires and in UK. Still strongly affirm the validity of liberation theologies as crucial in the process of social transformation and superior to North Atlantic theologies. However, liberation theology is to be understood as a continuous process of recontextualization, permanent exercise of deep hesitation in theology.[9]

Her program, summarized in the introduction was very clear:

> *Indecent theology* is a book on political sexual theology conceived as critical continuation of feminist liberation theology through a multidisciplinary approach that draws from sexual theory (Butler, Sedgwick, Garber), from postcolonial criticism (Fanon, Cabral, Said), from studies and theology of homosexuality (Stuart, Goss, Weeks, Daly), from Marxist studies (Laclau and Mouffe, Dussel), from continental philosophy (Derrida, Deleuze and Guattari, Baudrillard), and from systematic theology.[10]

8. Ibid., 15–18.

9. Ibid., 16–17, emphasis mine.

10. Ibid., 19.

She also defines her work as feminist theology, but in strong discontinuity with some of its streams, demonstrated either by breaking a style that leaves little room for the "ideological reconciliation" that other representatives of Latin American liberation theology have done. Her language subverts from the roots any efforts to "negotiate" the aspects that she considered crucial and defining, since she realized that they had not been radical enough to truly renew the complete theology:

> Theology is then seen in its true nature as a sexual project from its epistemological basis, based on a dualistic concept of sexual relations and their legitimating role. Can a theology of liberation and feminist liberation liberate if they still cling to these sexual hegemonic epistemologies.[11]

This "sexual project" must be radically deconstructed to demonstrate not only its patriarchal burdens but also its links to groups exercising control of power in all its dimensions. In most Latin American Christian communities, it is well known that this process has barely been done, although — nonetheless — it has significantly changed the direction of the new generations of thinkers and pastoral agents. However, it is not enough for the scope of this project.[12]

In the first chapter of *Indecent Theology* ("Indecent Proposals for women who want to do theology without underwear"[13]) Althaus-Reid harshly questions liberation theology, noting several of its problems of worldview and perspectives and noting that the scope of the first

---

11. Ibid.

12. Cf. Jung Mo Sung, "Teologia indecente em luto," in *Adital,* 27 (de febrero de 2009), n.p. [cited September 10 2016]. Online http://site.adital.com.br/site/noticia. php?lang=PT&cod=37485; y Leopoldo Cervantes-Ortiz, "Marcella Althaus-Reid", in *Protestante Digital,* January 31th, 2010, http://protestantedigital.com/magacin/9703/ Marcella_AlthausReid.

13. Ibid., 23–72.

theologians of liberation, men or women, was not enough to discern areas of human existence that had to be invaded by the approach that she was developed over time:

> It would be naive to consider that Liberation Theology was ever indecent, that is, that it broke away with the sexual imagery of Western theology through means of class analysis. Liberationists were in their own way right-wing Hegelian, by the way, who saw in the institution and the structures of the 'machista' heterosexual Latin American society the movement of a male God, of the poor, yes, but macho. [14]

Hence she repeatedly emphasizes the importance of the personal and sexual life of theologians that, in addressing certain issues, tended *to make decent* their perspective so as to be acceptable to their colleagues and readers within the churches. According to her, even this theology should be channeled through the course of indecency. Indecenting theology — to make it indecent as a systematic project — because it is a fact that we have lived under the influence, impact and custom imposed by a decent theology. Perhaps that was always the problem: trying to make decent a theology that — by definition — was not possible to be made so because it was still idealistic. The project of Althaus-Reid consisted of "talking dirty, telling the truth," as Rosemary Radford-Ruether summarized in a translated text in Chile:

> Her project of "indecenting" Christian theology offers a crucial new target for the analysis of theological symbols that unmasks its oppressive message and opens transformative views for human liberation and community buildings.

> For Althaus-Reid "decency" is a system, a sexual, social, political, economic and theological system that completely

---

14. Ibid., 38.

shapes the way we think and act in relation to ourselves and others, and in relationship to the natural world.

Decency is the manifestation of what she calls the "heterosexual matrix".[15]

To accompany Marcella Althaus-Reid in the project and in the way of her indecented theology is certainly difficult, because each step she is placing insights and findings to which there is no choice but to say, "Yes, it is true! Why has nobody said it before?" Systematic theology is shaken from its foundations in order to be re-elaborated with language that waives decency and opts for the — literally — naked truth. Nudity is a window for eroticism and openness:

The problem arises because it is easier to live without God than without a heterosexual concept of male. Both should be stripped simultaneously. The subversiveness of a religious system lies in its sexual subversions in that messy core of abnormal sexual narratives where virgins give birth and male trinities could mean the inconsistency of a single male definition, in the tension between patriarchal identity and difference. This stripping is the starting point of indecency in theology.[16]

Nudity, body, eroticism, indecency, as opposed to dualism. We are facing a new theology of corporeality, but one which does not look at the body as a susceptible abstract space in order to relate historically. On the contrary, it is a vehicle of moods, instincts, hormones, and desires:

---

15. Rosemary Radford Ruether, "Hablando sucio diciendo la verdad", *Con-Spirando*, n.p. [cited September 10 2016]. Online: http://www. https://es.scribd.com/document/153777566/Radford-Ruether-R-Hablando-Sucio-Diciendo-la-Verdad-Haciendo-Indecente-la-Teologi-a

16. Althaus-Reid, *La teología indecente,* 33.

The systematic theology belongs to this Western realm of grand narratives. Although it is constructed from a fictional, dualistic opposition between body and mind, the funny thing is that Christian dogma is based on body tensions. Therein, bodies contact with others, are flighty or aggressive or even lovers. Christianity, for example, is related to bodily functions (artificial insemination and the birth of Jesus-God, control aspects of sexuality, torture, starvation, death, and the return of the deceased body in the resurrection). It also includes personal relationships as the dogma of the Trinity, reflecting the social notion of what we can call the "medieval family" model with regard to hierarchical obsessions and darwinian tensions that are inherently masculine. Other dogmas elaborated, such as the life of the body after death, work with the same precision regulating bodies for a few concepts of sin that never cross borders of perceived bodily needs.[17]

It is a post-liberating theology that departs from the matrix of Latin American liberation theology and bites its tail, deeply self-critiquing:

This brings us to our current place in liberation theology as a centered decent authorship and the authorization/de-authoritization of the grand(iloquent) religious-political discourses of authority in Latin America.[18]

The spread of the traditional discourses has helped in training mentalities and consciousness:

These discourses have been collected in legal structures, scattered in proverbs and in popular art, incorporated into architectural designs and political functions, and have also designed spirituality in liturgical actions of political symbolism. Basically they are reflected in political events

17. Ibid., 33–34.
18. Ibid., 35.

such as the dismantling of the traditional beliefs after the conquest, tax systems, the control of land and property, and the legitimizing slavery and usury. These discourses are not only political but also theologically sexual. Christianity in Latin America imposed an economic order of sexual usury, of use of people in groups.[19]

Her argument in the chapter "The Indecent Virgin" sounds like a theologized and hypercritical continuation of *The Labyrinth of Solitude* by Octavio Paz[20] and some poems by Nicanor Parra with which she directly relates — especially the one that reads: "THE ETERNAL FATHER / ended up running away with a schoolgirl."[21] It is a very relevant and contextualized analysis of what is perhaps the symbolic presence for Latin American women, and not just Roman Catholics. In this line, the chain of ideas is irrefutable and raw, from the use of language in the starkest sexuality. This explains the "underground" ideological platform with which women are identified — or not — with the Virgin Mary, especially in her advocation of Guadalupe, and — at the same time — in the construction and reconstruction of their identity, a sexless one influenced by the Virgin:

However, this circle of empowerment is short-cutted because in worshiping Mary, women need to go through a spiritual clitoridectomy in the sense of mutilating their sensuality in order to identify with the Virgin, obtain her approval for their behaviors and never to question the political and social order created around such a religious ideology. It happens so because the Virgin and the vulva

---

19. Ibid., 35–36.

20. Cf Octavio Paz, *El laberinto de la soledad* (Madrid, Spain: Cátedra, 1993), especially the chapter "Los hijos de la Malinche". English translation: *The labyrinth of solitude and other writings* (New York, NY: Grove Press, 1985), 65–88.

21. Nicanor Parra, *Chistes para desorientar a la poesía* (Madrid, Spain: Visor, 1989), 134.

have been dislocated and separated, which represents a tremendous contradiction since the term 'virgin/virginity' often bring the mental image of a vulva, as a specific sexual location by means of identity.[22]

This form of female castration overrides the erotic-sexual-spiritual potential while prolonging the veneration of the Virgin, thus establishing the subjection in all orders. The female body image of each person becomes a denied space for vehiculating the links or the negotiation with the sacred in all its manifestations. The contents exposed in this way show an unspoken familiarity with the theology of the body of Brazilian theologian Rubem Alves — already quite old, since it goes back to the 1980s[23] — although clearly related to similar texts by Nancy Cardoso Pereira, the result of direct dialogue with her.[24]

Althaus-Reid amends the core of the "classical liberation theologians" as most of them have not understood poor women, symbol of the subjects exploited in all areas, including — of course — the sexual. That area of their life is completely denied and marginalized along with other areas:

> The stories of sexual desire among the poor are a vetoed chapter. [Gustavo] Gutiérrez said that poor Latin American women just care for the food of their children, but I say that we must also care — and in no little way — for our orgasms. If not, how do poor women end up having so

---

22. Althaus-Reid, *La teología indecente,* 75–76.

23. Cf Rubem Alves, *Variações sobre a vida e a morte ou o feitiço erótico-herético da teologia* (São Paulo, Brazil: Paulinas, 1981). In Spanish published as *La teología como juego.* (Buenos Aires, Argentina: La Aurora 1981), 23–55.

24. Cf Nancy Cardoso Pereira, "Mistérios da salvação", in Nancy Cardoso Pereira, *Amantíssima e só: Evangelho de Maria & as outras* (São Paulo, Brazil: Olho D'Água, 1999) and M. Althaus-Reid, "'Let them talk ... !' Doing Liberation Theology from Latin American closets," in M. Althaus-Reid, ed., *Liberation Theology and Sexuality,* 2nd ed. (London, UK: SCM, 2009), 5–17.

many promiscuous sexual relationships? Is promiscuity or, sometimes, the course of desire, the search for intimacy commonly unmet intimacy in the current conditions of sexual injustice?[25]

Genilma Boehler has summarized well, in a comparative analysis of the theology of Althaus-Reid with the poetry of Adelia Prado, an important current literary reference to a new vision of sexuality and faith taken from a self-critical perspective of feminity. Boehler has described these two authors as "indecent" by sharing a horizon of understanding.[26] She affirms:

> Althaus-Reid called decent theology that which denies the body and excludes life. The corporeal, claimed theology, (bi)sexed, she called indecent theology. Prado, in turn, in the structuring of his poems and prose, combines body, sex, God and the everyday, breaking, discussing, making a problem, making indecent. Both rearrange the concept of the term *indecent*, giving another meaning to the sacredness. Both work with eroticism revealing bias of thought emancipation of women in relation to political, economic, and religious-cultural aspects.[27]

At this moment, in light of pressing problems such as human trafficking — such social aberration or sin that has always been practiced — it seems that indecent theology would be the only Christian, biblical, and theological way to address it. Through its stripping and unmasking, a theology which is not afraid to explore the deepest personal motivations may be able to provide some light amidst such

---

25. Althaus-Reid, *La teología indecente*, p. 196.

26. Cf. Genilma Boehler, *O erótico em Adélia Prado e Marcella Althaus-Reid: uma proposta de diálogo entre poesia e teologia* (São Leopoldo, Brasil: Escola Superior de Teologia, 2010), n.p. [cited September 10 2016]. Online: http://dspace.est.edu.br:8000/xmlui/bitstream/handle/BR-SlFE/173/boehler_g_td95.PDF?sequence=1&isAllowed=y (Consulted: September 10th, 2016), 164.

27. Ibid., 149.

cruel situations. The remote altering of sexual praxis, dominated by the brutal profit in our societies continues to prevent people — particularly women — from meeting this form of spirituality that awaits them in their own bodies as areas of grace and revelation of the erotic love of God. Therefore, this is a way through which one can re-read the "texts of terror,"[28] namely, the Bible stories relating directly to sexuality which have been "sanitized" permanently and even used to impose models of marriage and family that original texts are far away from promoting.[29]

The indecent and "terrifying" aspect of these ideological approaches, which go beyond mere religious aspects, is that the rediscovery of erotic pleasure in Latin American societies, marked by a strong repression in their understanding of the body, has resulted in these societies being assaulted by mercenaries who imposed the sex trade as an aspect of economic globalization, without sensitivity towards children or teenagers at the understanding of sexuality earlier, violently and without any respect for their persons and their bodies.

This insensitive assault of child and youth sexuality is part of the crisis of meaning and significance that afflicts our societies, so that this theology, as proposed by Althaus-Reid, opens ways for a recovery of the free, joyous and liberating corporality, among other things.

References

Althaus-Reid, Marcella. *La teología indecente. Perversiones teológicas en sexo, género y política*. Barcelona, Spain: Bellaterra Edicions, 2005.

---

28. Phylis Trible, *Texts of Terror: Literary-Feminist Readings Of Biblical Narratives*. (Philadelphia, PA: Fortress Press, 1984).

29. Cf. Leopoldo Cervantes-Ortiz, "Un sermón 'indecente' sobre la familia actual», n.o. [cited September 10 2016]. Online: http://palabraviva.com.es/Contenido/Recursos%20Homileticos/Un%20serm%C3%B3n%20indecente.pdf. Originally published in *Lupa Protestante*.

Althaus-Reid, Marcella. "'Let them talk … !' Doing Liberation Theology from Latin American closets," Pages 5-17 *Liberation Theology and Sexuality*. Edited by Marcella Althaus-Reid. London, UK: SCM, 2009.

Althaus-Reid. "Living la vida loca: reflexiones sobre los amores ilegales de Dios y la defensa de la vida", *Revista de Interpretación Bíblica Latino-americana*. 57 (2016) No Pages. [cited September 10 2016]. Online: www.claiweb.org/index.php/miembros-2/revistas-2#52-63.

Althaus-Reid. "Who needs whom? Does The Church Need Theology Or Theology Need The Church? A Materialist Analysis of the Theological Industry And The Church Market." No pages. Cited October 2016. On line: www.issuu.com/centrobasilea/docs/bol21-ene-mar2006.

Alves, Rubem. *Variações sobre a vida e a morte ou o feitiço erótico-herético da teologia*. São Paulo, Brazil: Paulinas, 1981.

Alves, Rubem. *La teología como juego*. Buenos Aires, Argentina: La Aurora 1981.

Boehler, Genilma, *O erótico em Adélia Prado e Marcella Althaus-Reid: uma proposta de diálogo entre poesia e teologia*. São Leopoldo, Brasil: Escola Superior de Teologia, 2010. [cited September 10 2016]. Online: http://dspace.est.edu.br:8000/xmlui/bitstream/handle/BRSlFE/173/boehler_g_td95.PDF?sequence=1&isAllowed=y

Cardoso Pereira, Nancy. *Amantíssima e só: Evangelho de Maria & as outras*. São Paulo, Brazil: Olho D'Água, 1999

Cervantes-Ortiz, Leopoldo. "*La teología indecente*, de Marcella Althaus-Reid: un libro explosivo, antisolemne, (de)constructivo". en *Lupa Protestante*, 10 de julio de 2006, *www.lupaprotestante.com/blog/articulo-la-teologia-indecente-de-marcella-althaus-reid-por-lepoldo-cervantes-ortiz*.

Cervantes-Ortiz, Leopoldo "Un sermón 'indecente' sobre la familia actual.» No Pages. Cited September 10 2016. Online: http://palabraviva.com.es/Contenido/Recursos%20Homileticos/Un%20serm%C3%B3n%20indecente.pdf.

Parra, Nicanor. *Chistes para desorientar a la poesía*. Madrid, Spain: Visor, 1989.

Paz, Octavio *El laberinto de la soledad*. Madrid, Spain: Cátedra, 1993.

Ruether, Rosmary Radford. "Hablando sucio diciendo la verdad". No pages. Cited September 10 2016. Online: http://www.conspir-ando.cl/index.php?option=com_content&view=article&id=85:hablan do-sucio-diciendo-la-verdad&catid=38:con-spirando.

Sung, Jung Mo, "Teologia indecente em luto," in *Adital,* 27 (de febrero de 2009), n.p. [cited September 10 2016]. Online *http://site.adital.com. br/site/noticia.php?lang=PT&cod=37485;* y Leopoldo Cervantes-Ortiz, "Marcella Althaus-Reid", in *Protestante Digital,* n.p. [cited September 10 2016]. Online, http://protestantedigital.com/magacin/9703/ Marcella_AlthausReid.

Trible. Phylis. *Texts of Terror: Literary-Feminist Readings of Biblical Narratives.* Philadelphia, PA: Fortress Press, 1984

QUEER HOLINESS AND QUEER FUTURITY

ADRIAN EMMANUEL HERNANDEZ-ACOSTA

I

Queer holiness, as Althaus-Reid develops the analytical category in *The Queer God*, may be summoned to deconstructively mediate antagonisms surrounding futurity in queer theory. With queer relations to time at stake, resignification of holiness *à la Marcella* highlights the texture and depth with which queerness as social practice distances itself from a hetero-normative matrix lodged in theology — a distance effected not by an indifference towards political engagement, but by a provocation to dissent. This resignification of holiness, whose mood is de-colonial, throws the complexities of queer relations to time into stark relief by counter-intuitively imagining hell as the queer sacred. Such a resignification frustrates hetero-normative timetables encrypted in economies of salvation, while at the same time critically repeating an eschatological structure, which renews the relevance of salvation. More important, perhaps, than revealing and rehearsing a refusal of queerness to be theoretically, categorically, or politically — in the strict sense of the term — pigeonholed, queer holiness twists queer theory's relations to time. It affirms neither chasmic perpetuity nor redemptive circularity, but rather moments of prophetic intensification whose affective effervescence is not in vain (even) as it necessarily overflows.

Admittedly, deconstructive operations do not necessarily yield ethical affirmations. In fact, in their most violent interventions, they afford neither assurance nor recommendation. Nonetheless, the work of deconstruction is crucial to any conceptual trajectory bent on an ethical impulse. To this, Ernesto Laclau presses against temporal presuppositions and articulations of emancipation, pointing to the artificiality of any connection between the structure of futurity and the ethical impulse towards it. Insofar as futurity is structurally grounded in openness, an embrace of futurity cannot be decided upon such openness, even as openness constitutes a condition of possibility for any ethical impulse. Commenting specifically on relations with "democracies to come," Laclau explains:

> Precisely because of the undecidability inherent in constitutive openness, ethico-political moves different from or even opposite to a democracy "to come" can be made — for instance, since there is ultimate undecidability and, as a result, no immanent tendency of the structure to closure or full presence, to sustain that closure has to be artificially brought about from the outside. In that way a case for totalitarianism can be presented starting from deconstructionist premises. Of course, the totalitarian argument would be as much a *non sequitur* as the argument for democracy: either direction is equally possible given the situation of structural undecidability.[1]

Succinctly put, deconstructive operations return to moments ethical injunctions are decided and sedimented. The return to futurity's

---

1. Ernesta Laclau, *Emancipation(s)* (New York, NY: Verso, 1996), 77–78.

undecidability only intensifies a sense of responsibility with which one is charged in orienting oneself towards times to come. I will return to Laclau's notes on deconstruction's political implications after setting Althaus-Reid's orientation towards futurity within a larger discussion on futurity in queer theory. It is my contention that Althaus-Reid's category of queer holiness not only returns queerness as practice of dissent to moments of decision, it also invokes an ethical injunction by summoning de-colonial ghosts to re-encounters with undecidability.

Without further ado, then, the ethical impulse under consideration is the rehearsal of God's own deliverance incarnate. Whether leading God by a dog-collar or ushering Her into the penumbra of a dark, damp alley, Althaus-Reid ministers to a god still "in the closet." This paper does not use the widespread phrase, however, within the pervasively common binary of heterosexual/homosexual orientation based on the coordination of (perceived) genitalia, and which all too often refers to a homosexuality not (yet) disclosed. Rather, this paper uses the expression in a strictly Sedgwickian sense — that is, "in the closet" as in the forgetful disavowal of the failure always already present in attempts to embody hetero-normative prescriptions. As Sedgwick explains in *Epistemology of the Closet*, "Closetedness itself is a performance initiated as such by the speech act of silence — not a particular silence, but a silence that accrues particularity by fits and starts, in relation to the discourse that surrounds it and differentially constitutes it. [Likewise,] perhaps there exists a plethora of *ignorances*, and we may begin to ask questions about the labor, erotics, and economics of their human production and distribution."[2] In short, a

---

2. Eve K. Sedgwick, *Epistemology of the Closet*, (Berkeley and Los Angeles, CA: University of California Press, 1990), 3–8.

god "in the closet" is the God silent about, perhaps even ignorant of, Her queerness, a queerness to which Althaus-Reid ministers.

II

As the focus of her last chapter in *The Queer God*, queer holiness is a concept Althaus-Reid strongly desires to have linger in God's mind long after He leaves that gay bar at the outskirts of town or whenever he ends a passing visit in which He contorts under long lost spirits and cares for soon to be departed friends. While meditating on the practice of queer holiness, the theologian who refuses to wear underwear unleashes a litany of descriptions: a de-colonization of souls; a site of disobedience and disbelief; a counterinstitution; a social practice of irony and humor; a radical negation; a space for new ecclesiologies. More specifically, queer holiness is an "undoing of the colonial path of duplication, the dislocation of imperial strategies of holiness."[3] Moreover, it is "a demonology, or praxis of rebellious spirits" that engages in "the social practice of options and dissent."[4] Of course, the variegated textures and fluctuating intensities of queer holiness are responding to macabre iterations of the same — that is, a holiness held hostage to colonial epistemology, or, to evoke Enrique Dussel, the *conquiro ergo sum* at the heart of *cogito ergo sum*.

Though "colonial holiness" does not appear frequently as such in Althaus-Reid's exposé, her reader may trace its characteristics, which lay strewn throughout her work. She particularly traces two assemblages of colonial holiness: the sexual and the economic. With regard to the colonial assemblage of the sexual, she relates holiness to a larger imported structure meant to superimpose an imperial cul-

---

3. Althaus-Reid, *The Queer God* (New York, NY: Routledge, 2003), 154.
4. Ibid., 164, 170.

tural universe.[5] Althaus-Reid concludes "sexual redemption has been at the core of the political and sexual re-inscription of the Other in the imperial story of Christianity."[6] The construction of holiness as a path of sexual redemption is based on the conquistadors' model, not only in military enforcement and judicial application, but also and perhaps more importantly in epistemological approach. As Eduardo Mendieta posits in his expansion of Dussel:

> The Cartesian project of laying an unshakable ground of epistemic certitude led to the ethical and moral evisceration of the subject ... the pursuit of knowledge is accompanied by the constitution or construction of certain types of knowing subjects. Before there is knowledge, there is a knower ... The knowing subject is thus also a deculturing device. To eviscerate the subjectivity of the knowing subject demands this subject become dehistoricized, without a tradition, even a natural language ... It is the ventriloquist of nature.[7]

Hence, Althaus-Reid proceeds with deliberate pace in order to perceive the sexual assemblage of a holiness colonized by the conquistadors' epistemological model of certitude, supremacy, and transcendence. Not only does the "spirituality of the Other [remain] untranslatable"[8] within its framework, entire structures of salvation are imported to "rectify" what can only be understood as an aberration. And, given that Cortés only understands Montezuma's sodomy as a violation of sexual holiness, the directives of salvation as colonial rectification are towards the disciplined duplication of

5. Ibid., 155–156.

6. Ibid., 157.

7. Eduardo Mendieta, "The Ethics of (Not) Knowing: Take Care of Ethics and Knowledge Will Come of Its Own Accord," in *Decolonizing Epistemologies: Latina/o Theology and Philosophy* (eds. Ada María Isasi-Díaz and Eduard Mendieta; New York, NY: Fordham University Press, 2012), 247–249.

8. Althaus-Reid, "Queer Holiness," 157.

hetero-normative practice. Althaus-Reid plainly puts, " ... a different understanding of the sacred defines a way to construct intimacy and living relationships amongst people."[9] In short, colonial theology produces "selective salvation" whereby Christian subjects are recognized according to the services they render — that is, the intensity with which subjects subject themselves to disciplined duplication of sexual colonial holiness, or Christian decency.

Though regimes of hetero-normativity did not begin with Cortés, the distinct economic logic of this "modern/colonial gender system," to use a term by María Lugones, prompts Althaus-Reid to analyze the economic dimension of colonial assemblages of sexual holiness. When Cortés created the demand for salvation by constructing Montezuma within an ethically bankrupt epistemological framework, the Christian conquistador opened a market for the branding of colonial subjects with the Christian logo of sexual decency. Though deemed the illusions of heathens, other divinities became "real workforces [that] threaten the market."[10] Other incarnations of holiness are demonized and made illegal. Relegated to a "black market," intimacy untranslatable into colonial holiness hangs at the mercy of a necropolitical salvation,[11] one that would have practices of queerness ripped, scraped, and expunged for purposes of capitalist expansion.

These sexual and economic assemblages prompt Althaus-Reid to engage with prophetic urgency in the de-colonization of holiness. She stirs all sorts of queer spirits. And in this very stirring lies the strange came's intervention into queer theory's relations to time. A pivotal

---

9. Ibid. 157

10. Ibid., 155.

11. By "necropolitical," I mean what Achille Mbembe develops in his 2003 article in the journal *Public Culture*, entitled "Necropolitics," in which he defines the term as an analytic sensitive to the management of death within a given population. By "necropolitical salvation," then, I mean a theological assemblage that manages death along lines of (doctrinal) confession and (ritual) practice.

moment in Althaus-Reid's chapter on queer holiness deserves deli-
cate attention, for in it trembles futurity coiled with all its hope and
its fear. She concludes a paragraph thusly, "Holiness lost its queerness
with the conquest of the Americas."[12] The trauma of a perceived loss
is poignantly felt in such a dense yet concise confession. This trauma,
this unassimilated horror, then, leads her to suture the gap between
the present and a past decimated by the hetero-normative compulsions of colonial theology. In other words, she returns to the colonial
moment, with the hope that "indecent love *may become pedagogic …
for projects for justice and peace*" (emphasis mine).[13] The smeller of
lemon vendors deploys the curating disciplines of ethnology, eth-
nography, and anthropology to unearth, recover, and foreground this
lost queerness. *Zemis, Batuques,* and *Macumbas* are summoned from
both temporal and geograhic distance to aid in the coming out of
God. With the fierceness of grief, Althaus-Reid seems to take Frantz
Fanon's advice word for word. "The colonized intellectual who writes
for his people should use the past with the intent of opening the
future as an invitation to action and as a basis for hope."[14] To use
that which has passed, of course, is to make a past, to construct the
past itself. And this construction, as Fanon suggests, establishes as
its political vision the mobilization of a collective in futurity. What,
then, are the socially encrypted markers of this collective? What are
the parameters of this futurity? To what action and with what hope
does Althaus-Reid's queer holiness encourage return? These are central questions in discussions around relations to time in queer theory,
and if queer holiness is to rehearse the deliverance of God Herself, it
benefits from cross-examination. I bring, therefore, Althaus-Reid's

---

12. Althaus-Reid, "Queer Holiness," 156.

13. Ibid., 171.

14. Frantz Fanon, *The Wretched of the Earth* (trans. Richard Philcox; New York, NY:
Grove Press, 2004), 187.

queer holiness into intense interrogation with Lee Edelman's critique of futurity and the late José Esteban Muñoz's appraisal of its dire necessity.

III

I do not intend to reiterate the deadlock brawl between advocates and critics of futurity in queer theory, namely Muñoz and Edelman. Instead, this rather timely roundtable discussion puts great pressure on the efforts of both to synergistically complicate, refine, and advance the sensitivity with which Althaus-Reid's queer holiness relates to time. In turn, Althaus-Reid's ministry to a god still "in the closet" leaves queer theory not untouched. After all, like a passing but indelible glory, the irruption of queer ghosts haunt with an iridescent glow.

First, Edelman, Muñoz, and Althaus-Reid share a deep commitment whose mood is antagonistic, adverse. All three insist on the resistance of the here and now. More specifically, they dis-identify with the pragmatism of mainstream gay and lesbian politics. Muñoz evaluates this pragmatism as an "erosion of the gay and lesbian political imagination," which has "degraded the political and conceptual force of concepts such as freedom" and has moved "toward the goal of 'naturalizing' the flawed and toxic ideological formation known as marriage."[15] Not only has current gay and lesbian politics strayed far from gay liberation manifestos from the 1970s by groups such as Third World Gay Revolution, in Muñoz's assessment, the supposedly pragmatic strategy is hardly practical; for "gay marriage is not natural — but then again, neither is marriage for any individual."[16] Edelman

---

15. José Esteban Muñoz, *Cruising Utopia: The Then and There of Queer Futurity* (New York, NY: New York University Press, 2009), 20–21.

16. Ibid., 21-22.

takes a rather different approach to the same diagnosis. Confidently seated in the analyst's armchair, he walks gay pragmatism through its psychoanalytic underpinnings. For Edelman, "the Child remains the perpetual horizon of every acknowledged politics, the fantasmatic beneficiary of every political intervention," such that "reproductive futurism impose[s] an ideological limit on political discourse, preserving in the process the absolute privilege of heteronormativity."[17] In thoroughly Lacanian fashion, Edelman writes that since the realm of the Symbolic — that is, the site of politics, of order, and meaning itself — is in constant movement towards its own realization, "the Child embodies the telos of the social order and comes to be seen as the one for whom that order is held in perpetual trust."[18] Combined, then, compulsions to pragmatism dull and punctuate, for Muñoz and Edelman, the conceptual and political force of queerness.

Likewise, for Althaus-Reid, queer theology does not repeat a liberal protocol of multicultural (multigender and/or multisexual) inclusion. Instead, queer theology is a "theology from the margins that wants to remain at the margins.[19]" She leaves the young academic field a note:

> To recognize sexual discrimination in the Church and in theological thinking (by selective thematic of reflection or by de-authorization of other discourses) does not mean that a theology from the margins should strive for equality. Terrible is the fate of theologies from the margins when they want to be accepted by the centre! ... Queering theology is therefore a deep questioning or an exercise of multiple and diverse hermeneutical suspicions ... the gender paradigm, even if in dialogue with a liberationist one, has never been

---

17. Lee Edelman, *No Future: Queer Theory and the Death Drive* (Durham, NC: Duke University Press, 2004), 2–3.

18. Ibid., 9–11.

19. Althaus-Reid, *From Feminist Theology to Indecent Theology* (UK: SCM Press, 2004), 3.

enough to produce radical transformations. The problem is that gender paradigms tend to normalize theologies in the long term by subsuming differences into equalities.[20]

Queer theology, then, cannot remain within mainstream gay pragmatism, which is held hostage to either an impractical practicality or a desire to suture the ever-elusive gap of signification and realization. Moreover, queer theology does not seek the accommodating tolerance flagged by a rainbow above a steeple because of the compromises insinuated by such a gesture: the adoption of decency for the possibility of recognition and a diminution of hermeneutical suspicion resulting in critical myopia. Summarily, Althaus-Reid, Edelman, and Muñoz all orient themselves towards queerness, a resistance to these times and their colonial exchange system of queerness for homo-normativity, queerness for the Child, queerness for holy sexual decency.

How to best move in a resistant move is the question that once resulted in high collisions and severe diversions among queer theorists. Edelman's incisive analysis perhaps yields the most obstinate entrenchment. Yet, the refusal of futurity as the governing fantasy of the Symbolic provides a necessary challenge to the concept of queer holiness. For Edelman, queerness should not — given that it cannot — embrace the "governing compulsion, the singular imperative to embrace its own futurity in the privileged form of the Child."[21] Instead, it is a radical critique of the social itself by figuring "the bar to every realization of futurity."[22] In fact, "queerness attains its ethical value precisely insofar it accedes to accepting its figural status as resistance to the viability of the social while insisting on the inextricability of such resistance from every social structure."[23] This move

---

20. Ibid., 4.

21. Edelman, *No Future,* 15.

22. Ibid., 3.

23. Ibid. 3

presents a formidable challenge to Althaus-Reid's remembrance of the *zemis*, the *Batuque*, and the *Macumbas* as part of her attempt to resignify holiness. As mentioned earlier, the desire to resignify feeds off a trauma effected by a broken past. "Holiness lost its queerness in the conquest with the Americas." By rewriting the past of queerness she attempts to suture it with the present. Her desire is two-fold: 1) to relieve the grief produced by the colonial duplication of sexual decency, and 2) to somehow repeat the love of the lost queers. But, queer ghosts belong neither to the past nor to the present nor even to the future. Rather, they are, to use Laclau's phrase, "out of joint." "Anachronism is essential to spectrality: the spectre, interrupting all specularity, desynchronizes time. The very essence of spectrality is to be found in this undecidability between flesh and spirit."[24] Returning to Edelman, then, the very queerness of these "indigenous" ghosts lies in their refusal to endow the reality of a colonized sexual order with coherence and stability.[25] There is no reunion but the one Althaus-Reid attempts to knot for herself. It is important, however, to point out that while this psychoanalytic assessment cannot be dismissed as it provides a necessary, haunting insistence on the bad politics and ultimate impossibility of narrative temporality, the breach of signification need not be left alone. While Edelman "does not intend a new politics, a better society, a brighter tomorrow,"[26] Muñoz interjects, "[Though] the felicity of language ultimately falters, it is nonetheless essential."[27] Besides, queer ghosts twist the future on itself.

Where Edelman feels lacking, Muñoz senses excess. As he provocatively opens, "Queerness is not yet here ... we may never touch it, but we can feel it as the warm illumination of a horizon imbued with

---

24. Laclau, *Emancipation(s)*, 68.

25. Edelman, *No Future,* 33.

26. Ibid., 31.

27. Muñoz, *Cruising Utopia,* 10.

potentiality. The anticipatory illumination of certain objects is a kind of potentiality that is open, indeterminate, like the affective contours of hope itself ... queer cultural workers are able to detect an opening and indeterminacy in what for many people is a locked-down dead commodity."[28] For Muñoz, then, the indeterminacy of queer ghosts' temporality radically opens a surplus of possible futures that are not identical to the past; rather, they end up twisting relations to time. Indeed, Muñoz, not unlike Althaus-Reid, seeks an "affective reanimation to displace a disabling political pessimism."[29] This affective reanimation does not deny that the past is in the strictest sense irrecoverable, but instead of lingering despondently in the ensuing gap, queer holiness affirms the excess of possibility in the break. To the extent that decolonization requires resignification, Althaus-Reid's queer holiness will continue to experience vertigo as it peers into the deep between the living and the dead; yet like brooches, queer ghosts tenuously, gloriously, powerfully, clumsily pour among the young visions and dreams upon the old.

IV

Althaus-Reid avails herself of yet another tool besides the imagination of memory to minister to a closeted god. The classical deconstructive move she makes by disturbing the purity and necropolitical logic of the binary salvation/condemnation, or heaven/hell is perhaps the most brilliant moment of her reparation. This brilliance is in part due to its very simplicity. For Althaus-Reid, queer holiness could find no better site than hell, since no other position knows the practice of dissent better than hell. "Hell as a site of disobedience is the space where we not only find those who reject goodness, but those who

---

28. Ibid., 1, 7–9.

29. Ibid., 1, 7-9.

refuse to continue to be interpolated by the goodness of the capital-ist system in which we live and its current values."[30] In hell, salvation as duplication of colonial sexual decency is no longer required, and options really become available. Of course, this space is not called hell out of caprice. The ultimately unbreachable gap in all attempts of (re)signification makes this approach to decolonization somewhat of a hell. But, as suggested earlier, Edelman's correct insistence on the intransitive quality of the gap need not be left untwisted. Pre-cisely as a psychoanalytic intervention, Edelman's analysis may not solve queer holiness's shortcomings, but it may surely aid it in better coping with inevitable failure. Furthermore, hell is not only the most appropriate space for options; it is also, as a hub for queer ghosts, overflowing with bodies contorting in twisted relations to time.

Hellish relations to time are not only contrary to heteronorma-tive timetables of "reproductive futurism" or homonormative echoes of the same. Rather, the rhythms of queer temporality scramble colonial schedules of timely conversion, salvation, and eschatology. As Schneider explains, "What a queer vision! Hell is, for the most part, a hot, smelly, messy place. It is every bit the *body* in motion or in labor."[31] The corporality of hell is only confirmed by Althaus-Reid herself when she writes, " ... the imaginary of hell is part of a sophisticated body theology ... While Christianity may claim that there will be no sex in heaven, thus presenting us with the idea of the disembodied imaginary of holiness, in hell by comparison everything is related to bodies. There may be no-body in heaven, but there will certainly be some-body in hell."[32] To practice queer holiness as a hell-ish practice is to consecrate the very contradictions that emerge from

---

30. Althaus-Reid, "Queer Holiness," 167.

31. Laurel Schneider, *Beyond Monotheism: A Theology of Multiplicity* (New York, NY: Routledge, 2007), 97.

32. Althaus-Reid, "Queer Holiness," 167–168.

radical embodiment itself — that is, an embodiment at the limits of hetero-normativity temporality, which is theologically structured as the timing of salvations. With hell, then, Althaus-Reid teaches God how to dissent — that is, how to await its arrival through ghosts of long-lost queers, and how to persist in the embodiment of such dissent as a mounting in queer time.

Consider, for example, how the marvel evoked by the absence of Jesus's body, which the empty tomb figures, has historically been charged with immense theological effect. The lack of his body correlates to the excess of its meaning. From textual gestures towards post-70 CE Galilee to the French Jesuit Michel de Certeau's diasporic hermeneutics,[33] the theological density accrued by an absence has drawn disciples past and present into its captivating orbit. His present absence matters in the most literal of ways: Mary of Magdala's hair stands on edge; Salome's muscles, saturated with adrenaline, tense up and shake; waves of goose bumps rush over their skin. These flashes of trembling flesh, these traces of a time that is to come and yet is already here interrupts the finality and totalizing force of hetero-normative temporality. The temple may be destroyed, but Galilee awaits; we feel it in our very flesh. The kingdom of God is both here and now in our shaking, and then and there in our trembling. It is the work of queer holiness to harness trauma vis-à-vis a theological affirmation of temporal excess that brings futures into the present even as it defers their total materialization. In the words of Althaus-Reid, queer holiness is the "search for the Queer who is entombed in us."[34]

---

33. Cf. Michel de Certeau, "Mystic Speech" and "The Weakness of Believing: From the Body to Writing, a Christian Transit" in *The Certeau Reader*, ed. Graham Ward (Okford, UK and Malden, MA: Blackwell Publishers, 2000), 188-206, 214-243.

34. Althaus-Reid, *The Queer God*, 154.

The good news is that, as M. Jacqui Alexander recalls, these spirits, these concentrated energies, "do not like to be forgotten."[35] Rather, they return with "a call to remember, [to remember] embodied."[36] This is the pedagogic role of temporally indecent spirits: to attune a closeted God to the vagaries with which queerness consecrates all embodiment.

As promised towards the beginning of this paper, I conclude by returning to Laclau's notes on the political effects of deconstruction. The ethical impulse of queer holiness returns to a colonial moment of sexual decision, but it does so with a great cloud of witnesses. Their testimony bears witness to the temporal excess of embodiment, as they mount bodies and gods. To pursue *zemis*, *Batuques*, and *Macumbas*, among other long-lost queer spirits, is to plunge into a sea of temporal rhythms. Queer holiness brings the theologian to the precipice of hell, to the moments when she must decide to become yet again what she never was, a temporal contortion incarnate.

References

Alexander. M. Jacqui. *Pedagogies of Crossing: Meditations on Feminism, Sexual Politics, and the Sacre.* Durham, NC: Duke University Press, 2005.

Althaus-Reid. *From Feminist Theology to Indecent Theology.* London, UK: SCM Press, 2004.

Althaus-Reid. *The Queer God.* New York: Routledge, 2003.

Edelman, Lee. *No Future: Queer Theory and the Death Drive.* Durham, NC: Duke University Press, 2004.

de Certeau, Michel "Mystic Speech" and "The Weakness of Believing: From the Body to Writing, a Christian Transit" Pages 188-206, 214-243 in *The Certeau Reader.* Edited by Graham Ward. Okford, UK and Malden, MA: Blackwell Publishers, 2000.

Fanon, Frantz. *The Wretched of the Earth.* New York, NY: Grove Press, 2004.

Laclau, Ernesto. *Emancipation(s).* New York, NY: Verso, 1996.

---

35. M. Jacqui Alexander, *Pedagogies of Crossing: Meditations on Feminism, Sexual Politics, and the Sacred* (Durham, NC: Duke University Press, 2005), 289–290.

36. Ibid., 316.

Mendieta, Eduardo. "The Ethics of (Not) Knowing: Take Care of Ethics and Knowledge Will Come of Its Own Accord," Pages 247-264 in *Decolonizing Epistemologies: Latina/o Theology and Philosophy*. Edited by Ada María Isasi-Díaz and Eduard Mendieta. New York, NY: Fordham University Press, 2012.

Muñoz, José Esteban. *Cruising Utopia: The Then and There of Queer Futurity*. New York, NY: New York University Press, 2009.

Schneider, Laurel. *Beyond Monotheism: A Theology of Multiplicity*. New York, NY: Routledge, 2007.

Sedgwick, Eve K. *Epistemology of the Closet*. Berkeley and Los Angeles, CA: University of California Press, 1990.

PUSSY RIOT

<><><><><><><><><><><><><><><><><><><><><><>

Indecent Theology in the New Russian Revolution

JORGE AQUINO

THE REVOLUTION WILL BE SEXUALIZED

The role of sexuality as a pillar in the social orders and identity scripts of Western modernity has been well established in contemporary critical theory, at least since Michel Foucault's histories of sexuality and his turn towards understanding sexual differentiation as a construction of what he called biopower. Queer theory was born in the 1990s at the crossing of social movements for LGBTQ liberation and intellectual theorizations produced by scholars and public intellectuals such as Gayle Rubin, Eve Kosofsky Sedgwick, and Judith Butler. With Butler, the theorization of sexuality takes a turn toward interrogating the psycho-somatic dimensions of subject formation, as those processes — subsisting substantially in the unconscious — are inflected by socialized processes of ideological formation. Butler's work approaches the question of ideology mostly by way of crossing post-Freudian psychoanalysis with Althusserian notions of political subject-formation.[1] She further examines the phenomenon of activist strategic intervention in the social order by way of speech-acts and other political performatives that have the effect of resignifying dominant tropes of hegemonic (capitalist) ideology.[2]

This essay undertakes a case study of Butler's theorization of political performatives and the "psychic life of power" by examining the sexual theo-politics of the Russian punk band, Pussy Riot. I consider the band's transgressive performances as prime examples of what Marcella Althaus-Reid called *Indecent Theology*. This research seeks to establish a better understanding of how ideologies of sexuality are integrated into a subject as psychological process, and then how that process refluxes back into the milieux of collective social formation as expressions of a subject's political agency. The big prize of my research is to understand whether and how a sexually "indecent" theological performance can destabilize the stale social formations of the *kyriarchy*.[3] This is of critical importance to constructive theological work on questions of sexuality and gender. It also has power for informing anti-systemic social activism in a time of *de facto* transnational global governance by agencies and allies of neo-liberal capitalism, agencies all but indifferent to traditional forms of democratic activism from the popular classes.

---

1. Judith Butler, *The Psychic Life of Power: Theories in Subjection* (Redwood City, CA: Stanford University Press, 1995).

2. Judith Butler, *Excitable Speech: A Politics of the Performative* (Redwood City, CA: Stanford University Press, 1997).

3. I take the notion of *kyriarchy* from the work of María Pilar Aquino, who in turn takes it from Elisabeth Schüssler-Fiorenza. It signifies a more plural idea of patriarchy — one that recognizes how masculinism as a social privilege is soldered into forms of class, racial, and sexual privilege. See María Pilar Aquino, "Latina Feminist Theology: Central Features," in *A Reader in Latina Feminist Theology: Religion and Justice* (Austin, TX: University of Texas Press, 2002), 133–160, and Elisabeth Schüssler Fiorenza, *But She Said: Feminist Practices of Biblical Interpretation* (Boston: Beacon Press, 1992).

Pussy Riot became an international sensation after they burst into Moscow's Cathedral of Christ the Savior on Feb. 21, 2012 to stage a "punk prayer" to the Virgin Mary challenging Vladimir Putin's plans to run for a third term as president of the Russian Federation. Putin was subsequently elected to a six-year term as president, in effect nullifying, by legal technicality, the constitutional term limits that had forced him from the same office four years earlier. Now he is eligible to run for yet another six-year term and could remain as Russian Federation president through 2024. Pussy Riot, along with thousands of Russians, took issue with Putin's political resurrection and his heavy-handed style, especially the way he has coopted the Russian Orthodox Church hierarchy as a partner of state. Pussy Riot's punk prayer petitioned the Virgin Mary to "put Putin away," perhaps in the sort of psychiatric hospital the KGB would use to internally exile dissidents:

> *Virgin Mary, Mother of God, put Putin away,*
> *Put Putin away, put Putin away!*

The song complains that under Putin, liberty has been exiled to heaven and "gay pride sent to Siberia in chains." Putin, "their chief saint, leads protesters to prison under escort." The confusion of church and state in the Putin era is "the Lord's shit," marred by "the Church's praise of rotten dictators, the cross-bearer procession of black limousines." For women this is a sort of hell, where their only lot is to "give birth and love." The band called on the Virgin to wake up and seize her identity as a woman:

> *Virgin Mary, Mother of God, become a feminist*
> *Become a feminist, BECOME A FEMINIST!*

The women of Pussy Riot — "Nadia" (Nadezhda Tolokonnikova), "Katia" (Yekaterina Samutsevich), and "Masha" (Maria Alyokhina) — were charged with "hooliganism motivated by anti-religious hatred" and sentenced to two years in a penal colony for women.[4] The Pussy Riot spectacle generated enormous attention and debate around the world. To the liberal-minded in Russia and outside, the prosecution of Pussy Riot represented a patriarchal smackdown of women's rights, sexual freedom, and feminist art. Meanwhile the Russian establishment arrayed around President Putin painted Pussy Riot as a group of atheist blasphemers whose anarchic rant was maliciously intended to offend decent Christians and undermine the state. But as the case unfolded, it became abundantly clear that religious piety and patriotism were secondary in importance to the prurient interest that police, prosecutors, the press, and Orthodox Church leaders had trained on the sexualities and sexual politics of the defendants. The way the sexual aspects of their performance tended to arouse and unsettle figures in the establishment opens a portal into study of the revolutionary potential of theo-politics.

Understanding the theo-politics of Pussy Riot's intervention requires examination in several directions. First, I consider the hypothesis that Pussy Riot's *total performance* — from the womens' abortive appearance in the Cathedral of Christ the Savior, to their statements to police, their courtroom testimonies, and their subsequent interviews and statements — functioned as a "shock to the system" of Russian politics and the Putin regime. Second, I consider the specifically theological nature of their intervention by drawing from the Indecent Theology of the late Argentine-Scottish theologian, Marcella Althaus-Reid. Third, I offer some tentative conclusions about the shock value of the performance based on news and documentary accounts of Russian and international reaction. Part of the work involves assessing the performance's massive possibilities

---

4. Katia Samutsevich's sentence was overturned on appeal and she was released in October 2012.

for failure — in terms of whether its politics could be easily co-opted back into the hegemonic power grid, or neutralized altogether. Here I consider the risks of performative contradiction in Pussy Riot's intervention: Might the band's anarchistic dissidence be recaptured and resignified by capitalist markets and memes for 'appropriate' music, art, and political activism? Instead of a shock to the system, did Pussy Riot's performance risk being retranslated and reintegrated into dominant narratives about pop art, punk music, Russian dissidence, radical feminism, and transgressive sexuality?

JUDITH BUTLER ON THE MELANCHOLIC
INSTABILITY OF THE HETEROSEXIST ORDER

I begin by considering the psycho-somatic nature of the Russian body politic in light of Judith Butler's insightful and provocative discussion on the construction of homophobic male heterosexuality. For Butler, heterosexual identity is forged amid the Freudian dynamics of the *ego* and the *id*, and the emotional states of *mourning and melancholia*[5] that color the forbidding experiences that are constitutive of gender identity. Freud understood the formation of the ego in terms of a subject's object-relations with other people and with the world. Those relations are negotiated psychically in terms of what Freud called *object-cathexis,* the projection of psychic energy onto an object of desire — whether a person or an inorganic object — in a way that *attaches* the *id* to the object of its desire. Since many (if not all) of the objects of one's desire are sooner or later lost, however, a process of detachment has to take place on the level of the psyche. Butler notes that Freud's views on the psychic process of detachment underwent transformation based on his clinical experience. In 1917, when he

---

5. Butler, *Psychic Life of Power*, Ch. 5.

wrote "Mourning and Melancholia,"[6] Freud understood "that grief could be resolved through a de-cathexis, a breaking of attachment, as well as the subsequent making of new attachments."[7] But six years later, in "The Ego and the Id,"[8] Freud came to suspect that complete detachment from any psychic object was not really possible, and that the psyche was critically shaped by its inability to fully and finally grieve the lost objects of its desire. Instead of de-cathexis, lost objects are reestablished in the ego as *identifications*. Quoting Freud, Butler writes:[9]

> When it happens that a person has to give up a sexual object, there quite often ensues an alteration of his ego which can only be described as a setting up of the object inside the ego, as it occurs in melancholia. ... [I]t may be that this identification is the sole condition under which the id can give up its objects. ... [I]t makes it possible to suppose that the character of the ego is a precipitate of abandoned object-cathexes and that it contains the history of those object-choices.

How would such a figuring color the object-choices and ego formations of heterosexual/heterosexist culture? Butler argues that heterosexist culture orients gender to heterosexual desire after "enforcing the prohibition on homosexuality."[10] The violence of this proscription compels the subject not only to refuse same-sex attachments, but further to deny that s/he could ever have been moved by the prospect of such attachments. The unfortunate paradox of this

---

6. Sigmund Freud, *The Standard Edition of the Complete Psychological Works of Sigmund Freud*, ed. James Strachey, Anna Freud, Carrie Lee Rothgeb, and Angela Richards (London: Hogarth Press, 1953–1974), vol. 14

7. Butler, *Psychic Life of Power,* 134.

8. Freud, *Complete Works*, vol. 19.

9. Butler *Psychic Life of Power*, 133, quoting Freud, *Complete Works*, vol. 19, 29.

10. Butler, *Psychic Life of Power,* 135.

prohibition is that prohibition alone cannot destroy the elemental precocity of sexual attraction: While it may inhibit homosexual affect, an otherwise heterosexual person's repressed same-sex affections are mysterously, psychically reincorporated — sublimated and re-internalized — as *refused identifications* with the abjected objects of their foregone desire. Once repudiated, a foreclosed homosexual attachment resurfaces as an identification, one that becomes a structural element in the inner constitution of heterosexual ego and its gendered identity. A hetero man, variously subjected to the violent prohibition on same-sex affection, paradoxically grows to become

> *the man he "never" loved and "never" grieved;*
> *the straight woman becomes the woman she "never" loved*
> *and "never" grieved.*[11]

The passion that moved the attachment in the first place is not lost, but is recapitulated as a psychic process — a queer *id-entity* that participates in the formation of the heterosexual ego. As a subjective feeling, this buried identification is not neutered, but forever lives a mournful existence, wailing and wallowing in the mellifluous emotion-tones of melancholy. In effect, the specter of the refused object of desire has taken its stubborn place in the soul as an ineradicable psychic domain of homosexual desire, held within, almost invisibly, as "unlivable passion and ungrievable loss."[12]

> ... there is no final breaking of the attachment. There is rather the incorporation of the attachment *as* identification, where identification becomes a magical, a psychic form of preserving the object. Insofar as psychic identification of the object and such identifications come to form the ego, the lost object continues to haunt and inhabit the ego as one of its constitutive identifications.

11. Ibid., 147.
12. Ibid., 134–135.

If such abjected queer identifications are indeed constitutive of heterosexual gender identity, then heterosexualism must be a deeply ambivalent social formation — for "what is most apparently performed as gender is the sign and symptom of a pervasive disavowal,"[13] one that must constantly disclaim, *I long for what I am not,* instead of confessing that deep down, *I am what I long for.*

It is this psychic ambivalence and vulnerability to the queer in heterosexual culture that I want to examine in the theo-politics of Pussy Riot — considering them as exemplary practitioners of an *indecent* theology, as well as of the possibilities of revolutionary art in a time marked by what Guy Debord called the "society of the spectacle."[14]Althaus-Reid's theology celebrated both sexual transgression and sexual performance as intrinsic to a critique of patriarchal heterosexism in Christian faith-discourse. Her theology, reflecting on the *irruption of the sexual subject* in theology, can be meaningfully supplemented by further consideration of capitalism's ideological productions as *spectacles*, and of the spectacle itself as a fundamental capitalist commodity. Debord understood the ideological condition of his time (a year before the Paris uprisings of May 1968) as marked by capitalist subjectivities alienated by the mediatized spectacularization of reality. Mimicking the opening lines of Marx's *Capital,* Debord wrote, "The whole life of those societies in which modern conditions of production prevail presents itself as an immense accumulation of spectacles. All that was once directly lived has become mere representation." He understood the capitalist spectacle as both the image capitalist society projected to itself, as well as the productive system by which that image is projected. "The spectacle is not a collection of

---

13. Ibid., 147.

14. Guy Debord, *The Society of the Spectacle* (New York, NY: Zone Books, 1994).

images; rather, it is a social relationship that is mediated by images."[15] Debord makes for rather pessimistic reading; his brilliant analysis gives us a map of the ways and means of this spectacular prison of capitalist ideology and its subjectivations — but the map shows no exits. He is hardly alone.[16] Most of those who have written on capitalist ideology in the last two centuries founder on the question of how to overcome the discursive interpellation and psychic integration of subjects in modern global capitalism. One typical point of weakness is the perennially inadequate theorization of Butler's "psychic life of power." Another is that research on ideological formations tends not to take sexuality seriously enough. Even where considered an object of ideological formation, sexuality is seldom analyzed for its potential as the Achilles heel of any patriarchal order. This neglect of revolutionary sexual transgression is striking given the constant testimony of social movements marked by passionate sexual energy, provocative sexual stances, and broad demands for gender equality and sexual liberation. Many of the revolutionary moments of the last century have seemed charged with sexual excitement, anticipation, ecstasies, and erotic resistances of various sorts.[17] Today we can

---

15. Ibid., 12

16. One reads an indomitable pessimism throughout late Marxist writing on capitalist ideology, art, and subjectivation. Two signal examples are essays from Max Horkheimer and Theodor Adorno, "The Culture Industry: Enlightenment as Mass Deception," in Max Horkheimer and Theodor W. Adorno, *Dialectic of Enlightenment* (trans. John Cumming; New York, NY: Continuum, 2002), and in "The Postmodern Condition" in Fredric Jameson, *Postmodernism, or, The Cultural Logic of Late Capitalism* (Durham, NC: Duke University Press, 1991).

17. Among some familiar examples, Milan Kundera writes of the Prague Spring as a sexual and generational awakening, followed by a sexually repressive Soviet intervention (*The Unbearable Lightness of Being*, 1984); Reinaldo Arenas writes in the same register of the Cuban Revolution of 1959, a sexually liberating revolution that by the mid-1960s had fallen back into a Stalinistic repression of every freedom, especially sexual freedoms (*Antes que Anochezca*, 1992); Carlos Fuentes writes of Paris in 1968 as a cultural revolution in which the question of political liberation liberated sexual relations among strangers, and even between bourgeois couples whose

draw on queer theory and sexual theologies to consider the power of sexuality to subvert the ideological establishments of capitalism — though this remains mostly undiscovered country.

One important dimension of Butler's analysis of the melancholic condition of heterosexuality is her citation of its innate instability. The categorical proscription of an ineradicable psychic homosexualism opens a political vulnerability that is potentially destabilizing to the whole order of heterosexism. She reiterates that "gender is acquired at least in part through the repudiation of homosexual attachment," particularly precocious attachments for one's same-sex parent. But as we have seen, the refused homoerotic attachment is reincorporated into the heterosexualized gender identity as a foreclosed identification — one that forever holds the unlivable, ungrievable love one supposedly never had. Inasmuch as queer attraction should takes its place as a structural girding of a heterosexualized ego, that habitation would be self-contradictory and potentially volatile, and could develop into a fierce allergen. This abject, almost invisible identification

> contains within it both the prohibition and the desire, and so embodies the ungrieved loss of the homosexual cathexis. If one *is* a girl to the extent one does not *want* a girl, then wanting a girl will bring being a girl into question; *within this matrix, homosexual desire thus panics gender.*[18] (my emphasis)

If homosexual desire panics gender, can we take the next step and ask whether uninhibited expressions of sexual freedom can panic a sexually repressive and repressed political culture? Did Pussy Riot's activism — as a species of revolutionary, sexual theo-politics — de-

---

passions had long been chilled by interminable sessions of psychoanalysis (*Los 68: Paris, Praga, México,* 2005).

18. Butler, *Psychic Life of Power,* 136.

stabilize the Russian Federation's incestuous marriage of church and state? I will consider the question on a couple of levels. First, how does Pussy Riot practice a theo-politics of *indecenting*, as Marcella Althaus-Reid discussed the concept in her writings? Secondly, how does their performance actually transgress and displace the ideological order of Debord's *Society Of The Spectacle?*

MARCELLA ALTHAUS-REID'S
HERMENEUTICS OF INDECENTING

Marcella Althaus-Reid has to be recognized as one of the most productive, daring, and critical minds to write theology in the last century. Her writing moves relentlessly through the weaknesses of a number of fields — critiquing liberation theology from the standpoint of feminist theory or postcolonial criticism ... critiquing feminist theory for its silence on queerness and its "vanilla" Marianism[19] ... insisting that Indecent or Queer Theology is not necessarily a "homosexual theology," but a theology that seeks to overturn all hierarchization of sexualities.[20] Above all she was bent on smashing all the limits to liberation that she could identify in her tragically shortened career. Marcella's description of her Indecent Theology is straightforward and reiterated throughout her work.

> I deliberately use the term *indecenting* here in relation to the unmasking of ideologies. *Indecenting* is a term that reminds us that Liberation Theology's first act was that of troubling

---

19. Althaus-Reid, *Indecent Theology* (London: Routledge, 2001).

20. Althaus-Reid, "On Queer Theology and Liberation Theology: The Irruption of the Sexual Subject in Theology," in *Homosexualities,* eds. Marcella Althaus-Reid, Regina Ammicht Quinn, Erik Borgman, and Norbert Reck (London: SCM Press, 2008), 83–96.

the status quo, and that it was part of a provocative and heavily contested transgressive discourse.[21]

Liberation Theology posed a profound challenge to transnational, neoliberal capitalism and the oppressive class orders it had under-written since the time of New World colonialism. Indecent Theology likewise transgresses the smug relationship between heterosexist-patriarchal "decency" discourse in Christian theology and the colonial relations that discourse has historically underwritten. Indecent Theology works at deconstructing how moralistic Christian claims to gender propriety and sexual decency are articulated within a long-historical matrix — "a complex web of class, race, gender, and sexuality." Indecent theology takes its standpoint from the margins — sexual margins that are also socioeconomic ones — "to claim the marginal knowledge of God as a foundation for an alternative theological praxis of liberation."[22] Besides the Liberation Theology in which she was reared, Marcella's hermeneutics of the margins owes much to her formation in poststructuralist critical theory. There the question of marginality, and of counter-hegemonic enunciation from the margins, is not only a socio-economic condition or problem; it is actually a positive epistemological privilege, an insight from the underside — or the outside — of history. This is especially important in the case of the intimate socialization of gendersex identities, which are integrated amid a subject's partial surrender to the terms by which power has interpellated and subjectivized that individual.[23] The critical counter-interpellation of sexual ideologies is more

---

21. Althaus-Reid, "From Liberation Theology to Indecent Theology: The Trouble with Normality in Theology," in *Latin American Liberation Theology: The Next Generation*, ed. Ivan Petrella (Maryknoll, NY: Orbis, 2005), 25.

22. Ibid., 27.

23. Butler again offers powerful thinking on this question in her book on hate speech and linguistic injury in *Excitable Speech: A Politics of the Performative*.

complicated for subjects standing in a relationship of *détente vis à vis* the ideological system that has meted out their social identity. The "happy husband" or the "Stepford Wife" are unlikely to interrogate or contest their identities — unless, of course, the society where they have plied those identities should fall apart amid some unforeseen systemic crisis. But because a heterosexist order must constantly enforce the rote repetition of its rituals of gendersex relationing, its system will always-already be at risk of crisis. This becomes clearer if we take seriously the implications of Butler's observation on how the violently enforced contradictions of heterosexual formation portend risk to the sustainability of a heterosexist social order.

In brute historical terms, the decency ethos of Christian faith-discourse lies as a crossroads connecting the many provinces of Latin America's differentiated, violent, and self-conflicted sexual cultures. Marcella's recitation of "clues for indecent practices in theology" offers an economical hermeneutics of indecenting that informs a reading of the Pussy Riot case. These are essentially deconstructive principles and practices, which proceed by following a track of suspicion concerning the facial claims of ideological discourse, and then inverting/obverting those claims against the narrative experience of the marginalized faith community — the queer Christian underground. Its first principle is to acknowledge "the edges of the construction of the theological subject." It invokes questions about *who* is named as the normative voice in faith discourse. *Whose voice* is doing the speaking? Who are the *outsiders,* the *non-persons,* or the *outlaws* of the discourse? How does the slope of theological argumentation produce the marginalization or secondarity of certain subjects? Subjecthood should be read in terms of proscribed and truncated social agencies, recognizing that these roles are "established in a framework of power dynamics." Second, she insists that sexual ideologies be considered in tandem with racial and class ideologies, especially to recognize "the relationships between poverty and sexuality." Finally, such reflections are opened only after a community has learned "to engage in a theology of story where people can 'come out' as they are. ... [C]ommunion cannot happen among colonial subjects, only among friends." Furthermore, the Bible and church traditions ought to be read "sexually," with an eye to "exploring themes of God and sexuality beyond heterosexual metaphors. "We now need to denounce the heterosexual God embedded in dualistic values, narrow understandings of human relationships, and faulty perceptions of worlds divided between the center and the periphery."[24] Consideration of these hermeneutics of indecency opens insight into the sexual theopolitics of Pussy Riot's performance and subsequent prosecution.

'KILL ALL SEXISTS':
PUSSY RIOT AS *GENDER POGROM*

What sort of crime is *"hooliganism motivated by hatred of religion"*? And why should such a charge merit a sentence of up to five years in a penal colony? In a September 2012 interview with Russian television, President Putin cited the case against Pussy Riot as defending a compelling state interest. Insisting that the name of the band is intentionally "obscene," Putin said the prosecution presents important "moral" issues, particularly the defense of Russian religious faiths against intolerance and extremism. He noted that members of Pussy Riot had staged other spectacular public stunts, including "an orgy in a public place." (More on that performance in a moment.)

> This kind of conduct in a public place should not go unnoticed by authorities. Then they uploaded the video of that orgy on the Internet. Then they turned up at the Yelokhovo

---

24. Althaus-Reid, "From Liberation Theology to Indecent Theology," 36.

Cathedral here in Moscow and caused unholy mayhem —
then went to another cathedral and caused mayhem there
too. ... Russians still have painful memories of the early
years of Soviet rule, when thousands of Orthodox, Muslim,
as well as clergy of other religions were persecuted. Soviet
authorities brutally repressed the clergy. Many churches
were destroyed. The attacks had a devastating effect on all
our traditional religions. And so in general I think the state
has to protect the feelings of believers.[25]

The matter of transgressive public sex was a central theme of the
trial. The prosecutor opened by charging Pussy Riot with trespassing
in a cathedral area reserved for sacred rituals wearing "inappropri-
ate clothing ... revealing bare skin, thus violating cathedral regulations that shoulders and legs must be covered." Their neon-colored
balaclavas — which prosecutors caricatured as "provocative masks
with the eyes cut out" — also transgressed Article 213.2 of the Russian penal code, which states, "disrupting social order by an act of
hooliganism that shows disrespect for society and is motivated by
religious hatred or enmity."

Like all political offenses, Article 213.2 sanctions an ambiguous
crime. If the women of Pussy Riot had transgressed by "disrupting
social order," it would take some really panicked thinking to see
serious harm in their forty-second performance, which was quickly
broken up amid a whirlwind of police and angry churchgoers. The
most serious harm one sees are the expressions of shock on the faces
of the nuns and other Orthodox church ladies in the shrine. There
was no property damage. More likely the real offense was Pussy
Riot's ideological attack on Russia's patriarchal sexual order. What

25. Putin: Using Al-Qaeda in Syria like sending Gitmo inmates to fight," *Russia Today News*, n.p. [cited September 6 2012]. Online Sept. 6, 2012. Online at http://bit.ly/18BLVPy.

sort of an attack would this be? In so many expressions — their song lyrics, interviews, courtroom and jailhouse declarations — it is clear that the women of Pussy Riot understand that sex has power as an instrument of pleasure, of love, and even of spirituality. It is equally clear that they understand the provocative power of sexuality as a political and ideological weapon. In the 2013 HBO documentary, "Pussy Riot: A Punk Prayer,"[26] we hear Nadia Tolokonnikova turning the tables on her police interrogator — flirting, teasing, and taunting him with body language, the tone of her voice, and the substance of her responses. Such an up-front deployment of sexuality might seem paradoxical in the case of a band whose name a non-English-speaking Russian would not understand. When at one point the interrogator mispronounces the band's name (with subtle malice), Nadia corrects him, imploring, "don't fear that word, like the rest of the government." When asked for a translation of "riot," she replies, "uproar, *pogrom,* uprising of the oppressed masses, people who don't agree with the politics of the current regime." Later in the trial, when Katia Samutsevich was told that Pussy Riot's first CD release was to be titled "Occupy Red Square," she asked why it couldn't be called "Kill All Sexists."

Clearly the aura of sexual uprising provokes the band's many detractors. The "Punk Prayer" documentary follows a group of Orthodox hyper-faithful for their responses to Pussy Riot — including a collective of men who call themselves the Carriers of the Cross. These men, who bear the Orthodox cross before church processions, look like Russia's answer to the Hell's Angels biker gang, dressed all in black with t-shirts that read "Orthodoxy or Death." Their prayer to the Virgin Mary is more churchy — and sexist — than Pussy Riot's:

---

26. Mike Lerner and Maxim Pozdorovkin, dir., *Pussy Riot: A Punk Prayer* (United Kingdom: Roast Beef Productions, 2013), digital video disk.

Mother of God be joyful
know that God is with you.
You are a blessed wife —
and blessed is your womb.

There is the three-step patriarchal recipe for womanhood, doled up in four short lines: (1) be obedient to God; (2) be obedient to husband; and (3) be dutiful as mother. One of the men — an elder with a long white beard and white hair — speaks with concern of Pussy Riot's nefarious plot. "Nadia is carrying out a plan. I've followed her on the Internet. I've read what she writes and says," he says, speaking as though he were a deranged fan. He massages the fingers of one hand in the palm of the other as he speaks, his eyes darting from side to side. "There is a plan of action in place to destroy both church and state. It always begins the same way: attacks against the holy altars and against the throne." Another identifies Nadia as

> The main one: She is a demon with a brain. She's a strong demon. She's stubborn. You can tell by her expression; you can tell by her lips, by her mouth. It means she'll fight to the end. There have always been witches who would not repent.

During a 2012 prayer vigil, which Orthodox Patriarch Kirill had convened shortly after Pussy Riot's abortive Cathedral performance, one carrier of the cross opines that "'pussy' is a devious word. It means 'kitten,' but also 'the uterus.' There are some other possibilities. The best translation is 'deranged vaginas.'" He then comments that Pussy Riot is "fighting against a male view of the world. If they want to live without men, they should move to an island, or the Amazon or something."

An April 12, 2012, talk show on Russian television ("Special Correspondence") purveyed similar attitudes.[27] Its audience, stacked

---

27. Ibid.

with dour partisans of the Orthodox church hierarchy, depicted Pussy Riot as counter-partisans in an all-out gender war. The show's host described the Pussy Riot performance as "absolutely possessed," as a "'dance' with blasphemous screaming." He asks whether this performance was not an "act of war" against decent Russian society. "They messed with my faith," he says. "Am I supposed to forgive them? Or ... " — he smacks a fist into an open palm for emphasis — "should I first punish them, and then maybe forgive them, *if* they ask for it?" One audience member compares Pussy Riot with the Bolsheviks of the 1920s and 1930s who razed Orthodox shrines, including (in 1931) the original Christ the Savior Cathedral. Another says "they're real revolutionaries, real demons. They want to change our way of life." Hot volleys of applause meet each righteous pronouncement on the moral menace of Pussy Riot.

Apparently the provocative *gravamen* of Pussy Riot's performance was to proclaim and perform an anti-patriarchal view of sexuality before the altar of an important Christian shrine, in a time when President Putin had sealed a powerful alliance with the Orthodox church hierarchy. Clearly the question of sexuality was uppermost in the minds of government and church officials alike, who consistently showed an almost prurient interest in Pussy Riot. In her police interview Katia Samutsevich was asked "do you have kids," or do "you dream of marrying and having a child?" She cooly answers, "No I don't have such dreams. ... As children girls are told that they have to find a man and give birth to children. This pressure persists throughout life. In reality many girls don't actually want this."

"Including you?" the interrogator asks.

"Including me," she replies.[28]

---

28. Ibid.

Turning a perennially misogynistic question on its head, one could constructively ask: *What do the women of Pussy Riot want?* What dreams would they have — if not to marry and have children, like the Virgin Mary imagined by the Carriers of the Cross? Perhaps to frontally contradict the ideal of Christian womanhood boasted by the patriarchal Christianity of the Russian Orthodox Church. Asked in her police interrogation why she would "fight the Russian Orthodox Church," Nadia Tolokonnikova replied that the Cathedral of Christ the Savior "symbolizes the union of Church and State. That's not how it should be."[29] Masha Alyokhina reiterated this indictment of the idolatrous church-state partnership in her closing statement, explaining the lyric in the punk prayer, "Shit! Shit! God's shit!"

> It is this relationship we describe as "God's shit." I want you all to understand this: We use these words to describe a relationship, not religion, per se.[30]

Besides being incestuous, Russia's new church-state union is sexist. "The Patriarch stands at the altar. But a woman should occupy it," Tolokonnikova says during her interrogation. Referring to Pussy Riot in the third-person, she adds "They are feminists. As a member of Pussy Riot I believe that women should be allowed to run services and that a woman should stand at the altar, because she is not a sinful creature."[31] Among their other dreams: "We need to destroy the whole system," one balaclava-touting Pussy Rioteer says, in a clandestine group interview from the group's underground headquarters in June 2012. "It's rotten from head to tail. Only radical revolutionary ac-

---

29. Ibid.
30. Ibid.
31. Ibid.

tion can change anything. Talk and compromise gets you nowhere." Another chimes in: "Revolution, riot, riot, revolution."[32]

It is clear that performances of sexuality play a critical role in how the Pussy Riot collective imagines the riot becoming a revolution. Before forming Pussy Riot, Tolokonnikova and Samutsevich had participated in the Voina Collective, a Moscow shock-performance troupe. Voina (which means "war" in Russian) became notorious for two video productions — "Kiss Garbage,"[33] and "Fuck for the heir, Puppy Bear"[34] — in which Nadia Tolokonnikova played a starring role. "Kiss Garbage"[35] featured Nadia and several other Voina women approaching and stealing kisses in aggressive fashion right off the mouths of several shocked Moscow policewomen in highly trafficked public places. "Fuck for the Heir, Puppy Bear" was a low-budget, anti-government mock-u-mentary, staged as an orgy — with explicit acts of intercourse and oral sex by five couples of the Voina collective, including Tolokonnikova and her husband. The scene is shot in a Moscow biology museum before a throng of photographers, videographers, and several costumed comic figures, on the eve of Dmitry Medvedev's 2008 election as Russian Federation president. "Puppy Bear" nicknames Medvedev, playing on the *bearish* character of his surname (*medvyed* = *bear*). The heir for whom Puppy Bear would perform this fuck, presumably, is the *president-in-waiting,* Vladimir Putin.

---

32. Ibid.

33. See "Young Girls Kissing Russian Female Police Officers," Daily Picks and Flicks, Mar. 2, 2011, n.p. [cited September 10 2016]. Online: http://bit.ly/14YWmqP.
See "Voina Fucks for the Heir Puppy Bear," Live Leak, , n.p. [cited September 10 2016]. Online: http://bit.ly/125icul.

34. See "Voina Fucks for the Heir Puppy Bear," Live Leak, , n.p. [cited September 10 2016]. Online: http://bit.ly/125icul.

35. "Garbage" is a pejorative Russian nickname for police — uttered with the same anti-cop inflection as the English word "pig."

For the liberal-minded in the Eurocentric World — Western Europe, the United States, and perhaps Latin America as well — the Pussy Riot cause was morally easy to champion, particularly since images of the Voina performances did not get much spin in the Western media. Instead, Pussy Riot was depicted in the liberal bandwidth as three playful and rebellious young women taking their feminist agency in hand, using art and effervescent youth to challenge a corrupt autocrat and his sexist pacts with the Russian Orthodox Church. The reality is not so squeaky clean. "How many fans of Pussy Riot's zany 'punk prayer' in the Cathedral of Christ the Savior and Nadezhda Tolokonnikova's erudite and moving closing statement were equally thrilled by her participation, naked and heavily pregnant, in a public orgy at a Moscow museum in 2008?" asked Russian journalist Vadim Nikitin. He noted an earlier performance in which Voina had set fire to several police cars, and another in which the collective drew an enormous image of a penis on a St. Petersburg drawbridge.[36] This is not polite liberal politics, but punk anarchism with an uncompromising edge.

PUSSY RIOT AS INDECENT THEOLOGY

Pussy Riot's anarchistic punk bears strong critical resemblance — in its theological interests and its slash-and-burn style — with Marcella's *indecenting* project, as a reading of Pussy Riot's performances against Marcella's deconstructive hermeneutics shows. Pussy Riot's methodology of trangressive social activism directly targets the co-optation of sacred Christian power by the profane hand of a corrupt state. In their songs, their interviews, and courtroom statements, the young women of Pussy Riot consistently challenge the marriage of the Russian Orthodox Church as an establishment not only of the

36. Vadim Nikitin, "The Wrong Reasons to Back Pussy Riot," *New York Times,* Aug. 30, 2012, , n.p. [cited September 10 2016]. http://nyti.ms/125B3lC.

Russian state, but of Vladimir Putin's personal hegemony. They charge the church with conferring a false sacrality of *decency* on the Putin regime, which has derailed Russia's post-Soviet transition toward democracy, targeting dissidence in the manner of the old Soviet state within which Putin once played a critical leading role. Readers of Marcella's work will recognize in Pussy Riot's activism an innate recourse to what she calls the hermeneutics of indecenting.

Their work carries a powerful and consistent line of attack on gender oppression, charging that the power grid of both Russian government and of the Orthodox church is thoroughly inscribed with patriarchalism. We saw Tolokonnikova in her police interrogation contest the idea that the altar should be reserved only for male priests.

When asked whether she took communion in church, she replied that "we have different traditions in my family,"[37] suggesting that it is within her own agency as a theological subject, as a woman — not the patriarch or the police — to decide how she should engage the sacraments. The band's images of biblical women are also more feminist — even if Pussy Riot still must implore the Mother of God to "become a feminist" and be "with us in protest" ("Virgin Mary: Put Putin Away"). In "Putin Got Scared," Pussy Riot chastises "The Orthodox religion of a hard penis," proclaiming that

> *Madonna to her glory will learn how to fight*
> *Feminist Magdalene go demonstrate …*

Pussy Riot also went on the theological offensive in a media spin war that ensued with the church hierarchy after their arrest. They fought the government's attempt to frame conservative Orthodox believers as the faith's authentic theological subjects — the punk band's true victims — as if Pussy Riot were some sort of allergen

---

37. Lerner and Pozdorovkin, *Pussy Riot: A Punk Prayer.*

hostile to the life of the church. Not only have the women of Pussy Riot insisted on their Christian motives, they have found powerful support within the church.

> A huge number of Orthodox people are standing up for us. They are praying for us outside the courtroom, for the members of Pussy Riot who are incarcerated. We've seen the little booklets Orthodox people are handing out with prayers for those in prison. This shows that there isn't a unified social group of Orthodox believers as the prosecution is endeavouring to say. No such thing exists. More and more believers are starting to defend Pussy Riot.[38]

More telling even than this public support was Nadia Tolokonnikova's closing statement in the trial, in which she drew from the deep spiritual and intellectual roots of Russian Christianity with remarkable authority and insight for a person in her early twenties. She adeptly calls out the theological hypocrisy of "the state's leaders [who] stand with saintly expressions in church, but their sins are far greater than ours." But Tolokonnikova's richest theological reflections arise as she connects the liberation of womens' agency from patriarchy with the revival of "horizontal" relationships in Russian society, relationships whose atrophy supports the anti-democratic authoritarianism of the Putin regime. She cited a fundamentally spiritual motive animating the band's music. "We were looking for authentic genuineness and simplicity and we found them in our punk performances. Passion, openness and naivety are superior to hypocrisy, cunning and a contrived decency that conceals crimes." She cites this playful naivete as the antithesis of Putinism, which uses police

38. Adam Taylor, "Here's What Russian Punk Band Pussy Riot Said At The Conclusion Of Their Controversial Blasphemy Trial," *Business Insider,* n.p. [cited August 10 2016]. Online: http://read.bi/13zCDBq.

power in place of deliberative political processes to arbitrate difference in Russian society.

> We are absolutely not happy with — and have been forced into living politically — by the use of coercive, strong-arm measures to handle social processes, a situation in which the most important political institutions are the disciplinary structures of the state — the security agencies, the army, the police, the special forces and the accompanying means of ensuring political stability: prisons, preventive detention and mechanisms to closely control public behavior. Nor are we happy with the enforced civic passivity of the bulk of the population or the complete domination of executive structures over the legislature and judiciary. Moreover, we are genuinely angered by the fear-based and scandalously low standard of political culture, which is constantly and knowingly maintained by the state system and its accomplices. Look at what Patriarch Kirill has to say: "The Orthodox don't go to rallies." We are angered by the appalling weakness of horizontal relationships within society. We don't like the way in which the state system easily manipulates public opinion through its tight control of the overwhelming majority of media outlets.[39]

In contrast to those forces — repressive state power, a passive civil culture, the Patriarch's indecenting of the democratic right of protest — Tolokonnikova proclaims her very Christian faith in the charismatic power of honest words and the deeds of a transparent love. As militant as the rhetoric is, the women of Pussy Riot were never charged with material violence — only with transgressing socially accepted ideological limits in their art. Their trial is marked by repeated expressions of apology to those who may have felt injured or insulted by the performance, alongside an insistence that Pussy

---

39. Ibid.

Riot was not targeting Orthodox Christianity itself, but the corruption of Orthodox Christianity as it becomes institutionally embedded in Russian state power.

IN CONCLUSION: DOES IT BREAK WITH THE *'SOCIETY OF THE SPECTACLE'?*

While it is clear enough that Pussy Riot practiced a transgressive form of indecenting on the symbols of Russian religious and state power, is it equally clear that this activism had effects in destabilizing this *kyriarchal* regime? Consideration of the second point — whether indecenting is effective as revolutionary politics — presents a mixed picture, though it is still instructive to consider. Nevertheless, I conclude that Pussy Riot accomplished two critical goals of revolutionary art:

1) Its performance mocked and repudiateed the homogenized aesthetic that abets the marketing of pop culture, frontally defying capitalist commodification of art; and

2) Pussy Riot openly criticized not only the effects of power in patriarchal capitalist society, but the hierarchized social relations and distorting ideologemes by which those effects are produced.

Unlike many commercial acts that wear radical politics on the sleeve, Pussy Riot took its politics well past the limits of official decency and orthodoxy, mocking the Putin regime right in the heart of its ideological *sanctum sanctorum* — the Cathedral of Christ the Savior in Moscow. Its work represents the sort of art that is highly resistant to assimilation into the society of the spectacle.

On the other hand, Pussy Riot's activism and subsequent court case inspired a series of actions, statements, and gestures of solidarity from other performers, as well as diplomatic maneuvering pitting the United States and a few countries in Western Europe against Russia. The public support from more renowned commercial artists — Madonna, the Red Hot Chili Peppers, and Sting, among many others — often allowed those artists to strike politically correct identifications with the outlaw Pussy Rioters. None of those artists are particularly known, however, for risking prison and censure for their art; their politics is often just an exercise in product branding, to aid in marketing their art to self-righteous liberal audiences. Their criticisms of Putin landed like a few flies harassing a backyard barbecue. In this sense, the induction of the Pussy Riot case into the international capitalist entertainment circuits, and the twenty-four-hour news cycle, presented the greatest risk for the co-optation of Pussy Riot's radical message. Nevertheless, in her closing statements, Nadia Tolokonnikova insisted that Pussy Riot had destabilized Putin's neoliberal Orthodox hegemony with their fit of transgressive anti-capitalist art.

> Even so, I can now state — despite the fact that we currently have an authoritarian political situation — that I am seeing this political system collapse to a certain extent when it comes to the three members of Pussy Riot, because what the system was counting on, unfortunately for that system, has not come to pass. Russia as a whole does not condemn us. Every day more and more people believe us and believe in us, and think we should be free rather than behind bars.[40]

One could very well judge Pussy Riot's success or failure on the hegemonic question by simply noting the fact that Vladimir Putin remains in power, while the women of Pussy Riot did time in prison. On the other hand, one could just as well determine that Pussy Riot succeeded wildly — training international attention on the political

---

40. Tolokonnikova's closing statement, cited in Taylor, "Here's What Russian Punk Band Pussy Riot Said."

crisis in Russia and gaining global recognition for their ideology. If commercial success was also an antithesis of their performances, then Pussy Riot triumphed on that front as well; their music is sampled as much for its political content as for its aesthetic, a judgment less frequently made of commercial pop music. While Pussy Riot failed to enlist the Virgin's help to "put Putin away," it did show the way to a transgressive new theo-politics for punk music — and anti-systemic politics in general. Though there is no evidence that the women of Pussy Riot had ever read of Marcella Althaus-Reid, one can wonder at the spirit of Indecent Theology that seemed to inhabit their performances.

References

Althaus-Reid. *Indecent Theology*. London: Routledge, 2001.

Althaus-Reid. "From Liberation Theology to Indecent Theology: The Trouble with Normality in Theology." Pages 20-38 in *Latin American Liberation Theology: The Next Generation*. Edites by Ivan Petrella. Maryknoll, NY: Orbis, 2005

Althaus-Reid. "On Queer Theology and Liberation Theology: The Irruption of the Sexual Subject in Theology." Pages 83-96 in *Homosexualities*. Edited by Marcella Althaus-Reid, Regina Ammicht Quinn, Erik Borgman and Norbert Reck. London: SCM Press, 2008.

Althaus-Reid. "From Liberation Theology to Indecent Theology," No pages. Cited September 10 2016. Online: http://read.bi/13zCDBq.

Butler, Judith. *The Psychic Life of Power: Theories in Subjection*. Redwood City, CA: Stanford University Press, 1995.

Butler, Judith. *Excitable Speech: A Politics of the Performative*. Redwood City, CA: Stanford University Press, 1997.

Freud, Sigmund. *The Standard Edition of the Complete Psychological Works of Sigmund Freud*. Vol.14. Edited by James Strachey, Anna Freud, Carrie Lee Rothgeb and Angela Richards. London: Hogarth Press, 1953–1974.

Debord, Guy. *The Society of the Spectacle*. New York, NY: Zone Books, 1994.

Lerner, Mike and Pozdorovkin, Maxim. dir., *Pussy Riot: A Punk Prayer* (United Kingdom: Roast Beef Productions, 2013), digital video disk.

Nikitin, Vadim. "The Wrong Reasons to Back Pussy Riot." No Pages. Cited September 10 2016. Online: http://nyti.ms/125B3lC.

Taylor Adam, "Here's What Russian Punk Band Pussy Riot Said At The Conclusion of Their Controversial Blasphemy Trial." No pages. Cited September 10 2016. Online: http://read.bi/13zCDBq.

"Putin: Using Al-Qaeda in Syria like sending Gitmo inmates to fight." *Russia Today News*. No pages. Cited September 6 2012. Online: http://bit ly/18BLVPy.

PART II

EPISTEMOLOGICAL
FRAMEWORKS

SEXUAL DISSIDENCE, FAITH, AND RELEASE IN MARCELLA ALTHAUS-REID

GABRIELA GONZÁLEZ ORTUÑO

I.

Although the Latin American Liberation Theology is a commendable theoretical and practical effort, it is worth asking about its limitations. Would liberation be possible through work with the poor? Would an individual liberated economically also be considered liberated spiritually and bodily? What are the terms by which Liberation Theology measures/defines sin? What is the relationship among different genders such asmale/female/trans/degenerated[1])? What are the sexual parameters considered as correct in a society that seeks to "come closer to the kingdom of God on Earth"?

---

1. Although degenerate is considered an insult, I make a pun with the intention to refer to dissidents' gender, those who refuse to follow the guidelines of the binomial man-woman, who refuse to be defined as men and women through the appropriation of a word which in principle is pejorative. This is clearest in Spanish.

Of course, the first theology of liberation does not answer any of these questions. Even prestigious liberation theologians such as Enrique Dussel have very conservative attitudes towards homosexuality. Franz Hinkelammert may be, perhaps, the first liberation theologian who takes into account the issue of the relationship or spiritual/body liberation, although in a purely economic sense.

Despite the aforementioned, Liberation Theology was nurtured by the participation of non-Roman Catholic Christians, indigenous communities, women and homosexuals. Women — whose theological studies were slanted and whose meetings came to be held in basements — began to question the homosolidarity both within Liberation Theology as well as within the Base Communities, which by the end of 1980s began to blur:

> "The poor were ... constructed in an asexual theology and Liberation Theology. Women filled the requirement of the model of Maria machine. ... Her model of poor women excluded our transgressions, our vocations and our struggles to become what we wanted to be: poor women, but intellectuals active in theological practice, informed by studies and serious reflections."[2]

The themes of the reflexion in the Latin American theology of liberation began to change[3] and women in the biblical interpretations submitted to other viewpoints the possibilities of gender relations. The poor women became a talking point; they themselves were invisibles. The encounter between female theologians and feminists did not occur immediately in the Latin American theology of liberation due to prejudices on both sides. Disagreements and prejudices

---

2. Althaus-Reid, *La teología indecente. Perversiones teológicas en sexo, género y política* (Barcelona, Spain: Bella Tierra, 2005), 5.

3. Elsa Tamez, "Hermenéutica feminista latinoamericana, una mirada retrospectiva," in Marcos, Silvia, ed, Religión y género: Enciclopedia iberoamericana de las religiones (Madrid, Spain: Trotta, 2012), 43-66.

faced members of a patriarchal church against radical positions of feminism. According to Elsa Tamez, it was in the 1980s when they began to read and seek dialogue with feminism. The language among Latin American female theologians changed; they began to use feminist concepts, but it does not change the gender relations within the religious hierarchies.

We can observe a shift towards the late 1990s and the early twentiy-first century: female theologians engaged in ecofeminism and, thus, in many emerging popular struggles as neo-zapatism or the defense of natural resources. Female theologians and religious women spoke out against the few spaces of female leadership within Christian churches. Vatican authorities threatened some Roman Catholic religious women such as those belonging to Leadership Conference of Women Religious who had spoken in favor of the ordination of women or contraception. Women such as the Catalan nun Teresa Forcades had been attacked by conservative and radical left sectors since being enlisted in the fight against major pharmaceutical companies. For the political right, this irritates economic interests; for the radical left, it is a perverse influence of the Roman Catholic Church and its political interests and, therefore, in secular affairs.

It is noteworthy that the feminist Liberation Theology seeks to change the attitudes of the Roman Catholic hierarchy and of other Christian groups. However, this was not enough for some theologians self-declared as queer. Social homophobia is still a flag hoisted by the religious hierarchies from the idea of the body as a source of sin and sex as deviation of purity.

The theologians who call themselves queer not only have different sexual preferences; that is, they do not strictly adhere to a pattern to become a normalized gay or lesbian, but they are also sexual and gender dissidents. Marcella Althaus-Reid is the Latin American queer theologian in whose work we are most interested. Her work stands out from other theologians' by breaking away with the initial Liberation Theology and with feminist theologies. Her theological categories were developed from the liberationist method: look at, think and act since her reality. However, they go beyond that because for Althaus-Reid, "without sexual constructs there is no Other."[4] This is a knowledge located from the establishment of corporeal and sexual relations with the Other. From this place, we can transform social structures, not only churches and ways to exercise faith. In this way, the theological guidelines would shape "a sexual and political praxis … They shape epistemologies, visions of life and mystical projections linking the human and the sacred."[5] That is why for Althaus-Reid, it is better to speak from heterotopic places to which she arrives through perverted paths; that is, different ways, twisted, that challenge the sexual and social patterns of behavior established from the theological.

Her queer theology is extremely sensual, and her examples moved from the smell of lemons of the Bolivian saleswomen to the bodies in a salsa bar. They also range from a sado-masochist theologian to a gay elder Argentinean whose only partner [compañero] is Christ. This search for theological explanations bring us closer to the idea of a queer God; that is, a God which does not reflect the dominant male in the work of most theologians. Althaus-Reid struggles for a transvestite God, de-generate, neither sexist nor machista. Her proposal helps us to search at the margins for the seed resistance based on inter-gender and intersex relationships.

Thus, it is impossible to deny the body and its desires in religious practices when it is possible to see it in ceremonies, when speaking

---

4. Althaus-Reid, 31.

5. Ibid., 15.

of a virgin giving birth, a three-some God, or a Jesus of ambiguous sexuality who calls us love without limits. We can think of God as a power that is neither male nor female but queer; as a power that seizes every possibility of gender and degenerate.

Queer theology is based on a faith in Christ for heterosexuals, gays, lesbians, transsexuals, and the like, who " ... do not need to be exclusive but located in the space-time of the experience of a community."[6] This implies that the constructions of liberation are revealed before the limits of sexual carnal sins to demand love practices without borders. Finally, there is no mention of homosexuals or lesbians or gays or transgender persons in the New Testament. What for some may be a form of dismissal, ignore the fact that by not mentioning them, there is no condemnation either. The straight man is always subject to that. Therefore, the proposal of Althaus-Reid seek attend to what she called the radical principles of the Bible to encompass the Others: justice, peace, love, and solidarity, which, of course, have to be illuminated and redefined by the community.

Marcella Althaus-Reid, from the generation of her localized, critical, and decolonizing knowledge, was capable of destabilize the dominant hetero-patriarchal order that has built the modern/liberal/ capitalist model. Her philosophical thought is decentered, challenging the structures of rigid academic knowledge creation from a socio-sensual and sexual exploration. An heir of Liberation Theology — especially for her method — she also represents a breaking point with its homosolidarity tradition. She was also critical of feminist Liberation Theology, which she considered insufficient for sexual dissidents and for those who refuse to fit into rigid gender and sexual roles. Althaus-Reid challenges the parameters of sin and liberation,

---

6. Ibid., 267.

which for her are not located in sexual behaviors and parameters of normality, but the harm to others.

In order to approach to Althaus-Reid thought, I propose an exercise. The Gospel of Luke narrates:

> Do not go from house to house. Whenever you enter a town and are welcomed, eat what is set before you, heal the sick and say to his people: The Kingdom of God has come to you. But if you enter a town and they do not want to receive you, go into its streets and say, We tossed and left them in the dust of your town that clings to our feet. However, know it well: the Kingdom of God has come to you. I assure you that in the day of the trial, Sodom would be treated with less rigor than this city.[7]

The hermeneutic exercise from a conventional viewpoint would stop in the idea of the sole condemnation of those who reject Christ. A perverted interpretation would widen the spectrum of interpretation and would situate us in a non-conventional place; that is, from the interpretation departing from reality, from diversity of positions and lives.

Non-Christians may have more elements to be condemned than the sodomites may; sodomites did not deny Christ and there is no evidence of their hatred for others in the New Testament.

- Everyone who accepts Christ has the opportunity to enter the kingdom of God, regardless of gender or sexual practice.

- Goodness is rewarded; whoever is outside the kingdom of God is so because their lack of attention to the neighbor.

- Sexual freedom is not a sin. The sin is the lack of solidarity or ingratitude.

---

7. Luke 10:8–12, Latin American Roman Catholic Bible.

From an Althausian perspective, we could affirm that these are the options of interpretations for marginalization practices against the different. The inability to love the neighbor, that is, the construction of borders of inclusion/exclusion, is reprehensible, not the sexual practices considered outside the norm.

From perversions, or different versions, Althaus-Reid proposes to interpret beyond all traditional patterns that may lead us to maintain a blatant condemnation. The verdict would divert us from the principal Law: love your neighbor as one self.[8]

We can think of Jesus in the Gospel of Luke as someone who decided to be an outcast, outside the criteria of normality, but also from a perspective where sexual preferences are neither necessary criteria for the condemnation for anyone nor the determinant for salvation. In the Gospel we find also the answer given by Jesus to those who asked with which husband would a resurrected woman be, who had been married to seven siblings. The answer could be considered from the point of view of asexuality: none of them will take a wife or husband (Lk:20–35). From the viewpoint of Althaus-Reid, we could think about resurrected bodies who love each other beyond the limits of hetero-patriarchal standard.[9] After experimenting with the perverted hermeneutics of affection, sensuality, sexuality, and exclusion — that is, from our multiple Latin American realities — we find unsuspected ways of forming knowledge of corporeal and social liberation. The commitment to radical love as hermeneutic method and politic lib-

---

8. Franz Hinkelammert talks about the split between the mandate of love and the binomial law-sin in his work *Las armas ideológicas de la muerte* (Salamanca, Spain: Ediciones Sígueme, 1978) as two different forms of morality. While the first way results in life and resurrection, the second way — the law — would result in death.

9. In *Las armas ideológicas de la muerte*, after reading Paul, Hinkelammert states that bodies will resurrect with all their sensuality. Although he does not offer direct reference to the sexual, Hinkelammert affirms that bodies are resurrected with their needs. That is, his position is in favor of bodies, their needs and pleasures.

eration is what is considered eccentric, queer as Althaus-Reid called it.[10]

Althaus-Reid is a bucket of cold water. She was a disruptive thinker: Marx in a gay bar may shock many leftist thinkers; however, his thought shines in all those corners that critical thinking has obscured through patriarchal and westernized knowledge production. Although she was a philosopher of situated knowledge, who refers to specific problems, she did not anchor on particularism. Althaus-Reid helps us to see the interwoven relationships among class, sexuality, race, gender, and geographic location. It is a crossroads where we can position ourselves in order to understand the subjective constructions of a structural overview. Her vision of communities of exclusion — beyond the image of the poor to be liberated by the first Liberation Theology — denotes the various systems of power and support that cradle the current order for its reproduction. Queerness in her work does not simply adhere to the standardized homosexuality of the capitalist system.[11] Althaus-Reid appeals to the marginal, to the

---

10. There is a strong discussion about using the term "queer" in Latin America. On the one hand, for some it is a term that should be appropriated — such in the latinization cuir — in an effort towards decolonization (Viteri Maria Amelia, Serrano José Fernando and Vidal-Ortiz Salvador, "¿Cómo se piensa lo 'queer' en América Latina? Presentación del dossier," Iconos, 39 (2011): 47-60). On the other hand, feminism calls for more thoroughness in talking about gays and lesbians because they were labeled "queer". Queer also is considered as neoyorquism (Richard, Nelly, "Postfacio / Deseos de ... ¿Qué es un territorio de intervención política?," Revista Archivos de filosofía, 6 (2011): 465-481). There are also perspectives from other movements — such as the indigenous movement — which strongly criticized the coloniality of concept of queerness (ZäNä, Nxu, "Contra la teoría queer (Desde una perspectiva indígena)," n.p. [cited October 2 2016], Online: http://www.ciudaddemujeres.com/articulos/Contra-la-teoria-Queer). For more of this debate see González Ortuño, "Teorías de la disidencia sexual: de contextos populares a usos elitistas. La teoría queer en América latina frente a las y los pensadores de disidencia sexi genérica," Raíz diversa. Revista especializada en estudios latinoamericanos, 3:5 (2015): 179-200

11. Some authors such as Luis Martínez Andrade ("El enano en pelotas. Notas sobre la teología indecente," Revista Metapolítica, 73 (2011); 95-100) and Martín Cremonte ("Objeciones a la teología indecente de M. Althaus Reid & P. Moles," El títere y el enano, 1:1 (2010): 230-254) emphasize that one of the main weaknesses of the

eccentric, to what is alternative as another way of understanding the world.

II.

Now I would like to ask: Where does Althaus-Reid thought stand within postcolonial thought in Latin America?

I respond based on the idea of thinking the Christian communities that are built from the area of non-being; I mean from the marginalized Latin American communities, from the gender, race and sexual dissidents excluded. For this, we will compare the work of Althaus-Reid with the decolonial thinker Ramón Grosfoguel.

Ramón Grosfoguel[12] rescues the thought of Franz Fanon and builds a matrix where the exclusions are given from hierarchical markers based on the parameters of the Western viewpoint. These markers are constructed from the European arrival to the colonies, inhabited by those whose humanity has to be questioned, who are not considered human beings, and who reside in the zone of the unprivileged.

---

intellectual work of Althaus-Reid is not perceiving the issue of class struggle as central. Thus, she falls into the trap of using the concepts of identity and difference that can be "absorbed by the system." From my point of view, although Althaus-Reid has the central focus in the formation of the marginal from the standpoint of sexual diversity, she thinks from the intersection with other forms of oppression such as race, class and gender as a complex structure. This allows her — and allows us — to extend the landscape and see the devices of standardization and disciplining. Therefore, these two are operating from the current order. Furthermore, it also allows us also think of ways of organization that do not exclusively focus on the fight against economic oppression. The critiques of Althaus-Reid are related to the subjective ways by which we build knowledge. However, the construction of knowledge that incorporates experience, affection and faith is a challenge to the ways centered in the mind as only source of knowledge. It is a trap to assume that in practical and political theories there are no affective components or that they can be put aside.

12. Grosfoguel, Ramón, "La descolonización del conocimiento: diálogo crítico entre la vision decolonial de Franz Fanon y la sociología decolonial de Boaventura de Sousa Santos, disponible en CIDOB," n.p. [cited September 10 2016]. Online: http://www.cidob.org/es/content/downnload/29942/356572/file/97-108_Ramon+Grosfo

Colonies could be placed in the area of non-being. Grosfoguel refers to the exclusions regarding the wellness zone and describes the current order as a capitalist/patriarchal/Euro-centric/Christian-centric system. His main proposal is to think decoloniality through the construction of a cartography of exclusions.

However, the first disagreement with Grosfoguel lies in his idea of Christianity, since from its North American perspective it is clear that Muslims are marginalized. However, he does not stop at the faith of thousands of undocumented Roman Catholics, for instance. I argue that there is no single way of being Christian, as pointed by the Althausian Indecent Theology. Grosfoguel does not consider the danger of being Christian in territories such as Syria, where they currently face persecution. Therefore, he falls into the same error that he reviews: his view is focused on a vision of Westernized Christianity and on the privileges that this entails for some groups. From my point of view, it is possible to speak of Christianity in the area of nonbeing: persecuted Christians, the poor, homosexuals, and women, among many more. They do not adhere to the conformations of being modern/western/capitalist/hetero-patriarchal and that which is not counted into the matrix, although it is problematized.

It is impossible to regard Christianity as a unified and coherent entity. In this sense, it would be possible to talk about ways to be a Christian from outside the zones of privilege that Grosfoguel enumerates.[13] In spite of this, if we follow and expand his interpretation, we can affirm that there is no single way of living the Christian faith. On the one hand, some are in the zone of being, privileged, allied with right-wing groups that seek to maintain the existing order. On the other hand, there are other Christians who are in the zone of non-being, who have lived a syncretic process with African beliefs,

---

13. Ibid.

or other native peoples who adhere to their religious and political practices. For example, the Zapatista circles have churches. In other words, there are Christian groups who have joined political and social popular movements and who act against marginalization. On the contrary, Christians in the zone of being have adhered to the lifestyles of exploitation and hierarchy.

The Grosfoguelian matrix can help us locate the thought of Althaus-Reid because, although the former only enunciates the various borders of privilege and marginalization, the latter problematizes them. In addition, Althaus-Reid is able to analyze the logics of resistance of marginal communities in order to open the panorama of different ways of being in the marginal realm for the sake of modifying the current system. Like other decolonial thinkers, she maintains a proposed coexistence in equality more elaborated than that only framed within class differences.

As heir liberation theologians in Latin America, who theorized from the material conditions of life, Althaus-Reid does not work exclusively with poor communities in the area of non-being. Strictly speaking, her work is not confined to just denouncing either economic exploitation or the organization of peripheral dependence. On the contrary, Althaus-Reid developed her thoughts from her experience as part of the Base Communities. Her theology defied the model of homosolidarity from Liberation Theology and questions about a God in favor of sexual dissidents. From anticolonial and anti-patriarchal viewpoints, she proposes a radical love, a love without borders. That love goes beyond the liberation of the poor, which requires not only the liberation of souls but also of bodies and their sexualities. Althaus-Reid struggles to break the yokes imposed by narrow gender-role expectations. She shows that theological constructions entail the emergence of life patterns that generate both a sexual and political order. Althaus-Reid continues the feminist tradition of thinking that the private is also political. This amounts to saying that the area of non-being not only constitutes the border of privileges but also its own threat. This is not a matter of mass absolutely subjugated but rather of spaces where various relationships are created.

We can pause here to emphasize the dispute that has existed in Christianity regarding the use of bodies related to the concepts of love. First, the idea of love for God expressed from the resignation of the bodily pleasures in the earth — the limits of sin according to Saint Augustine, according to the idea of carnal impurity. Secondly, love of community belonging that is expressed in the struggles of resistance and emancipation that were considered heretic. Lastly, the love of God expressed in love for others through sexuality and gender dissidence.

In other words, inside Christianity, the construction of social and sexual diversity is not easy. This, coupled with the modern colonial order, has built Christian churches founded in hatred of the body, pleasure, and the Other, the different. From this Eurocentric view is hidden gender, sexual, spiritual, and political diversity. The Others were confining the area of non-being.

Althaus-Reid's anticolonialism denounces not just the conquest of territory and invention of a continent, she also denounces the of pain of the injuries committed against colonized women. This damage was ignored, for the men colonized were benefited by the patriarchal pact. The men colonized also maintain the subjugation of the difference as a means to build their own privileges. Althaus-Reid affirms that women colonized were reduced to sex objects. The settlers not only exploited the body for work but also for the control of gender and sexual norms. In this sense, her critiques converge with those of prominent Black decolonial feminist thinkers such as Ochy Curiel and Yuderkys Espinosa. They also delve into the idea of friendship and limitless love, without the restrictions of the hetero-patriarchal order. The female body and sexual alternatives become — within the colonial order — subsumed into dissident marginal suffering; thus female sexuality is placed in the non-being of the non-being. In these cases, sexual dissidents are denied even their faith. However, it is important to clarify that the faith denied is that one built by the colonizers. The faith of sexual dissidents remains alive in their daily lives and in popular religious practices. Althaus-Reid shows us that through popular religiosity, characters such as Santa Librada become a vehicle in which the poor accept and play with different sexual identities, with which they cohabit daily. Althaus-Reid makes us think clearly the coexistence of difference flowing in everyday *barrios* [neighborhoods]. In this sense, we even remember the character of Manuela in the writer José Donoso's novel, *The Place without Limits.* rmon[14] Manuela was a transvestite prostitute who attended mass every Sunday and was estimated by many people of town. The example of Manuela shows that the sexual preference or the construction of gender do not preclude the existence of faith.

Faith is a complex issue, one of many ways to build human beings. However — despite its apparent intimacy — faith is also able to act as a political articulation. In this way it is possible to detect subjectivities formed by seemingly contradictory elements such as Christian katarist indianists, Roman Catholic feminists, Christian prostitutes from Brazil, or queer movements devoted to Saint Sebastian, among many others. These movements are immersed within various struggles for sexual identity, the right to work, or their care for Mother Earth. In this respect, Althaus-Reid is the decolonial thinker who

---

14. José Donoso and Hugo Achugar, *El lugar sin límites. El obsceno pájaro de la noche* (Caracas, Venezuela: Fundacion Biblioteca Ayacuch, 1990).

does not despise or neglect faith. On the contrary, she leads us to rethink and to gauge its weight in regards to the construction of the order and the resistance to it.

In this respect, Althaus-Reid shows us that we should not deceive ourselves, as the colonizers are caught in their own trap. To marginalize the others is a form of restraint. The colonizers renounce to their desires for political power. The colonizers build dogmas of faith, which are the dogmas of performance, and build oppressed subjectivities — theirs as the first ones. These subjectivities are controlled from the structures of corporeal domination (the clinic), moral domination (the Roman Catholic Church), and legal domination (the stripping asset and wages). This confirms the capitalist hetero-patriarchal domination.

For Althaus-Reid, the patriarchal theology and its practices of homosolidarity are tools intimately linked with colonialism which are breed among many liberationists. For her, the decolonial problem is that it seems to indicate that the offense resides in a question of authority and not in a question of corporal damage or sexual violence. Native American men were diminished in their authority while the sexual abuse against women was obviated. These are never the focus of discussion by liberation theologians. Thus Althaus-Reid asserts, "What the European other obtained did not came only from exploitation of capital, but also by sexual arrangements."[15] Such agreements can be seen as patterns of behavior — of social order — in which women and their sexuality and their decisions appear only in last place. The conformation of sexualities impacts on the conformation of gender roles and in the processes subjetivizition, which in turn affect the social processes of hierarchization.

15. Althaus-Reid, *La teologia indecente*, 32.

The theological and philosophical thought of Althaus-Reid is developed not only through the scholarly study of Christianity or of Liberation Theology. It also refers to third-wave feminism and advocates for a theology of difference.

The development of theological knowledge — for her — occurs through experience and corporeal sensations as well as through sexual behaviors and the way faith is expressed as resistance to the modern capitalist-liberal system. That is why the emphasis on popular religiosity is essential to queer theology. Therefore, the popular piety of devotees to Santa Librada of the Deceased Correa offers us examples of instincts, knowledge, and corporeal experiences that the believers live about the sacred. It is a way to remove the hetero-patriarchal dogma through icons that have marginal characteristics for Christian churches: a female Christ woman and a deceased female saint with her breasts exposed:

All speech about religious and political authority hides knowledge repressed and exiled, left in marginal and indirect clues. It is a knowing that people dictate through counter religious and political symbols as well as methodological contradictions of the official versions ... they operate as scattered resistances that cannot be located neither in any future nor past utopia (theology).[16]

This is about the immeasurable excesses that the official devices of moral, economic, and politico discipline cannot grasp. These are the signs of faith that church institutions cannot comprehend. Facing the great theological and patriarchal canonical discourses, micro rhizomatic popular discourses resist and challenge the boundaries of class, race, and gender. The great rationality is cracked against the intuition of the difference and the sexual experience in the *barrios* [neighborhoods]. Althaus-Reid states, " ... the popular theology is

---

16. Ibid., 35.

pragmatic and materialistic, and close dealings with God on matters of survival in everyday life."[17]

This teaches us that it is not necessary to love God in one exclusive way, as there is no single form of exercise sexuality, as purity contradicts the natural.

The greatest legacy of Althaus-Reid is her eccentricity. We must learn from her ability to analyze beyond the apparent limits of exclusion. We must understand that idolatry to a dominant *macho* God erects an unjust system. She taught us that God might think differently — in a rhizomatic way — without limits for love. The love of our differences is where you can find the conditions to break the domination and or competition; knocking down them is the first step to change the current order.

What we face is a denunciation of the laceration of both the intellect and the body of poor women, of sexual diversity. However, we also have an exit from that situation: a liberation based on the rupture of narratives of class, gender, and sexual preference. It is not enough to worry about the food for the oppressed as the material is equally important to the construction of subjectivities. Therefore, to talk about a promiscuity of strategies in liberation struggles is not irrational. In the face of suffering and contemplation, we have the option of solidarity, contact, and sensuality:

the intimacy with others is of divine nature and — by far — the most divine commandment. The craving for proximity with others does not need to be sexual, but is closely linked to sexuality.[18]

Finally, strategies of resistance and struggle — the heterotopic places — are built from the corporeal and inter-subjective proximity. These are the key pieces to changing social relations based on

17. Ibid., 35.
18. Ibid., 135.

hierarchies that used the idea of sin to build places of privilege. The care, solidarity, reciprocity, and love are the basis to transform the order. These strategies bring us close to lovers and friends, make a community. The communities arise from the bodies, their needs and pleasures. This is the Marcella Althaus-Reid teaching.

References

Althaus-Reid, Marcella. *La teología indecente: Perversiones teológicas en sexo, género y política*. Barcelona, Spain: Bella Tierra, 2005.

Andrade, Luis Martínez Andrade. "El enano en pelotas. Notas sobre la teología indecente." *Revista Metapolítica*. 73 (2011): 95-100.

Cremonte, Martín. "Objeciones a la teología indecente de M. Althaus Reid & P. Moles." *El títere y el enano*.1:1 (2010): 230-254.

Donoso, José and Achugar, Hugo. *El lugar sin límites, El obsceno pájaro de la noche*. Caracas, Venezuela: Fundacion Biblioteca Ayacuch, 1990.

Hinkelammert, Franz. *Las armas ideológicas de la muerte*. Salamanca, Spain: Ediciones Sígueme, 1978.

González Ortuño, Gabriela. "Teorías de la disidencia sexual: de contextos populares a usos elitistas. La teoría queer en América latina frente a las y los pensadores de disidencia sexi genérica." *Raíz diversa* 3:5 (2015): 179-200.

Grosfoguel, Ramón. "La descolonización del conocimiento: diálogo crítico entre la vision decolonial de Franz Fanon y la sociología decolonial de Boaventura de Sousa Santos, disponible en CIDOB." No Pages. Cited September 10 2016. Online: http://www.cidob.org/es/content/downnload/29942/356572/file/97-108_Ramon+Grosfo

Richard, Nelly. "Postfacio / Deseos de ... ¿Qué es un territorio de intervención política?." *Revista Archivos de filosofía*. 6 (2011): 465-481.

Tamez, Elsa. "Hermenéutica feminista latinoamericana, una mirada retrospectiva." Pages 43-66 in *Religión y género: Enciclopedia iberoamericana de las religiones*. Edited by Silvia Marcos. Madrid, Spain: Trotta, 2012.

Viteri Maria Amelia, Serrano José Fernando and Vidal-Ortiz Salvador. "¿Cómo se piensa lo 'queer' en América Latina?" *Iconos*. 39 (2011): 47-60.

ZäNä, Nxu. "Contra la teoría queer (Desde una perspectiva indígena)." No Pages. Cited October 2 2016. Online: http://www.ciudaddemujeres.com/articulos/Contra-la-teoria-Queer).

PER-VERTING THE FOUNDATIONS

Epistemological and Methodological Challenges to the "Corporeality" of Latin American Liberation Theologies

NICOLÁS PANOTTO

In this chapter, I analyze some topics related to epistemology from the standpoint of Latin American Liberation Theology (hereinafter cited as TLL for its acronym in Spanish) and its various expressions in the continent. In the reasoning — as the title indicates — I address the term *corporeality* in two ways. On the one hand, I refer to the corporeality of the *theological subject*, which is not only that of the theologian but mainly the epicenter from which emerges the construction of the theological task for TLL. That epicenter is the place of the poor, which is precisely one of the most important contributions of this theological movement. Furthermore, it represents the historic location of a subjectivity, a context, and a specific locus which always cross and demarcate the constitution of the discourse on the divine.

On the other hand, I also refer to the *corporeality* of the theological as materiality, that is, in its ontological constitution. Again, as raised by TLL, historical contingency, power dynamics, hegemonic discourses, and social processes represent the constitutive "body" of any theological discourse. Moreover, this represents — as it has already been by TLL — a critique of the religious frameworks presented in an ahistorical way. Said silence legitimizes these religious frameworks' contingency and the power mechanisms — unaware at times — to which they respond.

Marcella Althaus-Reid radicalized these approaches in her work, to the point of demonstrating that TLL — at times — ends up falling into the trap that it denounces. Why? Because the meanings and definitions of history, subject, body, liberation, and the like, are also mediated from a specific *locus*. As we shall see in this case, that *locus* sets aside central themes such as sexuality, plurality of identities, heterogenous speeches, and faith experiences, among others. Basically, these elements have not altered various orthodoxies and traditions imprinted in Christianity, those preventing from taking the proposed criticism of the TLL to its last consequences.

Meanwhile, Marcella dares to examine the foundations. She touches those private parts of Latin American theology that are hidden due to modesty, despite the fact that they are as real as our bodies. The way she achieves this goal is by *perverting* those foundations through *indecency*. It is a provocation that allows us to open our eyes to a sincere coherence and radical stance departing from what TLL has historically proposed.

In this work I examine Althaus-Reid's deconstruction of the epistemological assumptions of TLL. From there, I rethink the known model "see, judge, act" proposed by this theological current from new contemporary approaches — especially from poststructuralist, postcolonial, and decolonial perspectives. Lastly, I re-read a particular case within TLL, namely, the work of Uruguayan theologian Juan Luis Segundo, as an example of how the new epistemological framework proposed by Althaus-Reid may be applied.

PER-VERTING THE EPISTEMOLOGICAL
FOUNDATIONS OF TLL

One of the main contributions of TLL was to present a new method of doing theology, which Gustavo Gutierrez summed up in his famous definition of theology as critical praxis. This simple statement brings to the table a number of core elements: first, that every theology is a response to a given context; second, that there is always a particular subject that makes that theology and is the *locus* of its work, in the case of TLL is the poor; and thirdly, that the biblical-theological tradition is built upon a combination of the types of relationships constantly developing between these elements. Finally, in order to understand and analyze these relationships, along with their dynamic, characterization and tensions, a framework of interpretation is required. In other words, it refers to the hermeneutic aspect, which is not an element but the methodological framework that fuses and gives "meaning" to these processes. In summary, every theology is embodied in a context and responds to a particular intentionality; it is biased in its subjective constitution, and it is relative as an answer to the interpretative particularities to which responds.

One of the theologians who has greatly worked on the subject was Clodovis Boff.[1] In his voluminous work of *Teología de lo político* [political theology], he embarks in a detailed work where he proposes a methodology and epistemology from a deep dialogue with Althusserian theory. Although it is impossible to extensively analyze his proposal, I will simply highlight some of his "intuitions" that are the foundation of his proposal in order to further the discussion with Marcella Althaus-Reid.

---

1. Clodovis Boff, *Teología de lo politico: Sus mediaciones* (Salamanca, Spain: Sígueme, 1982).

On the one hand, Boff's work — at least at that stage of his production — was based on a rational understanding of the epistemological. He departs from the following preoccupation: liberation theologians were not concerned with "rational justifications for their intuitions."[2] Therefore, he urged the existence of a "theoretical imperative" that should lead to build a "disciplined theology."

Hence, he explores the famous epistemological trio that has characterized TLL: to see, to judge, and to act. *To see* is the object of theology, which implies embodying and discerning the processes of time and history. That is part of a strictly political commitment involving the social sciences as a framework to read those experiences and contexts. Then, *to judge* as the hermeneutic operation where theology appropriates such reading and responds from the standpoint of the Christian tradition and the biblical witness. Last — but not least — *to act*. This represents the praxis as reflection and as a simultaneous political and theological *locus*. In conclusion, Boff discusses the epistemological criticism from two central propositions that must be present as hermeneutical poles where these processes are played: the "controversive reason" (critical and analytical agency) and the "architectural reason" (praxis and liberation).

Marcella Althaus-Reid states that she has a relationship between continuity with and disruption to TL, especially at its epistemological foundations. As already mentioned, one of her greatest contributions is to show the corporeality and sexuality as axiological epicenter. It is from this epicentre that she deconstructs socio-anthropological meanings, modes of sociability, redefinitions of subjects and identities, and the various dynamics emerging in the fields of economical, political, socio-cultural and theological task. Assuming all that as

2. Ibid., 17.

foundational, she questions these propositions of TLL, as I further analyze below.

Postfoundational Critique of Social Heteronormativity

Althaus-Reid poses heteronormativity as a closed understanding, orderly and restrictive of the social. Thus, she understands heteronormativity as the evocation of modern, colonial, and Western dualisms that remove the fields of experience, meaning and practices. This context anchors the construction of metanarratives onto various areas of life, which require clipping reality for its legitimacy. Heteronormativity is a set of ideological concepts, narrative and sociocultural constructions of bodily practices that attempt to curtail diversity, difference, and distinctiveness. "Homogeneity" — one of the most important adjectivizations of heteronormativity — involves silencing while imposing normativities. Hence, Althaus-Reid contested two central elements that influenced this heteronormativity in Christianity: the modern concept of linear time and the idea of the Western subject as the basis of social dynamics.

Here lies one of the most important concepts in the work of Althaus-Reid: the meaning of obscenity as excluded, as the imprinted excess in reality. Obscenity becomes methodology to discover per-versions:

> Per-version is nothing more than a name for a different interpretation, more rooted in reality than those representations and parodies of life of the people who seem drawn vignettes of colonial texts.[3]

The obscene, then, represents the complex process that permeates both social constructions as well as the constitution of the corporeality of subjects. That obscenity — what is different, excluded, and out of place — challenges the sense of order and normativity.

---

3. Althaus-Reid, *La teología indecente* (Barcelona, Spain: Bellaterra, 2005), 171.

This could be linked with the idea of the *ontological excess of the socio-political constructs*, an idea that has deeply influenced contemporary currents of philosophical and social analysis. Thus, this raises two elements. First, no socio-cultural construction can be sutured and complete in itself. There is always an "excess" of meaning or, from a Lacanian perspective, the possibility of symbolization of the Real beyond the reality as already constituted.[4] The context is never sutured — even less its possible ways of being. This excess is sometimes occluded by the provisions — heteronormativity in this case. It is in the naming of the "obscene" — as stated by Althaus-Reid — where what is evident is not only the forbidden, understood by the author as the dynamics of counter-power and resistance, but also the distinctive, the different, which enable the context to recognize the plural and the heterogeneous as they are.[5]

Second, the idea of excess repositions the notion of the subject. Alain Badiou has extensively worked this topic in detail. For Badiou, the concept of excess reconfigures the subject as a force figure. This is where Lacan and his definition of the Real as the symbolic excess comes into play, as aforementioned. Badiou recognizes the idea of torque as that which breaks replication, as well as the place where the "circularity without unity " reside as truthfulness. As Lacan asserts: "The subject is in internal exclusion of its object." From this perspective, the subject becomes throughout that which is lost, in mutilated truth of its representation. "Every subject is at the junction

4. Yannis Stavrakakis, *Lacan y lo politico.* (Buenos Aires, Argentina: Prometeo, 2007).

5. Ernesto Laclau, *Nuevas reflexiones sobre la revolución en nuestro tiempo* (Buenos Aires, Argentina: Nueva Visión, 2000); Jorge Alemán, *Soledad: Común. Políticas en Lacan* (Buenos Aires, Argentina: Capital Intelectual, 2012); Oliver Marchart, *Post-Foundational Political Thought: Political Difference in Nancy, Lefort, Badiou and Laclau* (Edinburgh, Scotland: Edinburgh University Press, 2007); Slavoj Žižek, *The Ticklish Subject* (London and New York: Verso, 1993), 83–127.

of a lack of self and destruction, of repetition and interruption, of emplacement and excess."[6]

The idea of excess is also a theological contribution. This is where the notion of the transcendent as that which exceeds the representations of the divine notably emerges as segmentations of meaning in history itself. As Caputo affirms, "The name of God is simply the most known and semantically rich that we have to referring to an endless excess and an inaccessible mystery."[7] In summary, the obscene as excess — as proposed by Althaus-Reid — is a central theological element in order to understanding the divine constitution which represents the diverse, the excluded, the segregated, while instances of historical transcendence. Furthermore, the final phrase while instances of historical transcendence is unclear. Is this unfinished? Or perhaps *while* should be replaced with another preposition; however, I am not sure what the author intends to say so I do not have a suggestion. Compared with the traditional approach of TLL, the excluded refers not only to an element, object, or person to whom God reveals Godself in grace, but also refers to a constitutive element of the divine in the historical revelation from its obscene underside.

---

6. Alain Badiou, *Theory of the Subject*, trans. Bruno Bosteels (New York, NY: Continuum), 165. Elías José Palti argues that this definition exceeds the idea of subject as *horlieu* (force) from the understanding excess in the very same work of Badiou. He states: "The subject in this case establishes a connection to the excess, but does not produce it. Invokes a Truth which he presupposes. A subject is essentially a 'local assessor' intra-situational repercussion of a long indiscernible generic truth which he simultaneously summons. Finally, a *militant* is but a bet on a chance encounter with an intervention's site event." *Verdades y saberes del marxismo* (Buenos Aires, Argentina: Fondo de Cultura Económica, 2005), 179.

7. John Caputo and Gianni Vattimo, *Después de la muerte de Dios* (Buenos Aires, Argentina: Paidós, 2010), 87.

Identities, Sexualities and the Political

The disruptive gap between TLL and postcolonial theology is the location of sexuality as "an unnatural conceptualization of identities in conflict."[8] Three central elements of the conceptualization of identity emerge here, as we find them in regard to contemporary political and cultural theories.[9]

First, political identities are distorted; this entails deconstruction of the essentialist ontology of the self proper (or the self *itself*) as articulated/understood/conceptualized in modernity with regard to the subject. Secondly, as a result, the meaning of pluralizing of social identities involves a denaturation of the unique social subject. Finally, the *locus* where such heterogeneity is inscribed always remains conflictive, because the intersection of the plurality is brewed within a dynamic of disagreement, dispute and tension as a struggle for meaning.[10]

Althaus-Reid explores these approaches linking the sexual and the political. The latter involves a daily commitment, where sex is the way to find identity and to question the dialectical binary oppression/liberation, which departs from a dominant hetero-patriarchal ideology. In this sense, to make evident the sexuality of the subject is to locate the body with its complexities, boundaries, and per-versions as an axiological point of departure of the constant redefinition of reality from the concept of identity. This redefinition of the place in history represents the essence of the political as a disruptive, alternative, and resistant dynamic countering to the prevailing powers.

---

8. Althaus-Reid, *Teologia indecente*, 18.

9. Nicolás Panotto, *Hacia una teología del sujeto politico* (San José: UNA, 2013).

10. Jacques Ranciere, *El desacuerdo. Política y filosofía* (Buenos Aires, Argentina: Nueva Visión, 1996).

In this regard, Althaus-Reid makes an interesting critique of the understanding of equality that promotes what is known as "liberal feminist theology." This theological movement is closely linked to a multiculturalist worldview, which includes the social as a set of isolated particularities rather than an interconnection or inter-culturality where identities com-penetrate. Rather, Althaus-Reid poses that this difference should be transformed into *an integral part of our theological praxis*. In other words, the opening exercise of this heterogeneity of constructions does not only imply a pragmatic and passive inclusion of individuals or ideas but also the constant opening of alternative spaces of reflection.[11]

I consider that this presents one of the central challenges to the epistemology of TLL. The centralization in the option for the poor as axiological epicenter enables the notion of subject in order to position itself as a focus of the theological work. This permit for the staging of a plurality of identities — women, indigenous peoples, African American groups, among others — with their own discursive constructions. My critique is that the heterogeneity of subjetivity, discourse, and the political as provenience from TLL does not cause an *epistemological twist* on its proposal. In other words, the pluralization was rather produced from a passive inclusion of narratives or as a simple pragmatic "result" deriving from a closed and a priori conception of the subject. It was not seen as a transformation in the theological propositions from the meaning that these dynamics awakened, and did not consider the place of difference, plurality and heterogeneity as epistemic starting points of the theological. Strictly speaking, it involved the application of an understanding of the subject to various fields, but not a redefinition of the meaning of

---

11. Marcella Althaus-Reid, "Marx en un bar gay. La Teología Indecente como una reflexión sobre la Teología de la Liberación y la Sexualidad," in *Numen: revista de estudos e pesquisa da religião*, Juiz de Fora, 11:1 e 2 (2006), 55-69.

the subject itself, especially with the theological importance of this movement.

"Indecenting the Production of God"

Overcoming the heteronormative order of the social and the curtailment of the sexual instinct of political bodies involves an exercise of *indecentment*. The decent construction of the social, the political, the religious, and the theological "has a regulatory function and [an] idolatrous" one. [12] This decency of social, moral and political formations are upheld by a "decent understanding" of the divine as legitimizing discursive framework.

Therefore, a deconstructive task involves the search for indecenting the production of the theological in both the biblical text and the discursive practices of individuals and communities. It entails seeking the constitutive heterogeneity of the theological and its production, which evidences the same plurality and heterogeneity of the context from which it originates. In this regard, an interesting proposal of Althaus-Reid is her idea of "transcendental viscosity," when paraphrasing Sartre. It refers to the "jelly" quality of the self that represents fluidity, transformation, and the process of change for both the divine and of the identities themselves. This is reminiscent of many contemporary approaches in TLL, such as the notion of *transcendental imagination* from Franz Hinkelammert[13] and the idea of transcendence as the "beyond" imprinted on History itself from Ignacio Ellacuría.[14]

---

12. Ibid., 68.

13. Franz Hinkelammert, *Crítica de la razón utópica* (San José: DEI, 1990).

14. Ignacio Ellacuría, "Historicidad de la salvación Cristiana," in *Mysterium Liberationis*, vol. I., eds. Ignacio Ellacuría and Jon Sobrino (San Salvador, El Salvador: UCA Editores, 1993): 328–329.

The Idealization of the Liberationist Method

Althaus-Reid defines the methodology of TLL as a "sweeping passion." She initially represented a transgression of the objectifications of systematic theology as well as ecclesial structures of power. However, over time she eventually kept the idealization of the epistemological foundation from which she departed, which in many points shares the same Western and modern parameters that she questioned in her discourse. Therefore, she affirms, "It has come the time for an analysis of the type 'see, judge, act' in theology as a material act of grounding Christianity in reality."[15]

Hence, Althaus-Reid takes a novel and provocative rereading of the epistemological trio "see–judge–act." She states: "The problem is that the TLL could not overcome the inherited idealism. The TLL has to take more seriously their materialistic base."[16] The base to which Althaus-Reid refers is related to the corporeality and its complexities. Moreover, she asserts that idea of the theological as a second act with respect to the confrontation with the social — as Boff has proposed in the work which I have analyzed before — has lacked a more responsive and "realistic" definition of the context. There is a central question that Althaus-Reid poses: "Is it possible that the time for seeing would also be the time for kissing?"[17] This complicates *to see* towards a more sensitive vision of the socio-cultural dynamic — not only the economics — of the corporeal, the sexual, the connectiveness, the relational, and the affective.

The judgment — discernment — is for Althaus-Reid part of a sexual and provocative reading of the biblical text. It is what she calls *indecent hermeneutics.* It is not the construction of a specific type of discourse

---

15. Althaus-Reid, *Teología indecente*, 188.
16. Althaus-Reid, "Marx en un bar gay," 61.
17. Althaus-Reid, *Teología indecente*, 180.

but the search and staging of the fissures that allow for alternative constitutions of interpretative and symbolic practices. "Indecent hermeneutics aims to find the path of methodological progress in our theological constructions. Rather, it is the art of pointing darkness, twisted categories and conflicting details appearing in disorder with or without persistence."[18] Hence theology is not a closed frame that is moving into an evolutionary a priori process. "The continuity of the hermeneutic circle of doubt and constant questioning of the explanatory narratives of reality precisely involves a process of theological discontinuity."[19]

Notwithstanding, Althaus-Reid also speaks of hermeneutics from the "radical principles" of the Bible, such as the concepts of justice, peace, love, and solidarity. Thus, the reflection in the community "floats freely" from the various specific ways that these narratives may take within the hermeneutical processes of the group. This is connected with the notion of *floating signifiers* in Ernesto Laclau as narrative frames whose meaning is not closured but rather concentrated in a pluralism of meanings in light of the contexts and subjects that apprehend and redefined it within the identity segmentation through which they circulate.[20] This leads to an intrinsic and dynamic politics; its floating condition opens for a hermeneutic spectrum which gathers a variety of subjects, settings and elements, while allowing for the redefinition of those same practices.

---

18. Althaus-Reid, *Teología indecente*, 158.

19. Althaus-Reid, "Marx en un bar Gay," 15.

20. Ernesto Laclau, *Emancipación y diferencia* (Buenos Aires, Argentina: Ariel, 1996), 69–86.

SEE, JUDGE AND ACT FROM
POSTCOLONIAL PASSION

The approach proposed by Althaus-Reid allows us to think of new epistemological foundations for the method "see–judge–act" of TLL, especially in a postcolonial tone. In line with the goal of this chapter, I propose the following questions:

1. What does *to see* mean in a context that is far from being homogeneous and which is governed by a vast body of hybrid and heterogeneous construction?

2. Is *to judge* a search of directive parameters of interpretation? Or is it the opening of an inclusive hermeneutic space and propeller of subversive otherness of meaning?

3. How do we understand *praxis* as a theological and political *locus* from which heterogeneity imprints the construction of identity and the plurality of gestures of resistance that subvert and question the complexity of the surreptitious mechanisms of power and traditional emancipatory practices?

From these questions as standpoint, I discuss some theoretical approaches and proposals that will serve to deepen the insights of Althaus-Reid.

Constitutive Otherness of the Social

The idea of otherness, hybridity or constitutive difference of the social proposed by postcolonial theory has a paradoxical dual function. The emphasis is generally placed upon the fact of the possible constructions of the plural from this understanding of context. However, the sense of difference, heterogeneity, diversity, and otherness also enables the analysis of the complexity of power dynamics, which are far from being neither homogeneous nor binary. The decolonial and postcolonial approaches allow for a relevant reading about the idea of colonization of power, knowledge and self — such as the work of Anibal Quijano.[21]

Moreover, the complexity of the power dynamic from a constitutive differentiality of the social also implies questioning its ontological status. In other words, the inscription of every power dynamic in a space cleaved by plurality deconstructs any absolute meaning. As Laclau affirms[22], the falsity of ideology is not deposited in the action of creating obnubilated consciousness in individuals, but rather defining itself as universal, an absolute and sutured statement. Nonetheless, it would never be as such because its inscription in a heterogeneous space defies the stiffness of its ontological status.

It is important to note that this absolute condition is not only a self-referential element but is also granted by what is excluded. In other words, subaltern subjects themselves could develop other narratives and practices of resistance if they also locate themselves in a different ontological space which concentrates power — for example, in understandings of absolute capitalism, the universalization of the neoliberal market, or the repressive omnipresence of globalization. Do we not legitimize the false closure of power dynamics by giving them an ontological status that they do not possess? Moreover, if we do not propose an alternative view to them, do we not run the risk of locating the emancipatory practices in the same place, thus retrofeeding — as Althaus-Reid affirmed — the same Western epistemologies, but now from the place of the excluded?

In such a way, to pose the constitutive otherness of the sociocultural involves deconstructing the power dynamics and promoting new forms of political action, that is, to institute new identities.

---

21. Anibal Quijano, "Colonialidad del poder y clasificación social," *Journal of World-Systems Research* (2000): 342–386.

22. Ernesto Laclau, *Misticismo, retórica y política* (Buenos Aires, Argentina: Fondo de Cultura Económica, 2000), 9-55.

Returning to Althaus-Reid, the obscene does not merely lie "outside" of the standard. On the contrary, the other, the alternative, the different, gnaws from within at what is instituted as a drive located on the contingency that constructs it. Here lies the importance of psychoanalytic studies — especially Lacanian — that have stimulated contemporary political theories.[23] The notion of excess — used by Althaus-Reid — represents the Real, which always exceeds any symbolization. Thus, it precludes the closure of the representation of the social as well as the constitutive lack of understanding of the subject. It is that notion where the unfulfilled desire is deposited, desire that always mobilizes the search for temporary and contingent identifications, maintaining the impossibility of sutural identity.

A Border Hermeneutics

The noted philosopher Walter Mignolo suggests — as the homonym of one of his last works — an *epistemic disobedience*,[24] closely linked to what Althaus-Reid proposed as indecent hermeneutics, as a way to demonstrate the obscenities that seek to silence the colonial system and as a means of the construction of alternative fissures. Firstly, the book expands the definition of *coloniality*. This concept refers to a complex matrix where various levels intertwined — as economy, authority, nature, gender and sexuality, subjectivity, and knowledge. Coloniality is also based on three pillars, namely, knowledge (epistemology), understanding or comprehension (hermeneutics), and feeling (aesthesis). On the other hand, there is also a relationship between coloniality and modern rationality, where the latter appeals to

---

23. Yannis Stavrakakis, *La izquierda lacaniana: psicoanálisis, teoría, política* (Buenos Aires, Argentina: Fondo Cultura y Económica, 2010) and *Lacan y lo politico* (Buenos Aires, Argentina: Prometeo, 2007).

24. Walter Mignolo, *Desobediencia epistémica* (Buenos Aires, Argentina: Ediciones del Signo, 2010).

a Totality that overrides any difference or possibility for construction of other totalities. Therefore, it requires a *decolonial* project as a *programmatic instance* of *detachment* or *delinking* — as shown in the work of Aníbal Quijano — of the categories of colonial knowledge.

Mignolo proposes a *strategy of detachment*, which involves denaturing the concepts and conceptual fields of coloniality. This does not mean ignoring or denying that which cannot be denied, but rather to use the imperial strategies for decolonial purposes. The *detachment* also implies disbelieving that the imperial reason can give by itself a liberating reason such as the decolonization proposals used by Marxism, which do not involve detachment but rather a radical emancipation, since this current offers a different "content" but not a "logical" alternative.

The project of a decolonization proposes a displacement of the theo- and ego-logic hegemony of the empire into a geo-political and a corpo-logic of knowledge-logic that arises from a de-classification and disidentification of subjects imperially denied. At the same time, it offers decolonial politics an epistemology that affect the political and economic control of neoliberalism and capitalism, both essential to the framework for the imperial project. The decolonization process begins when the actors who inhabit the languages and identities denied by the Empire become aware of the effects of coloniality upon the self, the body and the knowledge. This does not mean the call for an external element/actor/project but rather the inscription of an *externality* that embodies the difference in the *space of experience* and the *horizon of expectations* enrolled in the colonial space.

Here is the central proposal of the work: *border thinking*. This epistemology evokes the pluri-versity and di-versity of the dynamics between the spaces of experience and the horizons of expectations inscribed in a larger space of coloniality/modernity. Border thinking suggests that the decolonization will not come from conflicts over the imperial difference but rather from the spaces of experiences and the horizons of expectations generated in or from the colonial difference. Critical decolonial thinking connects the pluri-versity of experiences locked in colonial frames with the universal project of constant detachment of the imperial horizons. This constructs a proposal that goes beyond the implementation of a model within modern categories — right, center, left — to the staged demonstration of subversive inscribed spaces in the action of colonized agents between the fissures of the "system."

Hence a *border hermeneutic* leads us to twist the edges of the given meanings as well as to act from the fissures that represent any significant frame. Thus, positioning the hermeneutic at the borders of meaning signifies that its dynamics do not locate the creation of a type of specific discourse with a new actor. On the contrary, it opens that border to the possibility of including a plurality of narratives that are often silenced from certain regulatory principles that have resulted from the hermeneutical exercise. Returning to the concept of an empty signifier of Laclau, this hermeneutic goes beyond the dialectical synthesis that seeks to maintain the tension between thesis and antithesis in the field of all discursive construction.

The Political Drive of Popular Corporealities

To talk about corporeality of the subject — as emphasized by Althaus-Reid — involves an understanding of the *constitutive passion* of the political. Chantal Mouffe[25] is a feminist political theorist who delves into this issue. She is critical of a liberal rationalism — which could also be extended to the orthodox left — that forgets the affec-

---

25. Chantal Mouffe, *En torno a lo político* (Buenos Aires: Fondo de Cultura Económica, 2007), 13.

tive realm of collective identifications often seen as "archaic." In this sense, the political cannot inscribe itself in recognizing a plurality that agrees with values or interests that mediate the common good as a rational public construction or as an influence of desires and fantasies.

In the same vein, Ernesto Laclau contributed an important definition of populism.[26] He does not refer to a particular subject or social sector but to a political logic that emphasizes the heterogeneous constitution of the construction of the identity. There are several important elements of this theory. First is the discursive constitution of popular identity, not as isolated positions but as an equivalential chain between various narratives that converge on empty and floating signifiers. Second, the axiological principle of construction of populism is the demand (popular and democratic), whereby the *desire* of its satisfaction — which never ceases — ranks as the political drive to satisfy individual project construction. We must recognize, however, that Laclau did not have a complex understanding of the corporeal and of desire, which leads to Stravakakis'[27] critique that this author lacks a of sense of *jouissance*. Finally, the sense of hegemony — from a rereading of Gramsci — as a kind of construction of political identity of the people is compounded internally by a variety of demands that are strung around a signifier. However, it is where the internal plurality of the same identity — constitutive otherness of the subject, paraphrasing Lacan — opens to the transformation and constant dynamic from the attention to the various demands that constantly emerge from the people.

In short, the place of affectivity and passionality have to do with a *corporeal vision of the political*, which exceeds the site of the rational-

---

26. Ernesto Laclau, *La razón populista* (Buenos Aires, Argentina: Fondo de Cultura Económica, 2005).

27. Starvakakis, *La izquierda lacaniana,* 90–92.

ization and organization of a monolithic militancy as suggested by Althaus-Reid as one of the columns of her proposal. Moreover, this approach questions the strict location of politics in certain types of discourses and practices, such as nation-states, political parties, or nationalist narratives, opening the political praxis to every instance that would resignify both identity and meaning. She retrieves the disruptive political dimension, which comes from the people against that Other who imposes itself as the sole epicenter. In summary, subversion is taken from a sexual garment that subverts all rational order.

SUBJECTS, *BRICOLAGE* AND POSTFOUNDATIONAL THEOLOGICAL APPROACH: THE CASE OF JUAN LUIS SEGUNDO

As a simple example, I turn to the exercise of reading one of the classics of the TLL — which was one of the pillars of Althaus-Reid and also one of the most resisted by the "Fathers" of this movement — in order to resignify some central elements of the epistemology of TLL.

Criticism of the Marxist Critique

Juan Luis Segundo critiques Marxist approaches to the concept of ideology. Without questioning the division between structure and superstructure, he critiques the determination of the former exclusively to the economic realm. He also criticizes other terms, such as the ideological relationship with the interest, or the idea of antagonism and contradiction of Marxist dialectics. Of the latter, Segundo states that it "predicts inevitable events" and inexorable processes of history, leading to a kind of post-Hegelian idealism. He does not reject the dialectic, although he does reject its essentialism regarding the multiple socio-historical processes. In summary, Segundo relates

Marxism to the determinism of a science that he calls "digital language," which constrains the free actions of humankind to schematics of the relations of production.

In the same vein, Segundo questions TLL. Interestingly, by 1975 he had already disagreed with the idea of a "revolutionary process" as stated that Hugo Assman, who spoke of the need for Christian commitment to a "single revolutionary process" of the continent. Segundo differs from this proposal because — in his words — it "simplified with excess the reality of the revolutionary process."[28] Here we see reflected one of the biggest criticisms of the TLL by Segundo: its monolithic tendency. Beyond raising valuable critical proposals, he departs from a framework that emphasizes essentialized, established, a priori historical foundations. Segundo affirms:

> We could say, without fear of error, that [TLL] believed in constituting itself by shifting the accent of a salvation — considered unearthly — to he humanization of humankind, freeing it from all oppressions which, from within or from its environment, at the individual level or collective, infantilized and alienated it. But it happened that this new emphasis took the same old theological epistemology. In other words, it traversed to the theme *liberation* a childish, linear and Manichean type. Good and evil, grace and sin, had changed their names, or perhaps their location. Now they were called liberation and oppression, revolution and development. However, they remained opposing in the same simplified and absolute manner[29].

---

28. Juan Luis Segundo, *Liberación de la teología* (Buenos Aires, Argentina: Carlos Lohlé, 1975), 114.

29. Juan Luis Segundo, *Teología abierta*, vol. III (Barcelona, Spain: Cristiandad, 1983b), 272, emphasis in original.

Random-Grace-Freedom-Truth:
About the Disruptive Otherness of the Historical

Segundo understands the human being from a perspective of grace, the latter comprising as *opening of the fortuitous and the contingent.* Humans are not only "receivers" of the grace of God but are defined from grace in an act of both surrender and response. Grace — as made explicit by its etymological meaning — pertains to the opposition to that which is rigid and established as well as a commitment to what is new and dynamic.

Hence Segundo addresses the *principle of freedom* inherent in every individual. He defined it as the ability to interpret and give meaning. Therefore, the struggle for freedom is — in the words of Paul Ricoeur — a *struggle for interpretations*. Freedom is the *possibility* from an unspecified set of determinations. Freedom is a *given possibility* and *value* to be obtained, always playing among a greater number of determinism.

Freedom and grace take such dynamics because they are inscribed in a context plunged *randomly*. This represents an area of diversity, a *bricolage*. God Godself created the world as a space of multiple possibilities. It is the locus where each individual moves, as well as the source of all novelty. It is from this viewpoint that Segundo defines freedom as *multiplier of determinisms*. This is the context that God arranges for people as co-creators with the divine. Segundo questions the notion of "nature" as a limited or fixed entity that defines human beings. By contrast, he claims "nature" is the result of the free actions of individuals throughout history.

Subjects-Faiths-Ideologies in Tensions:
Towards a (De)Construction of the Political

In this context, Segundo defines faith as the *act of choosing*. It represents a framework of meaning from which it is perceived and gives meaning to our surroundings. Faith is therefore not something specific to the religious field but is a human characteristic. From that affirmation Segundo established the distinction between *anthropological faith* and *religious faith*. Faith always refers to a tradition as it departs from referential frameworks. By having such a condition, the language of faith is not abstract but symbolic. The specificity of religious faith resides in taking what Segundo calls "religious data," which are instrumental elements for faith to create a space for *learning to learn*.

This instrumentality is what Segundo understood as ideology. As aforementioned, freedom represents a (re)creative instance inherent to human beings. They depart from one or more frames of meaning (faith) in order to develop themselves, a process they cannot realize without the intervention of mediations that the hazardous environment and hearsay place at humanity's disposal. That is why — for Segundo — the problem of freedom is to learn a *method* in order to unfold the values chosen by the individual. This method is the *ideology*. Ideologies are chosen in relation to the functionality with respect to the frame of meaning (faith). Therefore, they — in Segundo's words — enter the realm of the hypothetical, and not of what is absolute. Thus, ideologies depend on their response to faith. Accordingly, they lose their place while remaining functional.

It is noteworthy to mention the following axiom: people act freely within a random area plagued by possibilities, choosing one or more frames of meaning (faith), which apply through concrete instrumentalities (ideologies), whose effectiveness depends on its functionality to faith.

Masses and Minorities

"Mass" and "minorities" are not a distinction between two particular groups. Segundo asserts that there are *mass behaviors* and *minority behaviors* in each individual and community. Individuals most of the time move within the mass, as they seek ways to economically use their energy, with the intention to resolve their problems immediately and with the least possible effort. This shows, then, that the emergence and growth of the minority depends on how it projects as mass. Therefore Segundo affirms, "all progress (minority) requires a general revolution, and all general revolution requires new laws, that is, to automate new behaviors. This is the great historical law — and if prefer ontologically — of all evolution."[30]

Revolution, then, represents an anti-mass attitude in service of the crowd. However, this revolution does not depart from a massified project whose structure reaches a homogeneous totality. On the contrary, it becomes real in the *moment* of individuals and communities. Christianity presents this characterization from its minority essentiality. This essentiality leads to a continuous suspicion and distrust of the forces that move the mass, including the belief that the people are a homogeneous and unified subject to their history as mass — as Lenin postulated.

This does not mean that Christianity is strictly minoritarian in its way to channel its social action. As mentioned above, in each individual and community both forms combine simultaneously. Christi-

---

30. Juan Luis Segundo, *Masas y minorías* (Buenos Aires, Argentina: La Aurora, 1973), 30.

anity tends to be a minority in its relationships and to be mass in its socio-political behaviors. This is done by not accepting this misleading detour of ambiguous methods that in this level — as well as in others — are required to be effectively liberating. For Segundo[31], the mass means unfreedom — as heteronormative was for Althaus-Reid. Therefore, the promotion of the minority — the obscene, the excess — involves mobilizing the concentration of energy use for a richer result. In other words, it focuses in the construction of a space of freedom that allows the development of individuals and their social context within, thus assuming the complexity of their environment in order to be able to face the inherent limits in a more effective way.

Freedom and Subject as Perversions

I summarize Segundo's approach developed so far in the following definition: *freedom is the inalienable characteristic that all subjects own, which reflects the divinity in them as co-creators with God in the world. This freedom is the intrinsic openness to context in order to create and re-create in the plural and multifaceted random space — or in the words of Althaus-Reid, the imprinted excess — which is found from a set of constraints — social, environmental, symbolic, and discursive. This dynamic is headed in the continuous choice of universes of meaning (faith) as frames of (re)signification of the context and action. From there, it constructs historical actions from particular forms and methods (ideologies), although contingent and hypothetical by the plurality of the (obscene) context in which they develop.*

As analyzed, the approach of Segundo, on the one hand, deepens the presuppositions of TLL. On the other hand, as a consequence of that, some of its basic premises must be questioned. The anthropological emphasis in his work should be highlighted. This anthropologization

---

31. Segundo, *Teología abierta*, vol. I, 253.

owes much to the turn of the subject at the time of the Enlightenment. According to Segundo, the history of Christianity restarts with the resurgence of humanism in the modern age, a point that at times has a disproportionate place in his work. That turn is not restricted to the concept of transcendental subject but — from an original proposition of science — from the theory of knowledge and from the neo-Marxist critique — proposes an anthropology that places the individual in a central location within the existential and social processes. However, it is *deconstructed* from the emphasis of *free movement* and not from an essence of the social. In other words, that freedom is precisely its essence and, as aforementioned, it represents openness, dynamics, motion, and continuous repositioning rather than a fixed nature. Moreover, the subject has a *central,* controlled, absolute, and sutured position, as it may be understood in modern anthropology. On the contrary, the subject is redefined and relocated in multiple spaces within the random context in which it inscribes.

It is at this juncture where we find several common points with the work of Althaus-Reid, and a considerable depth by the latter with respect to some of Segundo's presuppositions. Segundo dares to question the colonizer, modern, essentialist Marxist background, which is reflected in several key points of TLL. This opens a dialogue with other possible theoretical mediations to respond more sensibly to the complexities of the contexts. In turn, the notion of chance is linked very closely to the understanding of excess in Althaus-Reid's work, which culminates in the obscenities that inscribed subjectivities and which embody such excess in the place of the freedom of the subjects.

CONCLUSIONS

The proposal of Althaus-Reid per-verts the epistemological and methodological foundations of TLL when embodying them in the complex constitution of "obscene" body movements, from whose drive of desire crosses all socio-cultural, discursive, political, religious and theological normativities. Thus, each element of the epistemology of TLL is redefined as follows:

- *To see* becomes an act of corporeal sensitivity that goes to the most deep and intimate foundations of the repressive closure of normativities and the reality of the complexities of human interaction.

- *The political* as an object of theology is no longer a "project" or "program" in the sense of teleological orders where the same biblical and theological are routed many times as justification. On the contrary, it becomes an instance that enables a space of identity construction as a primary force for the promotion of a plurality of socio-cultural practices. Thus, its politicity is deposited in the hermeneutic exercise of the possibility of constant redefinition.

- *To judge* is not an analytic rational act but an opening to paths for the construction of meaning that always pass through the borders of senses, body, sexuality and their politics as well as social normativities. There believers *put the body* to interpretation and reread both their faith and their reality.

- *To act* gets pluralized from the same possibilities granted by this context, which is crossed by what is heterogeneous and diverse, radicalizing the disruptive dimension of the social practices, especially *politicizing the quotidian-ness of the subjects.*

- The *ontological status of the theological* is revalued from the understanding of the divine positioned in the gap of excess, of the Real mystery which does not curtail it but rather enables and promotes various productions around the economy of God. This resignifies these "radical principles of the Bible" — as Althaus-Reid declared — from a sense of incarnation more coherent to the complexities of existence, which is based on grace and divine pleasure in creation.[32]

- Althaus-Reid proposes a *narrative methodology* of the theological construction. Here we can remember the distinction made by Clodovis Boff[33] between academic, pastoral, and popular methodologies. However, Althaus-Reid manages to combine all of them, where popular and pastoral narratives and experiences enter into critical dialogue with the theoretical, which shows the corporeality of subjects in the very flesh of the theological.

References

Alemán, Jorge. *Soledad: Común. Políticas en Lacan*. Buenos Aires, Argentina: Capital Intelectual, 2012.

Althaus-Reid, Marcella. *La teología indecente*. Barcelona, Spain: Bellaterra, 2005.

Althaus-Reid, Marcella. "Marx en un bar gay. La Teología Indecente como una reflexión sobre la Teología de la Liberación y la Sexualidad." *Numen*. 11:1 e 2 (2006): 55-69.

Badiou Alain. *Theory of the Subject*. New York, NY: Continuum.

Boff, Clodovis. *Teología de lo politico: Sus mediaciones*. Salamanca, Spain: Sígueme, 1982.

Boff, Clodovis. "Epistemología y método de la teología de la liberación." Pages 103-113 in *Mysterium liberationis*, vol. I. Edited by Ignacio Ellacuría and Jon Sobrino. Madrid, Spain: Trotta, 1994

Caputo, John and Vattimo, Gianni. *Después de la muerte de Dios*. Buenos Aires: Paidós, 2010.

---

32. Jeorg Rieger, *God and the excluded* (Minneapolis, MN: Fortpress Press, 2001), 173; Cf. John Caputo and Gianni Vattimo *Después de la muerte de Dios* (Buenos Aires: Paidós, 2010)

33. Clodovis Boff, "Epistemología y método de la teología de la liberación" in *Mysterium liberationis*, vol. I., eds. Ignacio Ellacuría and Jon Sobrino (Madrid, Spain: Trotta, 1994) 103–113.

Ellacuría, Ignacio. "Historicidad de la salvación Cristiana." Pages 323-372 in *Mysterium Liberationis*, vol. I. Edited by Ignacio Ellacuría and Jon Sobrino. San Salvador, El Salvador: UCA Editores, 1993.

Hinkelammert, Franz. *Crítica de la razón utópica*. San José, Costa Rica: DEI, 1990. Laclau, Ernesto. *Emancipación y diferencia*. Buenos Aires, Argentina: Ariel, 1996.

Laclau, Ernesto. *La razón populista*. Buenos Aires, Argentina: Fondo de Cultura Económica.

Laclau, Ernesto. *Misticismo, retórica y política*. Buenos Aires, Argentina: Fondo de Cultura Económica, 2000.

Laclau, Ernesto. *Nuevas reflexiones sobre la revolución en nuestro tiempo*. Buenos Aires, Argentina: Nueva Visión, 2000.

Marchart, Oliver. *Post-Foundational Political Thought: Political Difference in Nancy, Lefort, Badiou and Laclau*. Edinburgh, Scotland: Edinburgh University Press, 2007.

Mignolo, Walter. *Desobediencia epistémica*. Buenos Aires, Argentina: Ediciones del Signo, 2010.

Mouffe, Chantal. *En torno a lo politico*. Buenos Aires: Fondo de Cultura Económica, 2007.

Palti, Elías José. *Verdades y saberes del marxismo*. Buenos Aires, Argentina: Fondo de Cultura Económica, 2005.

Panotto, Nicolás. *Hacia una teología del sujeto politico*. San José, Costa Rica: UNA, 2013.

Quijano, Anibal. "Colonialidad del poder y clasificación social." *Journal of World-Systems Research* (2000): 342–386.

Ranciere, Jacques. *El desacuerdo. Política y filosofía*. Buenos Aires, Argentina: Nueva Visión, 1996.

Segundo, Juan Luis. *Masas y minorías*. Buenos Aires, Argentina: La Aurora, 1973.Segundo, Juan Luis. *Liberación de la teología*. Buenos Aires, Argentina: Carlos Lohlé, 1975.

Segundo, Juan Luis. *Teología abierta*. Vol. III. Barcelona, Spain: Cristiandad, 1983.

Rieger, Jeorg. *God and the excluded*. Minneapolis, MN: Fortpress Press, 2001.

Stavrakakis, Yannis. *Lacan y lo politico*. Buenos Aires, Argentina: Prometeo, 2007. Stavrakakis, Yannis. *La izquierda lazaniana: psicoanálisis, teoría, política*. Buenos Aires, Argentina: Fondo Cultura y Económica, 2010.

Žižek, Slavoj. *The Ticklish Subject*. London and New York: Verso, 1993.

IDENTITY AS SEARCH AND
CONSTRUCTION OF MEANING
BY THE DISCOURSE OF THE PEOPLE

EMILCE CUDA

INTRODUCTION

This chapter is the result of a contribution from the field of Roman Catholic theology, to the international seminar "Pressing On: Legacy of Marcella Althaus-Reid," held as a tribute to the work of that author. Despite the theoretical differences that separate me from the thought of this theologian, I believe the debate about the possible paths to liberation and a better life for Latin American people is always fruitful. Therefore, I will not review her work. Rather, I offer a contribution in line with her theological-political reflections, albeit from another perspective.

Marcella Althaus-Reid, in her book *Indecent Theology*, introduces herself as an author of sexual political theology, which emerges from a liberationist critique of feminist discourse.[1] Interdisciplinary in

---

1. Althaus-Reid, Marcella, *La teología indecente* (Barcelona, Spain: Bellaterra, 2000).

nature, Althaus-Reid's work places Christian theology in dialogue with authors of philosophy and political theory such as Laclau, Mouffe, Derrida, Deleuze, Baudrillard and Gramsci. I will therefore expand upon her theological-political criticism by introducing elements of postfoundational debate from some of the authors chosen by the theologian.[2] In *Indecent Theology*, the author points to a de-hegemonization of theology. While I will not elaborate my argument departing from her sexual assumptions, I will expand by drawing from Laclau's theory of hegemonic construction. Without getting into that discussion, I will present the new trends of Roman Catholic theology as it is present in the latest document of the Latin American Bishops, *Aparecida*. The goal is to allow the reader to develop her or his own analysis and to compare possible advances and regressions, thirty years after Puebla. Finally, as a category on which Althaus-Reid focuses her criticism of the Roman Catholic proceed, the "poor" as the subject of liberation, I will talk about what it means today for the Latin American Roman Catholicism about political subjects in relation to poverty, also drawing from *Aparecida*.[3]

THE DIGNITY OF THE CHILDREN OF GOD AS ULTIMATE SENSE AS WELL AS TRANSCENDENT AND IMMANENT GROUND OF THE POLITICAL

"I have come that you may have life and have it abundantly" (Jn. 10:10). That is the core of the message that the bishops wanted to convey to the Latin American Roman Catholic people at the General Conference of Aparecida. In my view, it is the ultimate meaning that appears as both transcendent and immanent. The dictum "have life abundantly" referred throughout the document to the dignity of all

---

2. Ibid., 19.

3. Ibid., 42.

persons as children of God. Accordingly, one would have life whenever one is recognized in human dignity as a creature of God. That recognition needs, necessarily, the effective participation in politics, as a guarantee of that dignity. The Roman Catholic bishops promoted, as a condition for a dignified life, a culture of honesty as the counterpart to various forms of violence, embezzlement, corruption, and cultural relativism. They argue it to be a political task — which they call "missionary" — that does not belong to the clerical church but to the laity. That task is to be performed within the allocated republican rules in the democratic tradition of universal indirect participation, avoiding antagonism while producing reconciliation.

The problem, in part, which precludes dignity — that is, having life in abundance — according to the document, is the absence of a transcendent sense of life that would act in turn as an immanent social principle of unity in diversity. Foul today, according to the Roman Catholic bishops, is an ultimate sense that is capable of unifying "all these meanings of reality in a holistic understanding enabling [Latin American human beings] to pursue [their] freedom with discretion and responsibility".[4] Cultural relativism would then be the manifestation of a crisis of meaning, as if a previously transcendent-existential meaning present in the history of the Latin American peoples would have been replaced by multiple and fragmented immanent or quotidian senses. The *Document of Aparecida* proposes the search for meaning which would give unity to that diversity. Concurrently, the document affirms that in Latin America the unifying function — for example, the awareness of divine filiation — as something that gives meaning to the struggle for the recognition of human dignity has been done for centuries by popular religiosity.[5] That unifying func-

---

4. Conferencia Episcopal Latinoamericana, *Documento de Aparecida* (Bogotá, Colombia: CELAM, 2007), 42.

5. Ibid., 55.

tion has strengthened the Christian identity while placing it as the underlying common sense for diversity and multiculturalism.[6] Thus, the recognition of human dignity — whose transcendent foundation resides in the divine filiation — is a common vocation to Latin American peoples, which might work as immanent basis for the political community that results from their struggle for emancipation. The argument of the document of *Aparecida* would be: if God, in the person of the Son states, "I have come to give life to humanity and to have it abundantly" (Jn 10:10), then all human beings are called to live in communion as the Triune God. Therefore, the mystery of the Trinity — the unity in one nature of the three persons, the Father, the Son and the Holy Spirit — would make sense for Latin American peoples as they are one people with cultural diversity, united as a sacrament or sign of intimate union with God.[7]

For a moment, I turn to a reflection on the political that I have made on the pastoral constitution *Gaudium et Spes* (II.4), hoping to place theological categories from the theological field passable in conversation with categories of political theory in order to establish a dialogue of equivalence.[8] I will introduce categories from postfoundational thought about the meaning of the political, which can be useful for a post-colonial and post-conciliar theological reflection. As it is known, since Machiavelli politics has separated from morality and religion. Before Machiavelli, politics had its foundation in the ethical-legal or theological realms. Since publication of the *Discorsi*,[9] the political — for political theory — is grounded in a historical mo-

---

6. Ibid., 28–89.

7. Ibid., 108.

8. Cf. Emilce Cuda, "La comunidad política como fundamento de lo político en la *Gadium et Spes*," *Anatéllei* 28 (2012): 109–119.

9. Cf. Nicolás Maquiavelo, *Discursos sobre la primera década de Tito Livio* (Madrid, Spain: Alianza, 2000), 195.

ment, and is built — far from any transcendental principle — through a practice that produces knowledge from an action. The political practice establishes the political subject and the political itself, thus transforming the political, politics, and political subjects in pure autonomy. For Machiavelli, there is no political foundation beyond a knowledge-action as a pure discursive-performative practice.[10] While with Machiavelli the political was set free from all transcendent foundations and became an autonomous, political philosophy separated from political theory: the first sought to define essences and the second, the practice, produce knowledge of the factual. This distinction is rooted in the difference between "politics" and "political" — *la politique* and *le politique* in French — as introduced by Carl Schmitt and institutionalized by Pierre Rosanvallon.[11]According to the distinction made by Oliver Marchart, politics should be considered at the ontic or factual level, such as discourse, social system, or form of action. Alternatively, the "political" should be thought at the ontological level, as a principle of political autonomy or the institutional moment of the social.[12]

Postfoundational thought is characterized by a search — and not by a determination — of transcendent principles which can act as a contingent basis of the politics. This is different from both anti-foundationalists, who oppose all founding principles, as well as postmodernists for whom any principle is valid as foundational. In other words, postfoundationalists do not want to eliminate the founding principles, but rather weaken them, which is known as weak ontology. For example, the work of Vattimo, who avoided the possibility

---

10. Cf. Claude Le Fort, *Maquiavelo* (Madrid, Spain: Trotta, 2000), Chapter IV, 5.

11. Cf. Pierre Rosanvallón, *Por una historia conceptual de lo político* (Buenos Aires, Argentina: Fondo de Cultura Económica, 2003).

12. Cf. Oliver Marchart, *El pensamiento político posfundacional* (Buenos Aires, Argentina: Fondo de Cultura Económica, 2009), 22.

of an ultimate foundation, borders on political totalitarianism. Thus, the political is a time in which the political community is partially established, leaving open the possibility of change. Therefore, even if the idea of an ultimate foundation is eliminated, it does not imply that all transcendent foundation are eliminated as well.

For postfoundational thought, the transcendent foundation exists, yet it is transient and only appears at the time of the political, to be glimpsed at the moment of the institution of the social, foundation appear only for a moment, the moment of institution to then remove itself again. Whereupon, the foundation is always something to find through the political — understood as participating in the social space — which establishes ephemeral and shifting foundations, although never necessary. That absent and missing foundation renders impossible to closure a particular political and contingent time as absolute and necessary foundation. That reading of the political drives the ongoing search for the One, yet it always misses a core. As Derrida affirms, it always misses something,[13] which in my view is valuable in order to guarantee freedom as conceded by the political community; the same idea, that freedom in in the community, is also in *Gaudium et Spes*. Postfoundational thought seeks a transcendent yet absent foundation, whose absence allows for the operativeness of the political foundation. Therefore, the vacuum produced by the absence of an absolute foundation — the crisis — is indeed the space-moment where the political occurs. In other words, the absence of an immanent One positioned as an absolute foundation is a condition for the social to be instituted as a political community. This is in agreement with the categories of *Gaudium et Spes* for which an essential freedom of human individuals becomes the transcendent foundation, albeit

---

13. Cf. Jacques Derrida, *La escritura y la diferencia* (Barcelona, Spain: Anthropos, 1989).

undetermined and indeterminable. For the post-conciliar thought, freedom is the transcendent foundation of the political community, which is in turn the basis for the political. Concurrently, for postfoundational thought, freedom is also the foundation of the foundation. Freedom, for this position, is also the "original" relationship between the funding moment and the foundation. That is, freedom is a movement that retrieves and gives the foundation. Freedom is understood by Marchart as "positive freedom". In the same vein, Jean-Luc Nancy understood "freedom for" to be the negation of any determination that prevents the freedom. It implies empty space, the crisis, the difference.[14]

The pastoral constitution *Gaudium et Spes*, before introducing the topic of the political in its second part, begins — in part 1 — by talking about history as theater, which can be equivalent to the idea of antagonism. For Ricoeur, the political appears at the rupture moment between politics and the political.[15] Technically, the politics and the political is different Politics is like administration, the political is that I want to show in this article. For Arendt, the difference, it is the social difference, is possible in the social space as a word "among" human beings of a particular community, where the political still happens and society becomes the *polis*. That is, the city where the word in disagreement debates the conditions of freedom as a common good.[16] While Carl Schmitt takes the difference to the extreme in the dyadic friend-foe, for Laclau differentiation — as antagonism — is the moment when the dominant hegemonic foundation is challenged by a new signifier able to re-articulate the unsatisfied social protest.[17] For Jean-Luc Nancy, the social colonizes the political when

14. Cf. Oliver Marchart, *El pensamiento político posfundacional*, Chapter III, 4–5.

15. Cf. Paul Ricoeur, *Historia y verdad* (Madrid, Spain: Encuentro, 1990).

16. Cf. Hannah Arendt, *La condición humana* (Barcelona, Spain: Paidós, 1997), 19.

17. Cf. Carl Schmitt, *El concepto de lo político* (Madrid, Spain: Alianza, 1999).

the hegemonic norm invades civility as a space for debate, because "the political" is the operating community in the being-in-common, and "the society" is the negation of the political community, if upon which only needs are added.[18] The problem arises — according to Nancy — when society seeks community as communion in the unity of a party or political leader, thus immanentizing the foundation. That is when totalitarianisms would enfold. For Nancy, the political is the community, not a fixed identity, but as being-in-common — in terms of the council it could be named as a political community. It is the community in contention and in the dispute, putting the One as always extraneous. In other words, it is the community retreating — as that which is always expected to happen and therefore prevents the closure of a moment as totality — that ensures — said in conciliar categories — human dignity. Freedom is the ultimate transcendental foundation of the political, and the community that freedom originates is the partial foundation in the difference.[19]

ROMAN CATHOLIC MISSIONARIES: POLITICAL AGENTS OF PEOPLE AS POLITICAL SUBJECT

The *Document of Aparecida* denounces that Latin America witnesses a self-referential culture, on the one hand, exaggerates individual rights leavened aside the common good, leading to a "disregard for the other whom one does not need and to whom one does not feel responsible".[20] Moreover, that self-referential culture translates into an ethnocentrism, functional to economic exploitation which — contrary to all human dignity — prevents peoples from having abundant

---

18. Cf. Jean-Luc Nancy, *La comunidad inoperante* (Santiago, Chile: Lom, 2000); Oliver Marchart, *El pensamiento político posfundacional,* Chapter III.

19. Hannah Arendt, *¿Qué es la política?* (Buenos Aires, Argentina: Paidós, 1993), 46-69.

20. *Documento de Aparecida*, 46.

life. The document identifies that both exploitation and oppression are enabled by the social exclusion of those who are ethnically differ- ent — native Latin Americans, afro-Latin Americans, and immigrants. In this way, the document denounces the idea that ethnic identity is a factor for social subordination in our people, where non-Europeans,

> Are discriminated against in the labor market, in the quality and content of school education, in everyday relationships and, in addition, there is a process of systematic conceal- ment of their values ... [and suggests] to decolonize minds, knowledge, to recover the historical memory, to strengthen spaces and intercultural relations.[21]

However, it notes that if the outcasts burst into the social space, that action would transform them into social subjects, thus generat- ing protagonism for themselves through the creation of spaces for political participation. The *Document of Aparecida* identifies the so- cial process of reclaiming one's dignity as "participatory democracy," stating that it is produced as a result of an awareness of the power of these excluded sectors in order to generate change through the achievements of public policy that would reverse their exclusion.[22]

As a matter of fact, if the goal — proposed by Jesus and proclaimed in the message of the Roman Catholic Bishops gathered in *Document of Aparecida* — entails abundant life for all humanity, then "fidelity to the Gospel calls us to proclaim in all social Areopagus [...] the truth about and the dignity of every human being."[23] Therefore, the document states that the "Church" should promote universal citizenship,[24] and a culture of solidarity, because "the Christian life does not express solely in personal virtues, but also in social and

---

21. Ibid., 96.
22. Ibid., 69.
23. Ibid., 390.
24. Ibid., 205.

political virtues."[25] Yet, what do they understand by "Church"? For the Greeks, εκκλησία was the assembly of citizens. Therefore, in this case and according to my previous consideration of the universality of human dignity by divine filiation, "Church" ought to refer to all the baptized as citizens of the kingdom of God. However, it is unclear in the *Document of Aparecida* whether the term "Church" refers to all baptized, or just to the clergy. I believe that given the underlying postcolonial debate on subjacent cultural stereotypes as functional elements of centuries of exploitation, theologians specializing in topics under the realm of Roman Catholic Church magisterium teaching should clarify that concept. Theologians don't like to be outside the contemporary debates on the democratic process; this is the *Document of Aparecida* speaking about the boundaries of the republic citizens to all humanity, to "universal citizenship without distinction of person".[26] This distinction is very important because the document is committing itself to an intervention in social life. It is in the politics, in order to create the necessary conditions for a decent life. I consider it necessary to clarify the scope of that commitment, that is, to whom the *Document of Aparecida* is committed and to whom it is not.

To whom are the bishops speaking? To all the baptized, that is, the people? Only to the priests? Or only to the laity? In other words: Who is the political subject for Latin American Roman Catholic Bishops? In principle it would seem that the *Document of Aparecida* only understand the clergy to be the "Church," especially when it states that "the percentage growth of the Church has not kept pace with the population growth. On average, the increase of the clergy, and especially religious nuns, increasingly stirs away from the population

---

25. Ibid., 505.
26. Ibid., 414.

growth in our region" (AP 100) Moreover, the document also asserts that "the risks of reducing the Church to political subject have been overcome, concurring with a better insight into the seductive impact of ideologies" (AP 99). If the "Church" are the priests and religious, then does the *Document of Aparecida* condemn their political participation as political subjects, that is, as subjects of decision over the rest of the faithful? In my view, the teaching position since Vatican Council II — as I have shown in my comparison of the contents of the constitution *Gadium et Spes* (II.4) with postfoundational thought — intent to put the people as political subject, it is like free people to take their our decision.

I turn now to clarify the category of political subject. I define the category of political subject from the perspective of two authors from the field of political theory: Claude Lefort and Ernesto Laclau. From Lefort's reading of Machiavelli's *Discorsi*,[27] I notice that in order to define the category of political subject, it must first be differentiated from two other categories, namely "political actor" and "political agent."[28] A political actor, according to Lefort, is someone serving her own desires while ignoring the situation. On the contrary, a political agent is someone who acts in order to limit the desire of the Other from the practical knowledge of the situation. Instead, a political subject is someone who acts from the intelligence of the situation, understanding the political field as a relationship of forces, that is, desires. The political subject is, therefore, a situated subject positioned in the social and historical context with which they identify meaning, whether factual or logical. From within this context, the political subject produces a consistent theoretical knowledge and understanding of the situation in which it is inevitably immersed, as she is never as

---

27. Claude Lefort, *Maquiavelo* (Madrid, Spain: Trotta, 2010).

28. Cf. Emilce Cuda: "Actores teológicos como sujetos políticos", en SAT, *Discursos científicos y discursos teológicos* (Buenos Aires, Argentina: Agape, 2013), 293–302.

an external observer. The comprehension of the political subject is therefore the ability to understand conflict as a different process of corruption. The latter is understood as an accident that produces a deviation in the natural path of a supposedly preexisting vector as necessary, and therefore susceptible to correction or normalization. Understanding the conflict as a sign of emancipation process and not as a corruption of the established norm is what transforms a political agent into a political subject.

Thereby, any political subject becomes — from a lefortian reading of Machiavelli's *Discorsi* — an enemy of the established order through her attempts to foster a new relationship between authority and tradition, leading to the disenchantment of the people by the current hegemonic representation. On the other hand, the knowledge of the political subject is a knowledge-action. In other words, it is a knowledge built on action, in the practice of the political that draws from the knowledge of historical and current events. That knowledge — according to the reading of Lefort on Machiavelli's *Discorsi* — emerges from the action to explore the field of history and present, from a vision of social and power relations that are constituted discursively. Thus it turns the act of knowing into a practice of knowing. For the Machiavellian political subject there is no model; there is no foundation or essence of the political. For the Machiavellian political subject knowledge is acquired in practice, which indicates in each case the legitimate political decision based on the demonstration of a need — the need of the people is the legitimate *per se* for this tendency. Observation as a method is characterized by questions about the past that give reason and meaning to the present. From that observation, the political subject is able to articulate the present facts — in the light of tradition — in order to give them a new meaning. The political subject acts on the opportunity and as such becomes a political subject in that articulation — that is, in that rationalization of experience constituted by the event. Therefore, from this theoretical perspective, for the political subject the truth is not an objective knowledge that transcends the social and the political but a situated knowledge that evidences the need of the people as legitimate.

I propose the vision of another thinker, that of Ernesto Laclau. According to him, in the current populism, the moment of political emancipation does not refer to a dialectic between unity and fragmentation, by the action of a particular political subject — whether an individual or political party — who, like superstructure and from the cunning of reason, can restore the entirety, totality, or unity, of the social. By contrast, the social is always an open and contingent totality in which the political emerges — only for a moment — from antagonism. The political moment through which the new social unit is partly instituted is a product of the discursive practice of all the people as a political split, at one point, into two force fields that affirm and deny an identity. Therefore, the totality that appears as new hegemony is — for this author — the result of a discursive practice capable of articulating all unmet demands from a particular demand. That demand — as an empty signifier — becomes the nodal point able to establish equivalence between all unconnected social demands, dividing the social into two antagonistic fields. Therefore, for Laclau, the political subject is someone who emerges from a "discursive position of the subject," assumed for a moment by the social actor. In other words, they acquire their identity as a political subject to the extent that they are able to articulate their demands with all the social demands, becoming part of a chain of discursive equivalence that — through a negative way as-method — opposes any determination of their non-being.[29]

---

29. E. Laclau, *Hegemonía y estrategia* (Madrid, Spain: Siglo XXI, 1987), 142–143.

In the *Document of Aparecida*, the category of political subject seems to become clearer when it affirms that,

> Also verified in a relativistic mentality and religious ethics, lack of creative application of the rich heritage that contains the Social Doctrine of the Church, and sometimes a limited understanding of the secular character which is the proper and specific identity of the lay faithful.[30]

It seems, then, that the political task of creating the conditions for a decent life has been relegated to the laity, not the clergy. However, later on, when the document calls for "the formation of a laity capable of acting as a Church and competent interlocutor between the Church and society, and society and the Church,"[31] it appears that the political role is in the hands of the laity. Here, according to the classification made earlier based on the analysis of Lefort on Machiavelli's *discorsi*, one can infer that the political agent is the laity — not the political subject. Therefore, the missionary in the *Document of Aparecida* is the laity, a social actor who becomes a political agent and whose goal is to address the unmet needs of a Latin American people who suffer at the hands of injustice. The *Document of Aparecida* calls for the missionaries to be a sign of contradiction and novelty in a world that promotes consumerism and disfigures the values that dignify human beings.[32] This is clarified further when it states, "[L]ay Catholics must be aware of their responsibility in social life, they must be present in the formation of the necessary consensus and in opposition to injustice," even filling "the notable absence in the political, communicative and university, voices and initiatives of Catholic leaders."[33]

---

30. *Documento de Aparecida,* 100 c.
31. Ibid., 497a.
32. Ibid., 26.
33. Ibid., 19.

DEMOCRACY AND POPULISM

The participation of the laity as missionaries — or political agents, according to the definition of political subject given above — the *Document of Aparecida* suggests that it should be done within and in favor of the Republican structures, in the form of an indirect participatory and universal democracy. Now, while the Roman Catholic Bishops in Aparecida see it with approval:

> True democratic progress demonstrated in various elections [...nevertheless denounce in that a] rapid progress of various forms of authoritarian regression by democratic means that, on various occasions, derived in neo-populist regimest.[34]

The new Latin American democratic style, with social welfare policies against popular-needs-unmet by a model of liberal democracy which dominated the political scene of the twentieth century and became radicalized in the early 1990s–, is a sign that formal (liberal) democracy that dosen't work properly, and claims for a model of participatory democracy.

If the type of formal or indirect participation of liberal democracy is criticized, then: Does the *Document of Aparecida* refer to another model of participation, more direct, as the populists expressed in the streets in direct dialogue with their leaders, without falling either into populism as dictatorship, or antagonism as a method of conflict resolution, to a social constitution of new identities?

As can be read in the *Document of Aparecida*, the Roman Catholic bishops argue that when democracies — whether liberal or popular — are "radicalized [in] their positions, they encourage unrest and extreme polarization, and place that potential at the service of foreign interests than their own, which, ultimately, can frustrate and reverse

---

34. Ibid., 74.

negatively their hopes."[35] However, in other parts of the document, the Roman Catholic Bishops affirm that "there can be no true and stable democracy without social justice, no real division of powers without the rule of law."[36] They continue to assert, "[I]t is often forgotten that democracy and political participation are the result of the formation that becomes a reality only when the citizens are aware of their fundamental rights and their corresponding duties."[37]

I am interested in briefly considering what is denounced in the *Document of Aparecida* about the new democratic styles of "neo-populist" tone just because populism is the democratic trend from the 2000s onwards in the region. We must consider the policies of social inclusion, in response to popular demand, by the administrations of Lula, Kirchner, Evo, Bachelet, Dilma, Lugo, and Mujica. Regarding neo-populist democracies, the document declares that its "dialectic of opposition seems to prevail over the strength of solidarity and friendship... The unit is not built as opposed to common enemies but by establishing a common identity."[38] First I will discuss whether this point of contrast is relevant, and secondly, whether such a common identity — as one-way meaning — is likely to be built by mechanisms of friendship and solidarity while avoiding antagonistic moments.

I wonder, if it is possible, for the dignity denied to certain sectors of the population, the recognition of legal rights. Could this be done without confrontation or antagonism? Dignity has traditionally been denied by prejudices constructed discursively to facilitate exploitation. For example, the *Document of Aparecida* cited ethnicity as a cause of exclusion. In other words, the moment of institution of the

---

35. Ibid., 75.
36. Ibid., 76.
37. Ibid., 77.
38. Ibid., 528.

people is necessary to legitimate right time, which ultimately defines the state of justice.

I go back again to the pastoral constitution *Gaudium et Spes* in order to show an alternative interpretation of antagonisms to the one that seems to be promoted by the *Document of Aparecida*. Vatican II maintains that in the world is nothing but the theater of history;[39] awareness of social antagonisms is often concealed, denied, delayed, or simply ignored, thus preventing social awareness.[40] This conciliar theological positions allows the debate about antagonisms as the political moment. I will define "agony" as the time when the suffering becomes aware as conflict and it is no longer experienced as natural; thus the oppressed occupy the social space with the word of disagreement, as expressed by Laclau, Muffe, or Rancière.[41] The theatre of history, considered by *Gadium et Spes* as a tragic drama that becomes a consequence of the sin that enslaves it, finds in theology an eschatological resolution which is only possible in Christ. However, from political theory it finds its partial resolution through the discursive articulation of difference.[42] Dignity is made effective in living conditions that will make humanity aware. Dignity — which is nothing but freedom — has always been for Christianity the distinctive feature of humanity — and of each particular human being — because it was created in the image and likeness of a personal God. This freedom — which is the image of God in humanity — is manifested in social discourse.

---

39. *Gadium et Spes,* 2.2–2.

40. Ibid., 8.1.

41. Jacques Rancière, *El desacuerdo. Política y filosofía* (Buenos Aires, Argentina: Nueva visión, 2007); Jacques Rancière, *Los bordes de lo político* (Buenos Aires, Argentina: La cebra, 2007); Ernesto Laclau, Chantal Mouffe, *La razón populista* (Buenos Aires, Argentina: Fondo de Cultura Económica, 2005); Ernesto Laclau, *Hegemonía y estrategia socialista* (Buenos Aires, Argentina: Paidós, 2004).

42. Ernesto Laclau, *Hegemonía y estrategia socialista*, 149.

Returning to the appropriateness or the unsuitableness of antagonistic moments as a path for emancipation, I assert that in ancient
Greece a social conflict had its origin in the will of the gods.[43] If the
conflict of the Trojan War is viewed from Homer's account of Helen
and Paris, this idea becomes clear. Helena, satisfying their actions
with the promise of Aphrodite, reflects the will of the gods, only
subjects of history. This excludes Helena. Moral responsibility for
fidelity and the divine determination that is characteristic of her
actions prevents her from acting as a subject over the course of her
own life. That is, there is no story, thus condemning Helena to a given
fate determined by the will of the gods.[44] In the period of Athenian
democracy, drama takes the forms of tragedy or comedy as a new way
of representing social conflict. Therefore, it is worth considering the
difference between myth and drama, especially when we consider
that between the two, the idea of freedom goes from gods to men.
Thus inaugurating the historic times where human beings are the
subjects of history, leaving behind the mythical time. We could also
take the case of Sophocles' *Antigone*, where there arises the conflict to
obey the will of the gods or that of human beings. Creon, as a political
subject, from a leading role takes the social discourse and dictates
a law. However, only when another voice rises as social politics, as
subject, assuming the antagonistic role, is the social conflict made
evident and leads to the agonizing moment.[45]

Now, we must further understand the antagonism carried out by
marginalized social actors in current democratic contexts. Should it

---

43. Cf. Emilce Cuda: "Mito y realidad del discurso religioso en la ciudad democrática," *Proyecto* 61-62 (2013): 261-271.

44. José Martí, *La Ilíada de Homero. Edición crítica* (La Habana, Cuba: Centro de Estudios Martianos), 2004; Juan de Mena, *La Ilíada de Homero* (Madrid, Spain: Biblos),
1996.

45. Cf. Sófocles, *Antígona* (Madrid, Spain: Biblos), 1994.

be understood as mythical discourse? Or as antagonistic discourse? In other words, the question is whether that group of social actors becomes a people, and therefore the subject of history, by assuming an antagonist role. In the social arena, the agonists assume the antagonistic role by making the conflict visible and audible. They face a new discourse: the new democratic style, the populist style, and its: 1) agonism; 2) demands articulation; 3) antagonism or political moment when the social is divided in two after an empty signifier; 4) social justice; and so on.

In other words, antagonism designates a subject as free in social discourse and not as an innocent victim of fate. Agony becomes antagonistic, myth becomes history; that is real democracy in liberal modern societies. The antagonistic discursive is the moment of dignity recognition in the form of laws by the State of Law. Thus, religious discourse on social agents appears as a way to resolve the agonizing and antagonistic, and not as functional to their persistent exclusion. This scheme can illuminate the question about the role of religious discourse on the political actors in democratic contexts. In other words, religious actors become involved with political agents when assuming the antagonistic role of the social in defense of human dignity. Strictly speaking, when the non-word, the *ochlos* — as people who are not recognized in their dignity in the form of civil or social rights — burst the leading discourse hegemonized by the *demos*, in that moment the *ochlos* becomes *loas* — that is, in the people aware of its agonism. In the myth, his heroes are not political but executors of the will of another subject, and can only delay the inexorable destiny from being fulfilled, but never change it. Therefore, religious discourse becomes theological when freedom goes from the will of the gods to humanity, breaking the mythical story and allowing the history to begin.

References

Althaus-Reid, Marcella. *La teología indecente.* Barcelona, Spain: Bellaterra, 2000.

Arendt, Hannah *¿Qué es la política?* Buenos Aires, Argentina: Paidós, 1993.

Arendt, Hannah. *La condición humana.* Barcelona, Spain: Paidós, 1997.

Conferencia Episcopal Latinoamericana. *Documento de Aparecida.* Bogotá, Colombia: CELAM, 2007).

Cuda, Emilce. "Actores teológicos como sujetos políticos." *SAT* 1 (2013): 293–302.

Cuda, Emilce. "La comunidad política como fundamento de lo político en la *Gadium et Spes,*" *Anatéllei* 28 (2012): 109–119.

Cuda, Emilce. "Mito y realidad del discurso religioso en la ciudad democrática," *Proyecto* 61-62 (2013): 261-271.

Derrida, Jacques. *La escritura y la diferencia.* Barcelona, Spain: Anthropos, 1989.

de Mena, Juan. *La Ilíada de Homero.* Madrid, Spain: Biblos, 1996.

Laclau, Ernesto. *Hegemonía y estrategia.* Madrid, Spain: Siglo XXI, 1987.

Laclau Ernesto. *La razón populista.* Buenos Aires, Argentina: Fondo de Cultura Económica, 2005.

Laclau, Ernesto. *Hegemonía y estrategia.* Buenos Aires, Argentina: Paidós, 2004.

Le Fort, Claude. *Maquiavelo.* Madrid, Spain: Trotta, 2000.

Maquiavelo, Nicolás. *Discursos sobre la primera década de Tito Livio.* Madrid, Spain: Alianza, 2000.

Marchart, Oliver *El pensamiento político posfundacional.* Buenos Aires, Argentina: Fondo de Cultura Económica, 2009.

Martí, José. *La Ilíada de Homero. Edición crítica.* La Habana, Cuba: Centro de Estudios Martianos, 2004.

Nancy, Jean-Luc. *La comunidad inoperante.* Santiago, Chile: Lom, 2000.

Rancière, Jacques. *El desacuerdo. Política y filosofía.* Buenos Aires, Argentina: Nueva visión, 2007.

Rancière, Jacques. *Los bordes de lo político.* Buenos Aires, Argentina: La Cebra, 2007.

Ricoeur, Paul. *Historia y verdad.* Madrid, Spain: Encuentro, 1990.

Rosanvallón, Pierre. *Por una historia conceptual de lo político.* Buenos Aires, Argentina: Fondo de Cultura Económica, 2003.

Schmitt, Carl. *El concepto de lo político.* Madrid, Spain: Alianza, 1999.

Sófocles. *Antígona.* Madrid, Spain: Biblos, 1994.

PART III

INDECENT THEOLOGIES
PRESSING ON

OPPRESSED BODIES DON'T HAVE SEX

The Blind Spots of Bodily and Sexual Discourses in the Construction of Subjectivity in Latin American Liberation Theology

CLAUDIO CARVALHAES

INTRODUCTION

In Leonardo Boff's 1996 book *Brasas sob Cinzas*, he describes stories of the quotidian life of people he has met while traveling around Brazil, especially those among the poorest within the Brazilian population. In these stories, he vividly depicts the potency of death amidst the lives of banished people, their utter poverty, their lives lived in disgrace, and their search for dignity and honor. The reader is haunted and disturbed by these stories. In one of them, Boff recounts a visit to a poor house in which he baptized a child who was to die later the same day due to malnutrition. After he finished the baptism rite and before leaving the house, a woman suddenly asked him to go to her house next door. There, alone with this woman, he describes what happens:

After the baptism, a woman called me and conducted me to a small room in her *favela*.[1] Bare floor, this place had no furniture. Poverty inhabited every corner like an uttered scream of a dog. We were alone. Murmuring, she said to me: 'I have only met ugly, sick and skinny man in my life.' She then took off her clothes, showed me her naked body and confident, turned to me with her shinning eyes: 'I am still young, I am 35 years old (she looked like 60 years old), and I can make you happy for a moment. You are a well fed man, handsome and attractive. I only knew ugly, sick and skinny man. Give me this joy ... Please, make love with me! Only once, I beg!' I kept silence, a long silence, the silence of perplexity. Then I said: 'I am a religious person, I already have a commitment ... I can't ... I should not ... I don't want ... ' Her eyes turned down with deception. Later in my house, meditating on what had happened to me, I was filled with shame, shame of my own self. What an egoist I was. In my religious life, I learned that chastity was abstention and not a form of expression of a higher love. This unbounded love knows no limits. It's beyond right or wrong. This woman was purer than I was. She had the ability to offer herself and to love freely ... Had I known that chastity was something to be offered, as encounters without embarrassments, I would have made love with that woman. Not for pity but for a free decision and completely self-giveness. Chastity then would have been overabundance of love and not lack of love. If I was that kind of celibate man, I could have been a saint ... and could have sinned. For if I had sinned, I would have found God who makes sin become grace and grace become sin.[2]

---

1. Brazilian word for *slum* or *shacks*.

2. Leonardo Boff, *Brasas Sob Cinzas: Stories of the Anti-Quotidien* (Sao Paulo, Brazil: Ed. Record, 1996), 21–22.

This story is emblematic of and key to understanding the relation between Liberation Theology (LT) and the notion of the body, sexual practices and subjectivity. It is one of the very few times in LT literature that one can hear a poor person speaking about her/his sexual desires as concretely experienced by a renowned liberation theologian. Moreover, it is also stunning that a theologian would share such an experience, publicly risking himself to be judged in many ways. Nonetheless, in this very act of sharing this experience, Boff shows us how difficult it is to relate the theological task with the surprising events of life, with the other and with that which is violently repressed and forbidden in the other, i.e., the body and sexualities of the poor. Moreover, Boff's acknowledgment of his unprepared theology shows well how liberation theologians have been unequipped to deal with desiring bodies and sexualities amidst the life of the poor. No tools to deal with it, no eyes to see it, no theological categories to rationalize it, no human imagination to consider it. Perhaps the surprise of this woman's desire came to Boff as it would have come to any other liberation theologian. With this acknowledgement, Boff courageously risks all his theology. He *confesses* that he failed to listen to her voice, that he didn't understand her, that he was way too shocked by the crudeness of her flesh, of her desire, that frightening yearning and the *excesses* of a sudden naked body.

This is a pivotal example of what has been left out in LT, that is, to talk about the body and the sexual themes in the life of the poor: desire, sexual drives, unfitted sexual behaviors, sexualized notions of the subject, sexual (dis)orientations, transgressions, etc. These "categories" of thought have never been part of the discourse of liberation theologies in Latin America. The concrete body related to pleasure and sexual experiences were forgotten, hidden, denied, dismissed, seen as improper, neither necessary nor vital to the making of both theological discourses and its practices.

Moreover, in the history of Liberation Theology in Latin America (LTLA), patriarchalism, racism and homophobic tendencies have been constitutive elements that delineated the (un)conscious core of LT through its selective use of Material Sources, Hermeneutical Approaches, Political Theories, Economic Criticism, Phenomenological Lenses, and Theological Engagements. All of it is wrapped up in the limits of Reason alone. These "capital letter" engagements and choices have formatted the totality of LT discourses, creating blind spots of "lower case" aspects of human predicament that were never linked with the civilized use of reason: the body, the black people, the woman, daily life's disorder, children, relationships, and their complex relations to sexual practices. This binary system of thought has denied the possibility of difference and considered the subjectivity of the poor only in predetermined accepted social categories. Had LT engaged with *lower case* issues, the history of theology and the church in Latin America would have been much different from what it actually has been.

Liberation Theology became the umbrella that embraced all the "other" Roman Catholic liberation theologies such as feminist, black, indigenous, and later, earth/ecological liberation theologies. These "other" theologies, along with "other" sparse Protestant theologians of liberation were placed on the margins of the LT main movement. However, it was these theologies and theologians who where responsible for discourses that tried to touch on issues related to the body and sexuality more closely. Even though I am using the term Liberation Theology in Latin America, I am relying more closely on the Brazilian sources and evaluations of this theology.

This essay attempts to open a dialogue with the heritage of LT and looks to issues of sexual embodiment to find other ways to approach and relate to the reality of the poor. It does not have the poor participating in it but it tries first to dialogue with what has been said about and/or on behalf of the poor. In order to do that, it has first to undertake a critical revision of LT's resources and methodological system. New critical theories and philosophies have appeared since LT's emergence in the 70s, which offer different forms of thinking, re-creating, deconstructing, and reconstructing discourses, such as postcolonialism, new readings of Marxism, feminism, and races, queer theories, post-structuralism, critical, social and cultural theories, and so on.

In order to consider these blind spots within LT discourses, I believe one has to start with a critical approach to how the notion of subjectivity was created, recognizing first of all that the assumed subject (poor, desexualized, self-identical) in LT has made it impossible for the body and sexual identities to appear and/or to unsettle LT's discourses. Oddly enough, the notion of the subject in LT has in many ways mirrored and even reinforced the Western, European, Roman Catholic, colonized self that LT attempted to call into question. In other words, the *doubly colonized self* (by Europe and North America) in Latin America was never sufficiently disrupted in order not to serve as the ground for LT discourses. Only later on in the LT movement, due to some criticisms, liberation theologians started to mention in their footnotes some of the repressed/lower case forgotten issues: black and indigenous people, women, and the bodies of the poor.

After considering the notion of the self in LT, I will retrace some theological discourses on the body and sexual possibilities that can be found within the work of three LT thinkers and see how they engaged the body and sexuality and how the notion of the self in their theologies are constructed. The three LT thinkers are coincidentally, and perhaps meaningfully, non-Roman Catholic thinkers, namely: the former Presbyterian theologian Rubem Alves, the Anglican Jaci Maraschin, both from Brazil, and the Quaker Marcella Althaus-Reid from Argentina. I believe not only that they will give us perspectives on the historical creation and development of bodily and sexual discourses in LT, but also that they help us to open new streams of thought, to index new issues, becoming for us thinkers and partners in the necessary process of rethinking Liberation Theology in Latin America.

After examining their thought, I will pose difficult questions regarding the very substrate that grounds LT; namely, the use of the poor as the very subject of theology. By posing hard questions of *representation*, my intention is to unsettle the use of the category of "poor" as a given, uninterrogated theological mark and then try, as a conclusion, to offer new possibilities for LT to relate with the poor and their reality. My hope throughout this investigation is to pose challenges that might lead this movement in Latin America into new and maybe strange places of dialogue and creation.

THE SUBJECT IN LIBERATION THEOLOGY

In comparison to European and North American theologies, the main shift proposed in Latin American theology was to place the poor and their concrete situation at the center of every theological project. One had to start from "below", from reality and from there guide, illuminate and understand God's revelation in the Bible. The poor became the hermeneutical axis, the epistemic ground, and the social and theological criterion to access both human reality and God. Trying to dislocate the periphery to the center, this theology strived to be faithful to those who were excluded from society. LT wanted to make up what had been left out of the main theological discourses up to this point in Latin American history. This process of *listening to the poor* was LT's effort to shift the center of theological production from theological cabinets to the street, from conversations not with well-trained theologians but to the poor people in their location, from theoretical to practical ways of doing theology. That practice not only produced a "privileged subject" but also created a different way of doing theology. Enrique Dussel explains it thus: "There is a privileged subject who produces the theological discourse, and almost always, the theological discourse is marginal, implicit, spontaneous, resistant and it is the popular theology."[3]

In order to do LT, one has to understand the situation in which the poor are located and make sense of the reasons the poor are placed on the margins of the economic and social system. Thus, LT had to turn theology into a *second step*, a *second action* that would depend on a first act, which was the concrete and material analysis of reality. It was this analysis of reality that would give the poor tools to understand their situation and to see how this situation would determine their faith in God. Fed by socialist and Marxist movements around the world, LT adopted a Marxist reading of reality with strong emphasis on the notions of ideology, material reality, the power of the proletariat, and the understandings of *class struggles* as the very structure of Latin America societies.

Believing that the poor had become the new subject of their own history and of God's liberation project, liberation theologians made material life the source of theological thinking, rather than speculative, ahistorical spirituality, philosophy or theology. In that sense,

3. Enrique D. Dussel, "Hipóteses para uma história da teologia na America Latina," in *Historia da Teologia na America Latina* (Sao Paulo, Brazil: Paulinas, 1985), 188.

the church was not supposed to tell the poor what God wanted, but rather to encourage the poor to discover what God was telling them through their own lives and praxis as they read the Bible in community. Ortho-*doxy* was replaced by ortho-*praxis* in all the basic ecclesial communities; that is, daily life praxis was the way to interpret and get to the gospel and not the dogmas. The mediation of social sciences, not the theological canons of the church, was the source of this change in LT. However, as Clodovis Boff affirms in his seminal book explaining the difficult relation between praxis and theory:

> In fact, the ultimate originality of Liberation Theology relies not in its method, specifically in the use of social sciences, including Marxism. The roots of this method are in what bestow itself a 'spirit,' a 'new way' of using the method. And the roots are the spiritual experience of the poor.[4]

The poor, the *new subject* in LT, the agent of its own destiny, was to become conscious of his/her situation of oppression and injustice and then fight against it through a politically engaged faith. The educational method of Paulo Freire[5] was key in the pedagogical work of the catechists within basic communities which prescribed the following process to access reality: *to see, to judge, to act.* That sequence of looking at reality and its mechanism of oppression, the necessary decisions of what to accept and what to fight against, and the mobilization to change the situation was the process of making people conscious of their situation, what in Latin America was known popularly as *conscientisation.* Religion should be understood not as an ideological tool to hide injustice and oppression but on the contrary, as an instrument to detect the powers that organize and oppress society and to dismantle them.

---

4. Clodovis Boff, *Teologia e Prática. Teologia do Político e suas Mediações* (Rio de Janeiro, Brazil: Ed. Vozes, 1978), III.

5. Paulo Freire, *Pedagogy of the Oppressed* (New York, NY: Continuum, 2000).

The figure of the theologian was also transformed. Instead of sitting in their ivory tower, theologians were required to live among the poor and to understand their reality. The term used to describe this new theologian was taken from Antonio Gramsci's *organic intellectual*. Gustavo Gutierrez describes this theologian:

> Theologians will be personally and vitally engaged in historical realities with specific times and places. They will be engaged where nations, social classes, and peoples struggle to free themselves from domination and oppression by other nations, classes, and peoples. In the last analysis, the true interpretation of the meaning revealed by theology is achieved only in historical praxis.[6]

LT has created new hopes and new dreams of transformation. It has helped to create what is now one of the most influential political parties in Brazil called PT, the "people's party" that much later elected Lula as president of Brazil in 2004. However, in time, LT started to encounter problems within its own intellectual structure at the same time as it started to be bombarded from inner structures of power that once held control over the poor. The Roman Catholic Curia was not happy with the directions of the movement, especially its ecclesiology,[7] and started to explode the movement by moving archbishops associated with Liberation Theology from influential positions within the church throughout Latin America. Moreover, the political and economic situation in Latin America seemed to be too harsh to be transformed and the utopian thoughts that used to feed the grassroots movements (mainly Basic Ecclesial Communi-

---

6. Gustavo Gutiérrez, *A Theology of Liberation. History, Politics and Salvation* (Maryknoll, NY: Orbis Books, 1988), 10.

7. In his book *Ecclesiogenesis, The Basic Communities, Reinvent the Church*, (Maryknoll, NY: Orbis Books, 1986), Leonardo Boff argues for a church that starts from the people and does not depend on the hierarchical power of the church. This book compelled the Curia of the Roman Catholic Church to silence him for one year.

ties) were deprived of its powerful tools. The metaphysical use of the theological term *liberation* was not enough to hold the frustrations and the continuous lack of historical changes that were expected by the poor. On the other hand, Pentecostal movements started to grow everywhere with their promises of healing and miracles, appeasing somewhat the most immediate anxiety of the poor regarding their daily life's disorders such as illness, unemployment, difficult relationships, and lack of money. Even thought it is up for debate whether LT is dead or not, LT has definitely lost its strength with the end of Sandinism in Nicaragua, the implosion of the Berlin Wall in 1989, and the end of socialism in Eastern Europe. As a way to understand some of the *other* causes that provoked the collapse of LT from within, I will mention the following possibilities that are intrinsically related to the ways in which LT relied upon the category of the poor as its main subject.

1) Dependency on Social Sciences

What underscored the limits of LT was its over-dependency on the social sciences. Assuming that the first step of theology was to concretely understand reality, LT surrendered its discourses to social science categories, especially Marxist categories, and became a prisoner of its own historical interpretations. Since it was dependent especially on the use of class systems to understand the world of Latin America, the issues that rotated around LT were mainly political analyses, economic underdevelopment, and social revolution. These main social categories were then *translated* to the poor as lack of a decent life to live, lack of jobs, education, food, dignified life, etc., and all of that was encompassed under the main theme of oppression. As Frei Betto, a key thinker in LT in Brazil once said in an attempt to refocus the pastoral attention of LT:

One needs to think the pastoral work and elaborate reflections in dialogue with intellectuals, artists, scientists and
those that form opinion. In the moral area, the social moral
should also relate to the personal moral. Liberation theology has enlarged its defense to human rights of the poor.
The right of the poor are considered rights of God. Right of
life and the means of life such as: food, health, home, work,
school, education, social security, etc.[8]

Poverty, oppression, and injustice are so visible in Latin America
that one tends to locate human subjectivity under basic requirements
for human preservation and survival, that is, food, employment,
housing and health care. This visibility, however, made liberation
theologians close the grid of the poor's subjectivity around these
broad issues, forgetting to pay attention to what was less evidently
important in life. This totalizing social vision of the self overshad-
owed purportedly *negligible needs and activities* of human life such as
bodily pleasures, sexual and gender transgressions, carnival, obsessions, guilt, dance, moral constraints, disruption, drugs, fantasies, the
transitory, the erratic, relationships, battered women, tears, "cordial
racisms" (a racism neither contemplated nor confronted in the big
social analysis), spirituality, possession, trance and so on. As a result,
LT started to accumulate several blind spots within its own closed
structure and started to lose contact with the poor, their privileged
subject.

João Batista Libânio, a prominent Liberation Theologian, analyzing the situation of LT after twenty years said:

Liberation theology cannot be imprisoned in concepts
of social classes, not knowing the realities of the women,
children, black and native people ... In a meeting of SOTER

---

8. Joao Batista Libanio, SJ, and Alberto Antoniazzi, *20 Anos de Teologia na América
Latina e no Brasil* (Rio de Janeiro, Brazil: Ed. Vozes, 1993), 24.

INDECENT THEOLOGY • PART III. INDECENT THEOLOGIES PRESSING ON

(Society of Theology and Sciences of Religion — Catholic theologians in Brazil) in July 1990, the social scientists analyzed the theoretical aspect of Marxism used sometimes more and sometimes less by theologians. It was clear that such theoretical reference must not be broad only in is scope but also constantly revisited because of its insufficiencies, and among them the hypertrophy of class in detriment of cultural and sexual aspects of reality, its incapacity to analyze the power relation within the church and adapting macro-societal analyses, a lack of a critique to the state, the unknown realities that emerged in this new phase of capitalism, and etc. This gathering points to ways of social anthropology, sociology of the institutions, quantitative methods, of theory of action (A. Touraine), etc.[9]

LT use of *reason* became one with reality and one term could not be understood without the other. The main body of LT's work was done during the 70s and 80s. From the 90s on, besides some important works done here and there, LT became lethargic, less influential, enmeshed in constraints that did not ignite much novelty or serious conversations that would create new theological thinking. Libanio's analysis of LT and its self-criticism made in 1994 shows the increasing inadequacy and insufficiencies of LT. As they started to look for other possibilities of dialogue, the emphasis on social sciences was still the only way to access reality. There was no mention of feminism, body studies, sexual theories, race theories, everyday life, cultural theories, political identities, and so on. The notion of the poor as the main subject of LT was still under the broad categories assigned by old, self-enclosed systems of discourse.

---

9. Ibid., 23.

2) The Composition of the Liberation Theologians

The task of theology can also be understood not only by what is written but also by those who write it and from where they speak. The "who," "where," and "how" one does theology define what one includes in one's writings and what one forgets or doesn't add to one's theological production. In the case of LT, most of the theologians were white male, celibate priests of the Roman Catholic Church who got their graduate degrees mostly in Europe and Canada. Consequently, patriarchal constructions provided the framework within which these theologians created their thought. The metaphysical construction of the notion of liberation was still locked in binary constructs, which were related to big schemes of political, social, and economic structures of reality overshadowing the small, negligible experiences of women, children, black men and black women, indigenous, and queer people.

Even the term "liberation" meant pretty much what a white celibate man who studied in Europe understood of it. Women's struggles, domestic violence, racism, battered children, women's sexual exploitation, and indigenous problems were not so much part of the liberation theologian's radar as they were in the "hidden" reality of the poor. LT was not nuanced enough to account for differences of color, sex, or race among oppressed people. The Cannanites and Hagars of Latin America were not contemplated in most of LT discourses. They were disfigured figures of reality and only appeared as appendixes of theological work. Put differently, women, natives, and black men were only prosthetic implants in the poor's subjectivity that caused uneasiness in theological discourses. As for black women, gays, lesbians, transgender people and cross-dressers, they never even got to the appendix list of LT. They were left completely out of any picture of the poor's subjectivity.

For the most part, women were understood theologically through the male understandings of Mary, mother of Jesus. Libanio says that the feminine incorporated the aspects of Mariology that grew enormously and contributed substantially to the theological discussion. He writes: *"Mary is presented as a woman of faith, faithful and perfect disciple, a concrete expression of the preferential love of God for the poor. The women in our context feel proximity with Mary, poor woman, a people's woman"*.[10] As one can see, the characteristic poor women for most liberation theologians had to be faithful, passive and obedient, a *perfect disciple* who could only follow, never lead. The category of woman was self-enclosed in the image of Mary and ended up creating an image of an asexual virginal woman who never complained of anything, who was only fit to serve and to follow men's orders.

As for the African-Brazilians, the first books about them were written only in the mid-1980s. To my knowledge, almost all of this published material was written by men. There was not a single black woman writer in LT in the whole country of Brazil mentioned in the overall analyses of LT in Libanio's book. This is strangest contradiction and the most outrageous forgotten theme in LT, at least in Brazil; the almost complete absence of black people in the main works of this theology, especially if one considers that more than half of the Brazilian population (two hundred million people) is constituted by black people. It gets worse when one knows that the poor in Brazil are massively composed of black people who are living in *favelas* throughout the country. However, the nonexistent *presence* of black subjectivity in LT is the most evident *symptom* of LT's totalizing white patriarchal subjectivity.

Moreover, the native people of Brazil also occupy the last place within the grid of LT's index. A shocking proof of this absence is that

---

10. Ibid., 71.

the first native theological conference in Latin America happened only in 1991 when mainstream LT was facing its biggest challenges and was already at the end of its strength. In 1994 Libanio says: "Attempts to elaborate an aboriginal theology (natives doing theology) is just now occuring".[11] For the most part, the natives have been used as the counterpart of the *inculturation* dialogue, unfortunately a one-sided dialogue done by white liberation theologians who try to be kind enough in their Christian approaches to understand, describe, and set the tone of what indigenous people are and believe.

Moreover, the theological debate on inculturation also relates to popular religiosity and finds the same tone as Christian apologetic perspectives that subsume other religions within Christian categories (usually wrapped up in imposed "love and understanding") as means of evangelization. Libanio says:

> ... the reflection on inculturation is growing. The definitive text from Santo Domingo recognizes the manifestations of popular piety within the expressions of the inculturation of faith *even if they are superfluous or ambiguous* ... it also values the popular religiosity as privileged expression of the inculturation of faith, religious expression of values, criterion, behavior and attitudes that *are born from the catholic dogma and constitute the wisdom of the people, forming their cultural matrix.*[12]

The Roman Catholic matrix seemed to encapsulate every religious expression in Brazil in Christian perspectives. African and native religiosities, it was asserted, could only be accepted if understood by means of Christian concepts. Thus, Christian theology announces itself as a critical tool to judge and help popular religion to find the proper way of believing and ritualizing faith and to correct the trans-

---

11. Ibid., 132.

12. Ibid., 67 (italics mine).

gressions of the doubled religious other (poor and non-Christian) in their 'idolatrous" creations. As for Protestants, the role was to deny culture and demonize any other religion.

Thus, the minimizations of the forgotten other poor "Cananites and Hagars" are symptoms of the composition of the theologians who wrote LT. Let us look at the list of the main theologians in LT given by another white priest. Antoniazzi says:

> The production of the last twenty years has been domi-
> nated by a generation of theologians that goes from *J.B.
> Libanio* (1932) to *Leonardo Boff* (1938) and *Clodovis Boff*
> (1944). Among them, the ordained people are the majority.
> Some diocese's elders are among the new theologians (*A. J.
> Almeida, Vitor Feller, Luciano Lvall*) or from other countries
> (*J. Comblin*). In the last years, there is an important novelty:
> the appearance of lay theologians, men and women. The
> lay women theologians are in Rio de Janeiro, and some
> ordained people in spread out religious orders. The lay
> theologians are linked with the Pontific Catholic University
> in Rio de Janeiro.[13]

The theological grid is settled, the partners chosen, the names given, the issues granted and the hierarchy specified. Certain questions have been pressing against the grid: who are these lay men and women theologians? Who are the women theologians in Rio de Janeiro? Where are their *spread out orders*? What are their names? What are they doing? What year were they born? Have they published anything? What about the rest of the country? What about other people working with the poor? What about the poor? Aren't they *doing theology* anymore? What happened to their praxis? These mentioned theologians without names can be seen as a lure into what one does not really know or what one does not really care or see as

---

13. Ibid., 142 (italics mine).

important. Sadly enough, this is the present situation of the subjects who are writing theology in Brazil within LT: unknown. Unknown people writing about unknown people.

Can women, natives and blacks become more than subjects described in appendixes or points "d," "e," or "f" in their theological importance, having for the most part very little to say? What about gays, lesbians, and transgender people? What about non-religious persons or persons of other religions? Are they considered as poor or are only the Roman Catholic poor the 'real' poor? Who belongs to the critical mass that belongs to the theoretical category of the poor? Moreover, will a list of "others" be enough, a mere litany of exclusions? How then does one try to understand the subjectivities of the poor?

3) The Understanding of the Subject

LT wanted to encompass the whole reality of oppression and injustice in Latin America with a theological discourse. In order to do that, it elected some of those who were in the margins of socio-economic situation as *the* poor. In order to get to the notion of the subject, the criterion that grounded the decision of what was to be the category of the poor seemed *obvious*. The contingent of excluded people in Latin America was so great that those living in utter poverty were the clear-cut chosen people.

The idea of the subject was based on socio-economic terms as we see clearly in both Gutiérrez and Idígoras. In Gutiérrez, a theology of the human subject is based on the value of the human person as it is related to the notion of labor and to the access of the worker to what the worker produces. By condemning *alienation*, Gutierrez gets to the core of a human person's identity: "alienation is the absence that the worker suffers from the results of her/his work that ends up in division between the human person and the things he/she produces. Alienation is the opposite of a true human identity because in the situation of oppression, things are more important than persons."[14] In his *Theological Vocabulary for Latin America*, Idígoras defines the human person (the oppressed people) through socio-economic values as it relates to dignity. He says: "One must avoid abstract definitions of the person ... The concrete man (sic) realizes himself through socio-economic circumstances and in the progressive development of time ... In our countries in Latin America, we have the huge task of personalizing many of our brothers (sic)."[15]

This theology of the human person is the definition of human subjectivity. Subjectivity is understood in its material and concrete aspects and is represented here exclusively over and against its socio-economic conditions. However, this determination becomes an overarching concept, an *unmarked term*, without marks of sex, race and gender. The socio-economic subject is the chosen poor for LT and defines the theological discourse in ways in which the body, sex, race, and gender are always neutral terms.

This "poor" have no contradictions and can be fully understood and grasped. Moreover, the poor are fulfilled once the socio-economic situation is changed. The subject already carries in itself the specific conditions of agency. By regarding the poor as the center of every theological project, there seems to be no need to establish the limits or the impossibilities in which the poor would participate in this project, much less the ways in which this poor are to be represented in theological discourses. The written discourse of LT *over* the voice

---

14. Gustavo Gutiérrez, *Densidad del Presente* (Lima, Peru: Instituto Bartolome de las Casas-RIMAC e Centro de Estudios y Publicaciones-CEP, 1996), 39.

15. José Ignacio Tellechea Idígoras, *Vocabulário teológico para a America Latina* (São Paulo, Brazil: Ed. Paulinas, 1983), 373.

of the poor was to be a unified project, apparently faithful to everyone but actually much more faithful to LT's methodological categories than to the poor themselves.

The work of the theologians as *organic intellectuals* should be the re-telling of the stories of the poor and how the poor understood their reality and consequently God and the Bible. However, the stories of the poor were not always socialist stories, or stories that would carry the values and notions of LT. On the contrary, stories of the poor were also stories of immediate needs and narrow understandings of the structural situation that kept their lives in their miserable environment. The organic intellectuals *knew better* the structures of oppression and told the poor what they didn't know or the things they were supposed to know, want, and do. As a consequence, the stories of the poor started to be less and less described in LT books and instead, structured in doctrinal analyses that overtook the stories of the poor. Moreover, the writing of the stories told by the poor passed through ideological theological surveillances. Only selected positions could become theology. If this was not so, what would the theologians do when some poor people asked again for military intervention in Brazil? Or, would they respond theologically to improper sexual behavior such as extra-marital sex or sexual transgressions? Or, how could they keep the romantic idea of the poor when the poor approve the death penalty or even the end of human rights because they only protect bandits and murderers? What to do with these *wrong* positions of the poor? The theorization of the praxis of the life of the poor was soon to become somewhat idealized, and there was a subtle replacement of the poor as the *subject* who does theology by way of the organic theologians who knew better how to do proper liberation theology.

It is important to say that it was indeed necessary for LT to affirm and strategically honor the poor in different ways in order to move and shift the grid of theological structures. However, the strengthening of the poor ended up locking itself into another set of theological reasoning that imprisoned the poor according to the tenets of LT.

Thus, this poor, this encapsulated subject, could only do theology according to the tools presented to them. That's why Boff could not relate to that woman that wanted to have sex with him, even though I guess no theology would be able to teach us in advance how to react in such situation. Sex and sexual desires were not in the grid of LT or in the horizon of the stories of the poor told by liberation theologians. Thus, the stories of the poor were always permitted stories, stories of concrete material socio-economic scarcity easy to categorize: stories of oppression, no food, no home, no jobs. There were no reminders, as it were, of different absences in the life of the poor within LT discursive discourses.

LT believed that the process of conscientisation was the only way to a just world. They believed with Marx that once conscious of his/her own condition, the poor would become the master of his/her own history. In this process, there was a glamorizing of poverty by the intellectuals, and poverty, along with suffering, became a sort of privileged site for redemption. Slowly, poverty became beautiful, misery started to carry special blessings, and suffering became the only way to redemption. In no time poverty became the necessary condition for LT to survive and suffering became the concrete material for redemption. Without misery, LT had to disappear. As a consequence, many engaged theologians got good positions in seminaries, universities and social agencies, traveled around the world and enhanced their economic situations out of their work with the poor. Organic intellectuals fell in love with poverty, but they had the choice of leaving at any time.

The point I am trying to make is not that theologians should have chosen misery but rather, that the presence of misery in their theological labor ended up being vital for its own development and "success". Against the glamorization of the poor, Joazinho Trinta, one of the most important carnival creators in Brazil once said, "People like luxury. Only intellectuals like misery."[16] Along the way, and especially through its internationalization process, LT became an elitist movement that found spaces in seminaries and institutions throughout the world. This elitism can be seen in a main theological document developed later that is titled in Latin, *Mysterium Liberationis?*[17]

LT distanced itself from the poor and created a detached subjectivity to work from and with so that it didn't have to relate closely with the "non-theological" aspects of the nitty-gritty mess of the daily life of the poor, which included social immediacy, extreme violence, sexual transgressions, political detachment, and conservative religious positions.

Another critic points out to the construction of "the poor" as homogeneity, a defeat of difference or an essentialism grounded in essentialist theologies. I have mentioned it before and unfortunately have no time to develop it in here.

The framing of the poor's subjectivity attended to specific requirements from LT, a subjectivity that was caught up in social-economic strategies and engagements and homogeneous theological frameworks. Amidst this discourse of the poor's subjectivity, one blind spot

16. "Entrevista Joãozinho Trinta," Leia Brasil," n.p. [cited October 30 2015]. Online: http://www.leiabrasil.org.br/old/entrevistas/trinta.htm.

17. Jon Sobrino and Ignacio Ellacuria, eds. *Mysterium Liberationis: Fundamental Concepts of Liberation Theology* (Maryknoll, NY: Orbis Books, 1993). See a critique by Marcella Althaus-Reid in *Indecent Theology; Theological Perversions in Sex, Gender and Politics* (London and New York: Routledge, 2000).

was clear in the whole of LT literature, namely the absence of the body and sexual discourses. In the following part of this essay, I will examine the work of three theologians who have tried to deal with these absent issues.

THE BODY AND SEXUAL DISCOURSES IN LATIN AMERICA LIBERATION THEOLOGY

For this essay, I am considering the thought of three theologians (Rubem Alves, Jaci Maraschin, and Marcella Althaus-Reid) who have dared not to let issues of the body, desire, and sexualities slip away from theological discourses.[18] They created possibilities for others to think through these issues and have offered groundbreaking guidance for advanced studies. As I study their thought here, I do so by squeezing it into a nutshell and proposing an analysis of their work that includes both the *expansions* their thought has set forth in relation to what was normative in LT discourses, and also what I believe to be the *limitations* of their thought in relation to new understandings of the body and sexuality. I am well aware of the risks I run of being unfair to all of them, but I do it here with the purpose of keeping the dialogue flowing.

---

18. On the issues of sexuality from the most renewed theologians of LTLA we could mention Enrique Dussel. Amidst other projects, he tried to work on *an erotica Latin Americana* and the result couldn't be worse. In his own understanding of eros, he defends the idea of the *natural* relationship of man and woman, says that abortion is not natural and condemns homosexuality. Enrique D. Dussel, *Caminhos de Libertação Latino-Americana IV* (São Paulo, Brazil: Edições Paulinas, 1984), 211–213. See a consistent critique of Dussel's homophobia in the last chapter of Althaus-Reid's book *Indecent Theology*, 194–200.

Rubem Alves – The Unexpected Link between Theology and Desire[19]

Rubem Alves was one of the main Protestant theologians within Liberation Theology in Latin America. He studied theology at the Presbyterian Seminary in Campinas, Sao Paulo and later went to Union Theological Seminary in New York City where he became good friends with James H. Cone and Walter Wink. Right after his year at Union, he went back to Brazil and was persecuted by the Brazilian military dictatorship by way of his beloved Presbyterian Church of Brazil who turned him into the authorities as a "dangerous mind." For this reason, he returned to the United States and pursued his PhD at Princeton Theological Seminary under the advisory of Richard Shall. His book *A Theology of Human Hope*[20] is his PhD dissertation and one of the first seeds of LT thought. Back in Brazil, he wrote a seminal book on Brazilian Protestantism, which is still considered one of the most important books on this topic.[21] He also wrote a book on social philosophy and others on religion in Latin America.[22] He has published more than forty books.

---

19. Rubem Alves is a prolific writer. He has published more than 40 books and hundreds of chronicles, prose, poetry and aphorisms. For my purposes, I am using the following books: *Variações sobre a Vida e a Morte* (São Paulo: Ed. Paulinas, 1982); *O Suspiro dos Oprimidos* (São Paulo: Ed. Paulinas, 1984) and *Creio na Ressureição do Corpo. Meditações* (Rio de Janeiro: CEDI, 1984); articles: "*Des-:Livro, Contra o Método*; *Proseando, A Cozinha* and *Sobre Deuses e Caquis*," n.p. [cited August 1 2007]. http://www.rubemalves.com.br/.

20. Rubem A. Alves, *A Theology of Human Hope* (New York, NY: Corpus Books, 1969).

21. Rubem A. Alves, *Protestantismo e Repressão*. Ensaios 55 (São Paulo, Brazil: Ática, 1982).

22. Rubem A. Alves, *Tomorrow's Child. Imagination, Creativity and the Rebirth of Culture* (New York, NY: Harper & Row, 1972); *O Enigma da Religião* (Campinas, Spain: Papirus, 1984); *O Que é Religião?* (São Paulo, Brazil: Loyola, reprint 1999).

Rubem Alves helped at least three generations of theologians in Brazil to "loosen up their theological tongue."[23] He was one of the first theologians to diversify the forms of writing theology when no one knew or had the courage and/or creativity to do so. He blurred the field of theology not only with Marxisms, but he also introduced other strange partners to theology: poetry, literature, and psychoanalysis. Alves's theology has the body at the center of his thought, since for him it is in the body that everything starts. Theology is just a way of talking about the body. Here he defines theology:

> Theology is a way of talking about the body, the sacrificed bodies. It takes the bodies to pronounce the sacred name: God ... Theology is a poem of the body, the body praying, the body saying its hopes, talking about the fear to die, its dream of immortality, pointing to utopias, sword transformed in plowshares. Through this talk, the bodies hold hands and blend in a loving hug, sustaining them in order to resist and to keep walking.[24]

Using Marxist-psychoanalyst lenses, Alves says that the body does not float around without references in reality but it is always related to the larger world, as a continuation of nature and limited by society and its economy. His thought is indebted to Herbert Marcuse and the Frankfurt school of thought. He says: "I dare to ask: 'What is the purpose of having a free and just society if it does not provide space for the expansion of the body in pleasure, happiness and play?'"[25] He is also attuned to LT's glamorization of the poor. Criticizing the

---

23. Expression used by John Caputo to express his relation to Derrida's thought. See John D. Caputo and Carl Raschke, "Loosening Philosophy's Tongue: A Conversation with Jack Caputo," in *Journal for Cultural and Religious Theory* (2002), n.p. [cited October 30 2015]. Online: http://www.jcrt.org/archives/03.2/caputo_raschke.shtml.

24. Alves, *Variações sobre a Vida e A Morte*, 9.

25. Ibid., 34.

bourgeois view of the poor that says that the body is not a concern for the poor, he says:

> The poor smell bad, they don't treat their teeth, they are hungry more often and they cannot tune their sensibilities to classical music; besides, they are beaten up more often and they die earlier. For a flesh and blood person, this is the meaning of social class: what is possible and impossible for the body ... The (social) bodies are not the same, and also their gods ... The powerful are condemned to sing the love to power, while for the weak, they can only sing the power of love. I do not attribute special virtue to the poor. I am deformed enough by Calvinism, psychoanalyses and Marxism to do that. It is not their (the poor) option to sing the power to love. They are condemned to do it."[26]

For him, it is the body that makes us desire and dream dreams of transformation. For him, when negation is constantly imposed in daily life and these negations close down possibilities for the body to live an expanded life, the body becomes a site of resistance. In this process, the body imagines and creates new worlds, worlds that can hold dreams and make possible the actualization of the desires. "Imagination is the wing of the body and the body is the strength of imagination. Desire and power interpenetrate each other to give birth to hope ... That's how religion is constituted for those who love without power."[27]

His criticism has to do with the oppressors/colonizers who have tried to take away the perception of our bodies as a concrete and unified whole by imposing a relation to the body with an abstract realm of ideas:

---

26. Ibid., 34.
27. Ibid., 45–46, 65.

And now, as theologians we can revenge. Because we were humiliated when our traps were discovered, we pretended we were flying when we were only jumping. But now we have discovered that our detractors, embedded in a game called science, also entrapped us. Because there was an attempt to misguide us, they presented themselves to us as guardians of pure knowledge, without sheer beliefs or superstition, mirroring one hundred eyes, faithful reflection of their own objects, without desire or passion (Nietzsche) — and now we discovered that celestial or infernal beings do not exist in the world of the men (sic) ... No, there is no neutral world, the world is an extension of the body."[28]

The crossing point in which the theologian and the poor meet is the place of desire:

Where is the place of the theologian? It can only be the place of desire. It is there that hopes are born ... It happens however, that we become incapable of recognizing our desires ... Our desires are lost in a forgotten place imposed by the dominant order. What we love was interdicted because what the dominant order has offered us is not what we love. To name our desires is to recognize our condition of exiled people, out of place, u/topic, incarcerated in a present that represses the body, that carries an erotic-heretic project of liberation of life."[29]

Alves expands the notion of the self when he says that the project of liberation cannot be reduced to economical systems. One must understand that the body acts and reacts not only because it lacks bread, but is engendered by a larger process of desiring, even desires of unnamable things. In *O Suspiro dos Oprimidos*, Alves expands the

28. Ibid., 39.
29. Ibid., 201.

Marxist and economicist reduction of the body and evokes the need for the body to play:

> Life does not want to preserve itself only. Its intention is to express itself. It desires pleasure. It does not end in the process of eating, but includes the acts of laughing, dancing, singing and playing ... The question is the locus of the body. Where does the entire stimulus to dance come from?[30]

Moreover, using poetry and prose as resources for his theology, Alves worked with other possibilities for language, and turned the restricted focus of a social structured theological language, as seen in LT, into a looser language that opened up possibilities for issues such as the body and desire to appear. The body for him has a more serpentine way to get to things than theology's rigid set of categories of rational methods allows. He affirms: "My body does not understand the language of the method. Methods are rational procedures. But the body is a musical being. It only understands the language of aesthetics ... my body gets paralyzed, spelled and taken by the demon of gravity, dressed up with academic clothes."[31]

As a result, the theologian, who works within the boundaries of strict uses of reason, is replaced by the theo-poet, who works with the unfixed delimitations of the body through the freedom of language. For him, only the poets have the key to the human body and desire.

EXPANSIONS AND LIMITATIONS

Expansions: Alves expanded the notion of the self by widening the grid of theological language. Theological discourses were loosened up and became tools for dialogue with other fields, themes, and

---

30. Ibid., 177, 204.

31. Rubem A. Alves, "Des-Livro: Contra o Método," n.p. [cited October 2 2016]. Online: http://minhateca.com.br/Marcelahum/Galeria/DOC/Cr*c3*b4nica+-+Des--+Contra+O+M*c3*a9todo+-+Rubem+Alves,67459943.doc.

issues. Against Freud and Marx, he saw religion as a site for the body to find hope, resistance, and desire that could become revolutionary tools for the poor. His theological language helped Christian faith become suddenly beautiful and much more bearable for many people in Brazil, especially Protestants, which includes me; faith became more poetical than analytical, more mythical than literal, closer to the daily life than to the hierarchy of a given church. Methods were dependent on the ways in which the body moves and lives. He expanded the sources of theological partners, and finally, he brought the body to the center of the theological discourse, something unthinkable before him in any theological discourse in Latin America. In Alves, through sociological, psychoanalytical, theological and poetic approaches to the body of the poor, we learned the potentialities for resistance, the amazing sources of the human spirit, and the power of language to create worlds.

Limitations: Alves works in a faded Platonic framework that divides the body into inside and outside. Caught up in this binary, he looks more often to the inside of the body as desires somewhat replace the materiality of the unfulfilled body. For instance, truth lies *inside* of somebody rather than in and on the real marks of the concrete body. The body for Alves remains a sign of what the soul intends or yearns for and never becomes a site of material pleasure but casually expresses the concrete results of dreams, beauty, illness, and hopes. Paradoxically then, Alves's theological articulation of the body does not attend to much of the materiality of the body. The desires the body produces are related to feelings, longings, absence, and lacks of known and unknown things. The body and its desires are always trapped in nostalgic feelings of the past and of the future. The body is able to dream about the future and correct the past; it can connect with the present through the metaphors of food and garden, but it seems not so much able to engage with sexual desires. Alves uses the metaphor of the house to explain human life, and the privileged places of his house are the kitchen, the garden, and the room of mystery. The kitchen brings exhilarating experiences of the taste of food which gets to bodily senses; the garden produces nostalgia of immemorial times and hopes to plant trees for future generations; and the *room of the mystery* is the place in which the body keeps its most inner secrets and desires. Alves' house, however, does not have bedrooms, couches in living rooms or restrooms where the body could live its physical needs or sexualities. In Alves' house, desires do not relate to sex, i.e., his house is illuminated and beautifully described but there are not open experiences for sexual experiences. The body is correctly a language of demarcation, however not concretely experienced. Sexual experiences are hardly mentioned. Alves' body runs the risk of becoming a ghostly body, disembodied in its sexual possibilities. His theology of the body and sexuality helps construct a sense of the self in which race, gender, body and sexual practices are still denied by the sheer absence of its discourses. If they ever exist, they are always *absconditi*. In spite of his theological amplification of language, the sexual fluidity of the concrete body is still kept inward, fixed in unlocked rooms, and mostly untouched.

Jaci Maraschin – The Liturgy of the Body

Jaci Maraschin, like Rubem Alves, has also inspired more than three generations of students of theology including myself. He first studied theology in Porto Alegre, a state in the south of Brazil, then went to General Theological Seminary in New York City for his Master's, and then got his PhD in Strasbourg, France. He has published extensively but very little of his theological, liturgical, and artistic production has been published outside of Brazil. Maraschin had an enormous impact on theological education in Brazil when he was the general secretary of ASTE – Association of Evangelical Theological Seminaries.[32] He has worked with the World Council of Churches in various levels and has composed and published songs that have been published throughout the world. Once a theologian, Maraschin is now a poet, a musician and a religious thinker. He was a very important voice within the LT movement — especially in his writings on liturgy, on the body, and through the composition of songs. Influenced by LT, he has published the most influential theological hymnal in Brazil with more than 600 pages of popular songs that engaged theology, liturgical festivities and Brazilian culture in a way never seen before.[33]

Contrary to Alves, Maraschin's theology of the body is much more concrete and takes seriously the material contours of the body, including the bodies of the poor. In the midst of all sorts of disembodied theologies, Maraschin tried to recuperate a more positive notion of the body, stressing the need of the body to live a vigorous Christian faith, turning away the tendency to deny the body in Christian theology that used to see the body as impediment to the Christian faith. Here he defines his attempt to create a theology of the body:

> My experience in church and society has always been
> endangered by censorship and authoritarianism. The tradi-
> tional Protestantism, from which a great part of Anglican-
> ism comes from, never felt comfortable with the body and
> was always afraid of sexuality and eroticism. The church
> always talked about love but its love was more like altruism
> and renunciation than fruition of good and beautiful things
> in life. Many times I felt that, like Jesus who let himself be

---

32. Here the word *evangelical* does not have the same theological connotation as in United States. ASTE was not a conservative organization, but, on the contrary, one of the most progressive theological organizations in Brazil.

33. See Jaci C. Maraschin, ed., *O Novo Canto da Terra* (São Paulo, Brazil: IAET, 1987).

crucified, we, his followers, should also crucify ourselves making our desires bleed on the cross of this false morality that we all know too well. The church opted for Apollo when our bodies were siding with Dionysus, asking us to be flying angels when we were bodies made of flesh and bones. I tried to develop a theology of the body to protest against the de-erotization of life.[34]

After many articles, his theology was systematized in his analysis of the Constantine-Nicene Creed. In this book he tried to interpret one of the most important documents of the Christian church through the concrete bodies of the poor in Latin America through the lenses of philosophy, politics, ideology, hierarchical powers, daily life, and theological constrains that kept the life and the body of the poor away from fully embracing the Christian faith. In this book he asks: "What can baptism mean for those who are not used to taking a shower? What could Eucharist mean for those who don't have table, plate, glass or cutlery?"[35] In a disembodied culture in which Protestant theology was deeply influenced by pietism and conservative theological views, he kept calling people for a conversion *to* the body. That conversion to the body would certainly direct theology into different directions that would help to "construct a more fraternal society."[36] His concrete approach to the body made him known as heretic. Moreover, capitalism and globalization were for him spiritual enterprises that rendered the bodies of the poor spiritualized, that is, ideologically un-referentiated, un-codified. The conversion to a concrete body would imply a Christian faith radically attached to the body, its bones, blood, and tissues, as well as its sexuality and would

---

34. Ibid., 114.

35. Jaci Maraschin, *O Espelho e a Transparência. O Credo Niceno-Constantinopolitano e a teologia latino americana* (Rio de Janeiro, Brazil: CEDI, 1989), 246.

36. Jaci Maraschin, "Conversão e Corpo," in *Espiritualidade e religião na América Latina,* Estudos de Religião 4 (São Berbardi do Campo, São Paulo: IEPG, 1986), 6–83.

provoke political, social and economic awareness. He challenged Christian thought from a new paradigmatic notion of the body:

> When we realize that Christianity is the religion of the body par excellence, we should revise our liturgies and disincarnate hymns, our idealism located in heaven and our disincarnate religion. It is with the body that we worship God. But what body? How do we understand the body? Individualistically? Aside from other bodies? ... A theology of the body relates to sexuality ... it does not intend to establish the rules of the sexual game, but rather, to alert our contemporary society to the dangers of repression and to the fallacy of the isolation of sexuality from the larger context of society and history.[37]

Along with the notion of the body, he tries to talk about sexuality as a gift from God lived in the daily life of people. Going against the theological tides, he affirms that sexuality is a gift of life given by God. He deconstructs the ways in which main Christian theology relates to the body through platonic understandings of flesh, soul, spirit and spirituality. In an article entitled "Who controls my body?" he says it is not God who controls the body but life itself in its random movements. Churches had become mediations of life and body, and because of that, the Christian should always ask "what are the ways in which religion relates to the body?"[38] in order to perceive the ways in which the church controls the body and human sexuality.

It is especially through liturgy that he understands theology and the place of the body as it relates to faith. In a more recent article he talks about this relationship:

---

37. Jaci Maraschin, " Fé Cristã & Corpo," in *Fé Cristã: libertação do cativeiro para a esperança* (1986): 67–83.

38. Jaci Maraschin, "Quem manda no meu corpo?" *Jornal de Metodista* 1 e 2, (Setembro 1992): 1, 2.

The church centralized the liturgy of the sacrament on the
body and the blood of Christ. However, right away it forgot
that. Or at least, it was not consistent with what it used to
teach. When the church realized what the body and the
blood meant, it turned it into a spiritual matter. Body and
blood are earthly things and the church wanted to deal with
things from heaven. The church wanted to go beyond the
clouds and that's why it was suspicious of sexuality ... Liturgy moves around the space of human sensibility: vision,
smell, taste, tactile and audition. Jesus starts and ends his
ministry around the needs and pleasures of the body ... The
verb as flesh didn't fit within the limits of the dogma. Thus
Jesus was spiritualized ... When we relate liturgy with the
body in the celebration of the body and blood of Christ, it is
because the body is what we are. It is in this bodily quality
that liturgy becomes art in the body. That's why the church
invented processions, gestures, genuflections, holy kisses,
hugs, physical reverences and finally dances ... dance is
the erotic pulsing of the body in direction of the unknown,
thus, the ineffable. The liturgy that privileges the body
needs to perceive what this body shows and what it shows
in its surface or, in other words, in its skin. This surface can
be covered by veils and colors. But in this covering, it continues to be, is spite of all, the covered body that is always
able to be uncovered, thus revealed.[39]

He continues his critique when he asks "why the litanies of the
churches do not mention the problems of sexuality in their prayers
and the songs sung in church do not express the human gratitude
to God for the gift of orgasm ... "[40] Moreover, he attempts to find a

39. Jaci Maraschin, "Meia Hora de Silencio: liturgia na pos-moderinidade," in *Liturgia Anglicana*, Inclusividade: Revista Teologica de Estudos Anglicanos, 6 (2003):135–
136, 140.

40. Maraschin, "Quem manda no meu corpo?," 1.

theology that would imagine the idea of sexuality through the understanding of the virginal birth of Jesus:

> The Spirit acts to create a new life in the world through that woman (Mary) ... Maternity was freed from the weight of patriarchalism and on the other hand, even sexuality itself was freed for the confinement of the procreation process. That's why the symbol of Mary and its virginal maternity can be a place to imagine a new world of sexuality where the patriarchal traditional limits start to erode by those who prefer not to marry, by those who transgress the normative rules of monogamy, by male and female homosexuals and by transsexuals.[41]

He also thinks that both the understanding of the poor and the theological option for the poor has to be expanded beyond the economic grid. He is one of the first to attest to the fact that the option for the poor had to include those who are not traditionally considered as poor:

> But the humble (it would be better to say 'the humiliated') are also the women, the black and the homosexuals in our patriarchal society. Are we ready not only to make a preferential option for the poor and oppressed in its economic sense of this term but also, along with our sisters and brothers, to opt for liberation both in the church and it the world.[42]

Finally, he also expands human sexuality as he tries to expand the understandings of the body. In an attempt to define his notion of sexuality he writes:

> The limits of sexuality are the limits of the body. It starts in any part of the body and never ends. It goes from one

---

41. Ibid., 2.

42. Ibid., 2

place to another. It gets the head in delirium and trembles in the dorsal spine. Sometimes it gets concentrated in the genitals; collapses with the sexuality of other bodies; gets blurred and enmeshed. It makes what we are. It fills the world with lyricism and enchantment. It enters the labyrinths of desire; explodes in the trickster places of libido; fulfills itself in Pleasure.[43]

EXPANSIONS AND LIMITATIONS

Expansions: In his attempt to fight against abstract uses of theology, Maraschin helped many students of theology to engage the body in their theological discourses and especially in their liturgies. The practical result of his theology has been the free association between theology, the body, and Brazilian culture, its music, dance and festivities in unthinkable ways. When sexuality was a forbidden theme especially in Protestant theology, he gave to it a theological framework, affirming it, relating it to the materiality of the body and pleasures, connecting it to the core of Brazilian culture and rescuing it from mainline theological discourses that used to relate it with notions of sin. He does not like to be called a theologian anymore but rather a religious thinker, since he sees the field of theology as something that has already ended. Nonetheless, he gives us many hints into new possibilities for theological and religious thought and discourses.

Limitations: Maraschin's notion of the self works within the contours of the body, including its sexualities and possibilities. However, his ideas are spread out in various articles and show scattered comprehensions of the body but do not offer a consistent approach to a possible *politics of the body* which would entail a more expanded analysis of these political contours. In other words, while he does

---

43. Jaci Maraschin, "Os Limites da Sexualidade", in *Movimento popular. O Desafio da Comunicação,* Tempo e Presença 229 (March 1988): 26–27.

analyze theoretical and practical approaches such as colonized structures of oppression and exploitation of the body, a more sustained political, economic and specially racial, analysis of the processes of silencing and manipulation of bodies and sexualities are missing. His work is made of a series of many spread articles, only hinting at his thought, somewhat focusing it, and half way articulating/working through various directions that never offer a fully grounded thought with lingering effects. Thus, we keep asking what these possibilities can do to the theological discourses, what it can open or close, what politics it accesses or dismantles, what structure it displaces, what laws it breaks or what theological thoughts is spurs. But perhaps this is the way many Latinxs writers do their work.

Marcella Althaus-Reid

Althaus-Reid is an Argentinean theologian who was raised as Quaker in a Roman Catholic setting. She studied theology in Buenos Aires in one of the most important theological schools in Latin America, ISEDET. Althaus-Reid's theological thought as seen in her groundbreaking work was the first thorough attempt to undo and redo LT using tools taken from postcolonialism, post-Marxism, and especially queer theology.[44] Her awareness and powerful critiques of the "unquestionable western subject,"[45] including the ways LT was constructed, give her an expanded notion of the self as she tries to relate LT, the body and sexualities:

> The poor was a hasty concept. It referred mostly to the male-perceived peasant world of the poor, not to the urban poor, and to the Roman Catholic poor. It reflected the homogeneous tendencies inherited from the Western frame-

44. See Althaus-Reid, *Indecent Theology.*
45. Ibid., 16.

work of thinking theology ... Sex was out of the question, but a sexual shadow covers many triumphant writings with doubts and ambivalence. Not only did 'the poor' subsume women, it also subsumed lesbian, gay, transgendered and bisexual people ... The poor, as in any old-fashioned mor- alizing Victorian tale, were portrayed as the deserving and asexual poor.[46]

Inhabiting the same methodological approach of LT (praxis over doxa) she deconstructs this theology by finding in the *first step* or *first act* of theology not only sociological, economic, or political aspects of reality but also, and mainly, bodily and sexual threads, which she problematizes with unsettled sexual identities that compose and disrupt the reality of the poor in Latin America. Moreover, in her theological process she affirms that economic, political, social theories, and sexual identities are all interrelated and interconnected with "theological frames of support."[47] She brings to the attention of liberation theologians the notion that theological definitions of the body and sexual practices, explicit and not, which include its pos- sibilities and constraints, are the core materials that construct and define reality and its connection to life in general. She remembers that the interpreted self, including its bodily and sexual aspects, are always related to super-structures, i.e, the social, economic, and political configurations giving to it the very ground for its formation and determination. Her main goal is to undo these structures of thought through "disseminated resistances"[48] taken from materialist sexual approaches to the subject.

The emphasis of sexual identities in the making of theological frameworks turns theology into a sexual act, a way of dismantling

---

46. Ibid., 30.

47. Ibid., 176.

48. Ibid., 20.

not only Christian systematic or dogmatic theology but a way of disrupting and, to use her own word, *per-verting* the established norms of behaviors, thought, rituals, and life in all its particularities. The sexual theological framework is not only able to change purely theological assumptions but also able to change social realities.

Althaus-Reid starts by correctly accusing LT of being heterosexist, masculinist, and patriarchal. LT shares the same patterns of European theological grounds which maintain the body and sexualities of the poor outside of the theological, cultural, racial, gendered, economic, and social grid. The body and sexualities cannot be considered along with theological structures that leave the body and sexualities outside of the permitted grid, creating blind spots of thought and practices.

Althaus-Reid recuperates a sexual and bodily language that was dismissed altogether by LT, which includes not only desires but sexual desires, desires of the flesh, lust, secrecy, kisses, smell, obscenity, sexual perversion, bodily fluids, gays, lesbians, cross-dressers, transgender persons, fetishism, sadomasochism, sensuality, etc. With this language she expands the critical and culturally contradictory site of the human body, emphasizing the many ways in which women's bodies and sexualities have been controlled and constrained. She aims to break down binary systems that structure Western thought and consequently theological systems that keep women, their bodies and sexualities on the down side of the hierarchical dualisms of male/women and mind/body.

One way of dismantling this binary structure for her is to establish the body as the paradigm that relates and blurs sexuality and economics as well. She says that a body paradigm

> is therefore pertinent in theological analysis, and does not need to come from the European Other, but from the lemon vendors, who embrace in their lives the economic and sexual connotations of the survivors of the destruction

of the Grand Narratives of Latin America. The paradigm is an indecent paradigm, because it undresses and uncovers sexuality and economy at the same time.[49]

Regarding sexuality, she means "a site of bodily and emotional preferences which defines a sexual and/or gender identity."[50] As for the notion of the self, she refers to Rosi Braidotti:

> Rosi Braidotti has considered how the subject is defined at the crossroads of multiple variables (sex, gender, race, class, etc.) and by the interaction of both material and discursive practices. In theology, this interaction is an intertextuality and intersexuality.[51]

Althaus-Reid is at the edge of disseminating resistance and indecency against the ongoing and preposterous colonization of the subject as she invites theology to risk moving around non-defined and perverted notions of sexual identities, sexual performances, of bodily and sexual practices in general.

In *The Queer God*, she continues to deconstruct theological terms and reframe theology through a critique of white heterosexual patriarchal frames, undoing theological postulates and popular understandings of Christian beliefs and dogmas. However, in this book, she does not see heterosexual theology as her univocal enemy in *Indecent Theology,* but engages her theological hermeneutics with "Queer Theory, non-heterosexual and *critical Heterosexual Theology.*"[52]

In this book, she continues her project of disseminating unthinkable ways of thinking about God and human sexualities, identities, relations and practices. This time she brings more stories from Latin

---

49. Ibid., 19.

50. Ibid., 109.

51. Ibid., 82.

52. Althaus-Reid, *The Queer God,* (London & New York: Routledge, 2003), 2 (italics mine).

American people, especially indigenous people, and tries to challenge pervasive "colonial assumptions"[53] that determinate what and who Latin Americans are or are supposed to be. She tries to use new understandings of sexuality as a way to break down solid systems of thought and create new and expanded definitions of religion, economics, and social and sexual constructions. She says: "The point is that, although religions are made for, or around, clear sexual classificatory patterns, sexuality limits or opens up the horizon of religious systems."[54]

Her theology assumes notions of ambiguity, intranslatability, and un-representation. This un-site of theology creates a kind of strange God for the well-known structures of love and knowledge. This Queer God, foreign and unfamiliar at first, can be realized in the midst of the poor and indecent people in their own, radically communal and overwhelming hospitality.

EXPANSIONS AND LIMITATIONS

Expansions: LT has in Althaus-Reid a dangerous and at the same time dazzling companion: dangerous because she disrupts the core of LT thought, and dazzling because she presents LT to unfolding folds of thought and theological possibilities. Her inter-disciplinary work brings together unthought possibilities from which LT can recreate itself. Her expanded notion of the self not only calls LT's methodology into account regarding its blind spots, but also entraps it through twisted uses, cleaving moves, and by tearing apart its grounded system. There is much to think in and through her work and even more to see it actualized.

---

53. Ibid., 116.
54. Ibid., 160.

Limitations: As a way to engage in a lengthy dialogue with her groundbreaking work as a new radical form of LT, I will use most of this space to make a longer critique. 1) Her work in *Indecent Theology* runs the risk of reducing the limits of the subject only to the realm of non-heterosexual instances. An Indecent Theology is only possible through the exposition of non-heterosexual obscenities: sado-masochism, exhibitionism, and hard-core sexual acts. Any *unadventurous theology* that escapes this grid of queer experiences remains systematic theology, thus evil. 2) The "new poor" in her theological system are only made of gays, lesbians, cross-dresser, and transgender people. Only they live in the margins and are properly able to be indecent, obscene, deviant, and perverted, central requirements for an Indecent Theology. 3) The glorification of the poverty by liberation theologians is mirrored in the same glorification of the sexual, perverted stories of the poor in Althaus-Reid's examples. By emphasizing and centering perverted sexual habits of poor people over and against normative sex, she runs the risk of switching the binary normative/perverted sexualities upside down. The binary is not undone, just replaced. 4) Perhaps because she comes from Argentina, a country with a relatively small population of black people, she lacks a thorough analysis of race in her work. Coming from Brazil, I must say that a race analysis should be at the core of any Indecent Theology.

A QUESTION WAS LEFT OUT:
CAN THE POOR SPEAK?

LT was a product of modernity, grounded in a great scheme of grand narratives. In spite of its newness, of its indigenous voice, of its emphasis on the lives of the poor in Latin America, its structure mirrored the same limits, boundaries, and repression imposed by Western

European colonizing thought, so much so that LT wanted to re-tell/ re-write the whole structure of theology through its fundamental doctrines.[55]

However, due to the growing globalized process of exclusion seen throughout the world, one cannot simply abandon LT as a thing of the past. On the contrary, it is more than urgent and necessary to think about different ways to dialogue with this theology and find other paths and partners in a possible new theology that continuously engages the poor. As a starting point for new dialogues the question that one should continuously pose is: What has LTLA left out of its various discourses? While LTLA was, on one hand, deeply preoccupied with the oppression and concrete needs of the poor in Latin America, at the same time it reproduced the same power/knowledge compound of the colonizer's thought in various ways, either forgetting, not knowing, silencing, hiding, or leaving some aspects of the poor's possible subjectivity outside the realm of its main preoccupations.

One can relate LT's assumptions concerning the body and sexualities to what Foucault says of modern Puritanism. He said that " ... modern Puritanism imposed its triple edict of taboo, nonexistence and silence."[56] It is not difficult to see how LT's use of reason enforced this triple edict throughout its praxis and discourses: it never depicted sexual stories in their theological task of listening to the poor. Oppressed bodies don't have sex, don't make love. Poor people were always too busy working or searching for jobs, crying, resisting, suffering from all kinds of oppression and being faithful to Christ and to the church in order to have sex or waste time having any kind of bodily pleasure and/or sexual imagination. The theological silence

---

55. See Jon Sobrino and Ignacio Ellacuria, eds., *Mysterium Liberationis: Fundamental Concepts of Liberation Theology* (New York, NY: Orbis Books, 2004).

56. Michel Foucault, *The History of Sexuality: An Introduction,* vol. 1 (New York, NY: Vintage Books, 1990), 5.

reinforced the idea of non-existent sexual practices among the poor and ignored the idea that sex was an important aspect of human life, re-avowing the taboo of sexuality and its sinful relations to pleasure as well as restricting the understanding of sex to means of reproduction. Through this theological silence, LT regulated what was *the* theological discourse in relation to the body and to sex. Again, the story of sexuality in LT can be seen as an analogous to what Foucault said in his history of sexuality: "What is at issue, briefly, is the overall 'discursive fact', the way in which sex is put into discourse."[57]

Along with the necessary movement between critique, expansions, limitations, etc., done in this essay and the important contributions these three thinkers have made to the theological thought in Latin America, I want now, briefly, to call attention to the "discursive fact" that grounds the theological work of LT in general, even the work of the three mentioned theologians analyzed here, in regards to the poor as a subject of history and the construction of its subjectivity.

The task of LT was the faithful reconstruction of the world through the point of view of the poor, the new subject of history. From this perspective, the subjectivity of the poor, the material and non-material components of that which belongs to the life of the poor in general and specifically were created and solidly defined. This effort was done without any awareness that this project of describing the poor could entail certain impossibility at its core. There was too much trust and certainty that the poor could be simply grasped, understood, explained.

In all its processes, and because the poor were *the* subject and the core of this theology, there was a question that remained unasked by liberation theologians, namely: Is it possible to talk about the poor? Liberation theologies in general never asked whether the very

---

57. Ibid., 11.

notion of the poor was possible, never considered their discourses about the poor as weak, compromised, mortally wounded, impossible in inescapable ways. On the contrary, the very notion of the poor went for the most part uninterrogated. Eventually it became a given. The social tragedy was such that just the mentioning of the poor was enough to give grounds to any "honest", (read unchecked) theological construction. LT never paid attention to the fact that in defining the poor, and consequently its subjectivity, it erased other variables of gender, race, class, sex, and other unsaid perspectives, forgotten themes, silenced desires, and unthought presences. By defining the poor, they also decided what was important to them regarding sex and bodily pleasures, which turned out to be in LT literature nonexistent practices. They thus reified taboos that had been constructed by the Christian church in Brazil since the *conquista* by way of silence.

Another pressing question should be asked: Can the poor speak? Here one should meditate on the well-known words from the South Asian thinker Gayatri Spivak, "can the subaltern speak?"[58]

The colonization process along with the new imperial "globalatinization"[59] of the world has made the poor and the understanding of poverty more scattered and more undefinable than ever before. The definition of spiritual poverty and material poverty provided by Gustavo Gutierrez in 1969 has become too simplistic and must be re-examined. Who are the poor today? Those who live in abject social conditions? Those who are homeless? Those who live under the stress of war? Women? Those who are black in Brazil or black women in the US? Those who are gay, lesbian, cross-dressers, or

---

58. Gayatri Chakravorty Spivak. "Can the Subaltern Speak",? in *Marxism and the Interpretation of* Culture (eds. Cary Nelson and Lawrence Grossberg; Champaign, IL: Univ. Of Illinois Press, 1988), 271–316.

59. Jacques Derrida, *Acts of Religion*, ed. Gil Anidjar (New York, NY: Routledge, 2002), 50.

transgender? Those who are physically challenged? Those undocumented in other countries often called illegals? Those who suffer in hospitals? Those who have their identities silenced? Prostitutes in Amsterdam or in Brazil? The drug addict in Switzerland or Colombia? Those who live in the *morros* of Rio de Janeiro or in the *favelas* of Sao Paulo? Those who suffer from AIDS and hunger in Africa or in Asia? Those who lost their loved ones on September 11th or the uncounted families who lost loved ones in massive attacks by the US in Iraq? Those who have lost their jobs in Singapore or the immigrants unemployed in France? Those who work at Dunkin' Donuts in Massachusetts or in the sweatshops in Papua New Guinea? The boy who was born in the shanty town in the Northeast part of Brazil and will never have the chance to go to college or the boy who gets his highest degree at one of the top Ivy League university in US but gets cancer? The girl who sells her body on the street of Peru or the girl who is battered by her husband in Africa? Who are the poor today?

The recent explosions of identities and the excessive confidence in the notion of "experience" as the core and sole criterion for theological constructions have turned the field of liberation theologians into a dead end; that is, small groups breaking down from other small groups, creating smaller communities that try to preserve their identity at the expense of isolation by increasing and exclusion. Thus, minority groups fight for some ink to publish their own voices and can only connect to other groups that do not incur any possibility of collision/challenge of their own identity. How to understand these scattered discourses? How to avoid silence? How to be *honest* to excluded minorities? How to engage with their subjectivities without imposing others' categories upon them? How to include them all in a course syllabus or in a theological agenda?

Twisting our previous question, how do we take the poor as the subject of any theological discourse? Is it possible to "know" them? Is it necessary or is it a must? Is not the process of understanding also a movement of power and control? How do we describe the lives of the poor *properly*? What are their experiences? Can a theologian write about her/his experience and make it account for most of her/his people? What to do or how to speak of unclaimed and unspeakable experiences that lie at the heart of someone's communities? What about the *inhuman* experiences within human experiences? How do we re-count them? How does one account for a subjectivity when experiences are ambiguous, forgotten, forbidden, fearful, traumatic, impossible to grasp? Are these untold stories part of the poor's subjectivity? In a possible wide spectrum of many possible experiences, which are the ones that should be kept? How can we be fair to everyone? How does one know what are the necessary aspects of the lives of the poor without selecting and choosing for oneself? Is the telling of the stories of the poor enough? Is it possible to translate them with fidelity? What tools should one use to tell their stories/histories/herstories? Moreover, how to deal with the "them" in relation to the "us"? What is "us" and what is "them"? What to do with the voice of the poor? Can one listen properly? Do they speak? Can they speak? To what extent are their voices my voice or is my voice attempting to be their voice? Trying to wrap up these questions into one, the question becomes the question of representation: Is it possible to re-present the poor? Lyotard says:

> The unrepresentable is what is the object of an idea, and for which one cannot show (present) an example, a case, even a symbol. The universe is unrepresentable, so is humanity, the end of history, the instant, space, good, etc. The absolute in general says Kant. For to present is to relativize, to

place into contexts and conditions of presentation, in this case plastic contexts and conditions.[60]

Unending understandings of the self, conflicted politics of representation, explosions of identities, indefinable sexual performances, untranslatable cultures, reversed anthropology, internalized/blurred colonized laws, an increasingly exclusive economic market, shrinking spaces of differences, the growth of conservatism and fundamentalism, radically opposed theological positions, all of these aspects severely and inescapably influence the work of the *organic theologian*.

Again, questions related to the body, sexualities, and theology are posed to us as exploded ways into our knowledge construction; that is, we work among the ruins of ourselves and our opaque ways to see reality and ourselves. Then the question becomes: is it possible for the body to be apprehended and theologically described? How can sexual experiences be collected and re-told? What is revelatory about the human experience and what hides from being revealed? How can we create ethical discourses without reinventing metaphysical approaches to the poor? How can we make a theological account of this all-too-concrete life of the poor when one cannot escape the solipsism of language or the meta-regulations of the undecidable? From a feminist perspective, this difficulty with the body is clear and devastating:

> The body has, however, been at the center of feminist theory precisely because it offers no such 'natural' foundation for our pervasive cultural assumptions abut femininity. Indeed, there is a tension between women's lived bodily experiences and the cultural meanings inscribed on the female body that always mediated those experiences ... the female

---

60. Jean-François Lyotard, *The Inhuman* (Stanford, CA: Stanford University Press), 126.

body (is) a contested site — a battleground for competing ideologies.[61]

Spivak also reminds us about the representation of the figure of the woman:

> Between patriarchy and imperialism, subject-constitution and object-formation. The figure of the woman disappears, not into a pristine nothingness, but into a violent shuttling which is the displaced figuration of the 'third-world woman' caught between tradition and modernization.[62]

In her own examination of the notion of the subaltern in her postcolonial studies, Spivak says that the subaltern cannot speak, especially women. The subaltern's voice is enmeshed in such a way with the voice of the colonizer that one can only try to find the voice of the subaltern by deconstructing the code and the voice of the colonizer in the colonizer's own texts. Spivak's project is not to give up representation but to try to get to the voices of the subaltern through the deconstruction of western canonic philosophical texts.

Liberation theologies have never dealt sufficiently with such questions. They have always assumed "reality" as such and have taken for granted their ability to re-present, translate, or determine whatever the poor want or desire, suffer or expect. So much so, that the discourses of LT have become a self-reflexive and self-determinant theology. After some time, LT didn't even need the poor anymore. The subject was all figured out in known categories.

---

61. Katie Conboy, Nadia Medina and Sarah Stanbury, eds., *Writing on the Body: Female Embodiment and Feminist Theory* (New York, NY: Columbia Univ. Press, 1997), 1, 7.

62. Spivak, "Can the Subaltern Speak?" 306.

CONCLUSION — THE WRITING OF THE SELF AND ITS (IM)POSSIBILITIES

The question of representation lies at the center, if there is a center, of any theological enterprise. How to re-present that which might have never been presented or might be excessively present? How to give an account of the exploitations of bodies and sexes throughout Latin America? How can we relate these bodies and sexualities to the interplay of notions of capitalism, of races, of culture, of gender, of identities, of globalization, of homogenization, of multiculturalism, of democracy, of fragmentation, of theologies, etc.?

As I have argued, the body and sexual discourses are not "immediate" aspects of the poor's subjectivity. What then might mediate this aporia? How can we face this impasse?

On the one hand, the notion of the subject is not a given and its irreducible materiality precludes full apprehension and description. In this *khoral*[63] space, the self is not *there*, as a presence waiting to be represented or properly described by our theologies. The notion of the self is left irreducibly open, since no discourse can exhaust it completely, making the work of the theologian very difficult as it asks for different closures made from different starting points. The self, therefore, is like possible worlds made of breaks and emergences and the complications of its possibilities. Jean-Luc Nancy affirms, "the world as possibility, or the world as chance for existence (opening/ closing of possibility, unlimitation/disaster of possibility)."[64] These possibilities of the world, of the self, and of subjectivity have to deal with its incongruence, ambiguities, paradoxes, impossibilities, limi-

---

63. *Khora* is a word found in Plato's writings and used by contemporary writers such as Jacques Derrida and Luce Irrigaray. *Khora* is an unnamable place, verifiable but never defined.

64. Jean-Luc Nancy, "Introduction," in *Who Comes After the Subject?* eds. Eduardo Cadava, Peter Connor, and Jean-Luc Nancy (New York and London: Routledge, 1991), 2.

tations, mistakes and its overflowing outcomes which make language fail to grasp, to interpret, to reiterate or to represent. Nancy says:

> There is nothing nihilist in recognizing that the *subject* — the property of the self — is the thought that reabsorbs or exhausts all possibility of being-in-the-world (all possibility of *existence*, all existence as being delivered to the possible) and that this same thought, never simple, ever closed upon itself without remainder, designates and delivers an entirely different thought: that of the one and that of the some one, of the singular existent that the subject announces, promises, and at the same time conceals.[65]

The recognizing of the subject and all its possibilities in the world are caught up in a web of promises and annunciations that are always engaging with that which creates a different thought that conceals itself. On the other hand, the endless crossroads in which the self gets materialized cannot just be suspended in *aporias*, in indeterminacies and sheer impossibilities. Whatever we make of the self, even its effacement, will turn into self-defined structures that will constitute both imposed limits to the description of the self and also the appearance of experiences known and yet to be discovered. The notion of the self, if possible, will always have to be fluid and open to unending definitions. The attempt is to deconstruct the notion of "the poor" by bringing about provisory identities, unpacking this unmoved colonized self and offering other possible configurations. In that sense, the theological work will necessarily be a work of continuity and discontinuity, of links and dis-ruptions. The life of the poor in its subjectivity, incongruence, vices, blurred interiority and exteriority, hopes, passions, sexual adventures, economic trials, and experiences *in general*, lies in this movable grounds of risky materiality as mentioned before in Althaus-Reid's use of Braidotti's

---

65. Ibid., 4.

perspective on the multiple variables of the self and the interaction of material and discursive practices.

To fight injustice, suffering, and oppression in Latin America, new approaches to LT will have to be critically able and creatively skilled to discover *per-verted* and *disfiguring* ways of life amidst life. Its theories and propositions will have to be inscribed "in the infinity of the transformation of 'realities'."[66]

It is in between impossibilities and possibilities, within metonymies, intertextuality, intersexuality, and interstitiality[67] that the work of the theologian, as it relates to the subjectivity of the poor, should be done. The un-represented self does not render itself a-historically or non-referenced. The self has always been a construct, represented and exploited since immemorial times in various forms, values, norms, and perspectives. These representations cannot remount to an original self or to a proper notion of the subjectivity. The self, as well as God, democracy, the good, etc., is always the re-presentation of a re-presentation, rendering the present impossible. The represented self constructed and imposed by the *conquistador* over the colonized bodies and minds of Latin American people has been the one of the most powerful and devastating *dis*-figurings of the self

---

66. Lyotard, *The Inhuman*, 22.

67. Mark C. Taylor's understanding of interstitiality can help us here: "What is required is to think in terms of interstitiality rather than oppositionality. The problem is that language is structured, as the structuralists have taught us, in terms of binary oppositions. Hence it is impossible to articulate that what we are attempting to think ABOUT directly. Our discourse must be, in Kierkegaard's terms but with a different twist, indirect ... the interstitial is the domain of alternation (one of the nuances of altarity) where the sacred oscillates in an approaching withdrawal and withdrawing approach. The interstitial is neither here nor there; it is not present and yet not absent ... this is what the about that religion is about implies — no more than implies because, of course, it can never be specified, determined, articulated, or fixed." In Mark C. Taylor and Carl Raschke, "About *About Religion:* A Conversation with Mark C. Taylor," *Journal for Cultural and Religious Theory*, n.p. [cited October 30 2015]. Online: http://jcrt.org/archives/02.2/taylor_raschke.shtml.

in the last 500 years. It created the self according to its own image and self-understandings and established a necessary *other* in order to keep the sameness of its self protected. The understanding of the other shaped reality, economy, politics, health, sexuality, law, theology, money, and inner perceptions that carried a world that didn't belong to the colonized.

As new theologies try to deconstruct it, one gets confused/disconnected/detached/lost/dizzy with the sound of one/many voices, sometimes criticizing, sometimes being appropriated and/or assimilated, or appropriating the other without knowing; sometimes including issues, topics, senses, understandings that were left out, sometimes denying what could be a site for possibilities, sometimes forgetting to affirm and never being able to get rid of the internalized deformation of 500 years of intense destruction. The deformation is part of our constant process of formation. The world economic order sets the poor in disorder, as the one to blame and to eradicate as if we are going in the wrong direction. The represented *self*, constructed and imposed by the *conquistador* over the colonized bodies and minds of Latin American people, has still affected the ways in which we see ourselves. That violence is such that our discourses cannot remember what we once were, IF we once were. We cannot understand anything without the colonizing discourses that continue to render ourselves almost incognito. This elicits a sense of having never actually been born, but rather, having always already been made; it is a feeling/sense/cognito that can only be understood by the title given to us *a posteriori* by somebody else and placed on a label somewhere (always) else in our marginal history. Our selves are engulfed in the noises of the voices of the other and every time we speak we have to scream. In spite of it all, to not undo this structure is to let our selves, whatever these selves might be, be endlessly re-appropriated, re-presented by *the Other,* allowing processes of destruction, devastation, exploitation and death. The same other colonized self is always ready to take advantage of *the o/Other.* New constructions of LT need to keep doing their job: nagging, disquieting, destroying, and deconstructing the unmoved notion of the colonized self in unlimited ways in order to create new possibilities for the poor to express, live, and experience life in a more expanded way. In a sense, this project relates to what Spivak says of Derrida:

> Derrida marks radical critique with the danger of appropriating the other by assimilation ... He calls for a rewriting of the utopian structural impulse as 'rendering delirious that interior voice that is the voice of the other in us.'[68]

However, this politicized approach to the self, this dis-appropriation of the other by ways of assimilation, this attempt to re-present an (im)possible Latin American self always comes with a reminder: whatever notion of subjectivity that might be constructed must be done with/for the poor in a more responsible manner, with a certain awareness of the constant blind spots that one will leave unattended. Unmistakably, the poor of liberation theologies is always and already partially represented, a chosen poor in some of its particularities, a poor that always relates to our own precarious understandings, opaque visions, and erring systems.

"The poor" is always a trap in theological linguistic tools. Ultimately, the poor can neither be described nor represented, neither affirmed nor denied, neither embraced nor rejected. New liberation theologies have to be honest with its continuous but failed endeavor and leave aside any self-righteous endorsement as being true representatives of the poor. To talk about the poor is to work with blurred hermeneutics and to attempt any presentation is to write unfair

---

68. Spivak, "Can the Subaltern Speak?" 308.

theologies, because of its impossibility. Theology should be then the activation of differences, and to err in these new theological events might be seen almost as a given, however a given that never leaves us powerless! I would say that new liberation theologians should be like Lyotard's philosophers or artists:

> The text he (sic) writes, the work he produces are not in principle governed by preestablished rules ... (they) are working without rules in order to formulate the rules of what *will have been done*. Hence, the fact that work and text have the characters of an *event* ... it must be clear that it is our business not to supply reality but to reinvent allusions to the conceivable which cannot be presented ... Let us wage the war on totality; let us be witnesses to the unpresentable; let us activate the differences and save the honor of the name.[69]

Perhaps now, with what we have learned with Leonardo Boff's situation, and without the fixed horizon of LT's methodological categories, theologians can re-act differently with unnamed women and men. Perhaps now, we might even start by naming that woman, an unspeakable name that will evoke millions of other unnamed women, in spite of all the complications of the proper. Perhaps, now, by adding another twisted floor of desire to our Marxist materialistic tools, we might engage not only with the surroundings of all her social poverty and deprived life, but also with the constant shutting down of her desires, the yearnings of her concrete body. Perhaps, now, we might learn with Maraschin to pray and ask and thank God for our orgasm, so that our theologies might include the pleasures not listed in our theologies. Perhaps, now, we might take each ex-

---

69. Jean-François Lyotard, "Note on the Meaning of the Word 'Post' and Answering the Question 'What is Postmodernism?'" in *Continental Aesthetics. Romanticism to Postmodernism: An Anthology*, eds. Richard Kearney and David Rasmussen (Massachusetts and Oxford: Blackwell Publishers, 2001), 370.

perience with its horizons, concealments and many possibilities of closures as rapture, an unforeseen, uncontrolled movement that changes our theologies and our ways of thinking and living in our bodies completely, radically, without remainders or solace. Perhaps, now, we can start a new liturgical procession with the poor, holding together an overflowing chalice of desires and absences, potentialities and miseries, contradictions and desperation, political betrayals and small gestures of redemption, death and unexpected epiphanies of our daily lives, trying endlessly to give contours to our lost graces. As we work with these contours, we must be aware of the beautiful muse singing that offers total fulfillment, sang and proposed by the malleable traps and paradoxes of the mighty capitalistic market. And as we go, we will keep trying to pay attention to that which we keep denying, forgetting, forbidding, destroying. Perhaps, now, through the theological liquids and excretions of our bodies, kisses and sexualities, we perform our subjectivities of becoming.

Perhaps, we might gain a twisted eye and ear not only to see and hear the unnamed woman differently, but also to see and hear the ways in which life appears and demands, sometimes scarcely, sometimes abundantly, sometimes hidden, sometimes blatantly in and through our bodies, desires, sexualities, and our blessed as well as anguished materiality.

My harsh critique of the first generation of liberation theologians does not eliminate the obligation to keep going back to them, since they have given us the first tools to create a liberation theology in Latin America. Thus, returning always again to Leonardo Boff, his traces help us to move forward and backward regarding the poor and our organic theologies. First, we must remember to keep a long silence of perplexity before the O/other. Then, we should know that our theologies will always be ill-equipped, provisory, mistaken, always begging to be remade. Thus, every time we encounter the poor we have to go back to our theologies and re-write everything we thought we once knew. Every time we meet the poor we must ask for forgiveness, confessing our mistakes, our failures, our horrors, and our joys, the impossibilities of our grasp and how it would have been done if only we only knew how to encounter the O/*other*, that which is not myself, and yet, fully part of myself. Then, perhaps we might begin to become faithful through our failures and a little more consistent with our theological practices and thoughts through our often glorious well-meaning intentions, embarrassing arrogances, preserved distance and ashamed miscomprehensions.

References

Althaus-Reid. *The Queer God.* London & New York: Routledge, 2003.

Althaus-Reid, Marcella. *Indecent Theology; Theological Perversions in Sex, Gender and Politics.* London and New York: Routledge, 2000.

Alves, Rubem A. *A Theology of Human Hope.* New York, NY: Corpus Books, 1969.

Alves, Rubem A. "Des-Livro: Contra o Método". No pages. Cited October 3 2016. Online: http://minhateca.com.br/Marcelahum/Galeria/DOC/Cr*c3*b4nica+-+Des--+Contra+O+M*c3*a9todo+-+Rubem+Alves,67459943.doc

Alves, Rubem A. *Protestantismo e Repressão.* São Paulo, Brazil: Ática, 1982.

Alves, Rubem A. *Tomorrow's Child. Imagination, Creativity and the Rebirth of Culture.* New York, NY: Harper & Row, 1972.

Alves, Rubem A. *O Enigma da Religião.* Campinas, Spain: Papirus, 1984.

Alves, Rubem A. *O Que é Religião?* São Paulo, Brazil: Loyola, 1999.

Boff, Clodovis. *Teologia e Prática. Teologia do Político e suas Mediações.* Rio de Janeiro, Brazil: Ed. Vozes, 1978.

Boff, Leonardo. *Brasas Sob Cinzas: Stories of the Anti-Quotidien.* Sao Paulo, Brazil: Ed. Record, 1996.

Caputo, John D. and Raschke, Carl. "Loosening Philosophy's Tongue: A Conversation with Jack Caputo." *Journal for Cultural and Religious Theory* (2002) No pages. Cited October 30 2015. Online: http://www.jcrt.org/archives/03.2/caputo_raschke.shtml.

Conboy, Katie, Medina, Nadia and Stanbury, Sarah, eds. *Writing on the Body: Female Embodiment and Feminist Theory.* New York, NY: Columbia Univ. Press, 1997.

Dussel, Enrique. *Historia da Teologia na America Latina.* Sao Paulo, Brazil: Paulinas, 1985.

Freire, Paulo. *Pedagogy of the Oppressed.* New York, NT: Continuum, 2000.

Foucault, Michel. *The History of Sexuality: An Introduction,* vol. 1. New York, NY: Vintage Books, 1990.

Gutiérrez, Gustavo. *A Theology of Liberation. History, Politics and Salvation.* Maryknoll, NY: Orbis Books, 1988.

Gutiérrez, Gustavo. *Densidad del Presente.* Lima, Peru: Instituto Bartolome de las Casas-RIMAC e Centro de Estudios y Publicaciones-CEP, 1996.

Derrida, Jacques. *Acts of Religion.* New York, NY: Routledge, 2002.

Libanio, Joao Batista and Antoniazzi, Alberto. *20 Anos de Teologia na América Latina e no Brasil.* Rio de Janeiro, Brazil: Ed. Vozes, 1993.

Lyotard, Jean-François. "Note on the Meaning of the Word 'Post' and Answering the Question 'What is Postmodernism?'" Pages 47-50 in *Continental Aesthetics. Romanticism to Postmodernism: An Anthology.* Edited by Richard Kearney and David Rasmussen. Massachusetts and Oxford: Blackwell Publishers, 2001.

Lyotard, Jean-François and Geoffrey Bennington. *The Inhuman: Reflections on Time.* Stanford, CA: Stanford University Press, 1992.

Maraschin. Jaci C., ed. *O Novo Canto da Terra.* São Paulo, Brazil: IAET, 1987.

Maraschin, Jaci. *O Espelho e a Transparência. O Credo Niceno-Constantino-politano e a teologia latino americana.* Rio de Janeiro, Brazil: CEDI, 1989.

Maraschin, Jaci. "Conversão e Corpo." *Estudos de Religião* 4 (1986), 6–83.

Maraschin, Jaci. *Fé Cristã: libertação do cativeiro para a esperança.* São. Bernardo do Campo, Brazil: IEPG, 1986.

Maraschin, Jaci. "Quem manda no meu corpo?" *Jornal de Metodista* 1-2 (1992): 1-2.

Maraschin, Jaci. "Meia Hora de Silencio: liturgia na pos-moderinidade." *Liturgia Anglicana,* 6 (2003):135-140.

Maraschin, Jaci. "Os Limites da Sexualidade". in *Movimento popular. O Desafio da Comunicação,* Tempo e Presença 229 (March 1988): 26–27.

Nancy, Jean-Luc. "Introduction." Pages 1-8 in *Who Comes After the Subject?* Edited by Eduardo Cadava, Peter Connor, and Jean-Luc Nancy. New York and London: Routledge, 1991.

Sobrino, Jon and Ellacuria, Ignacio, eds. *Mysterium Liberationis: Fundamental Concepts of Liberation Theology.* New York, NY: Orbis Books, 2004.

Spivak, Gayatri Chakravorty. "Can the Subaltern Speak?." Pages 271–316 in *Marxism and the Interpretation of Culture*. Edited by Cary Nelson and Lawrence Grossberg. Champaign, IL: Univ. Of Illinois Press, 1988.

Tellechea Idígoras, José Ignacio. *Vocabulário teológico para a America Latina*. São Paulo, Brazil: Ed. Paulinas, 1983.

"Entrevista Joãozinho Trinta," Leia Brasil." No pages. Cited October 30 2015. Online: http://www.leiabrasil.org.br/old/entrevistas/trinta.htm.

PERVERSION, ETHICS, AND CREATIVE DISREGARD

Indecency as the Virtue to Ethical Perversion

ROBYN HENDERSON-ESPINOZA

INTRODUCTION

Marcella Althaus-Reid's work has given theologians and ethicists a way to pervert theology. We do this via Indecencia (Indecency), a method that privileges fleshly narratives and furthermore puts material flesh on bodies that have been displaced and wasted by the over-dominant segments of power structures.[1] Indecent Theology's point of departure is fundamentally about suspicion, and it concerns the ideological use(s) of tradition and the traditional understandings that emerge from a Decent Theology — a theology that is stabilized in the Center for the consumption by the dominant members of so-

---

1. Place and displacement are important aspects of developing a postcolonial theory of space and place. The margins of the margins, in Althaus-Reid's language, are places of displacement, but instead of considering these places vile and dispensable, I consider these places important places for perversion to emerge, necessary, too, in the sense that these places are productive and engage in the proliferation of perversion.

ciety that further stabilizes norms, values, and actions. For a variety of theologians, queer theologians especially, the framing of an Indecent Theology is, and has become, a way to consider the larger frame of theology and ethics as a queer enterprise, a multi-dynamic and multi-vocal transgressive movement of *praxis and reflection*[2] whose starting points are the margins of the margins, valuable places of networked displacement. This multi-dynamic transgressive movement also has a *normative horizon*;[3] that horizon is the ongoing efforts at perverting decent theologies and ethics. Moreover, Indecent Theology is a theology whose purpose and end is a radically enfleshed praxis-oriented ethic starting with the stories of people's lives, their experiences, and does this without censorship; its points of departure are the margins of the margins of all living things.[4]

The Theology that Althaus-Reid introduced us to is queer in many ways. Chiefly, her work is a non-normative and transgressive expres-

---

2. I borrow this language from Nancy E. Bedford. She, in 2005, gave me the language of praxis and reflection relative to feminism. Her definition of feminism is "I understand feminism as a multifaceted movement of praxis/reflection that has the varied flourishing of women of all ages and conditions as its immediate goal, abundant life for all of creation as its ultimate vision, and the dynamic equality and mutuality of women and men of all ages as its normative horizon." She went on to say to me the following: "Sure, that is mine. Normative horizon refers to the fact that it does imply a metanarrative of justice, not only a particularist vision. If you look at that handout from the FT class, you'll see that I contextualize the comments. I want to avoid the discourse of 'equality,' understood as 'identicalness' without losing the need for things like equal rights before the law." This definition became important during a Feminist Theology class at Northwestern University/Garrett-Evangelical Theological Seminary. This definition helps me see a creative opening for an Indecent Theology after Althaus-Reid.

3. While the language of normativity and/or normative and horizon may seem problematic, since I am attempting to disrupt the stasis of normativity, here, as Bedford outlines in her definition of feminism, normative horizon helps give shape and form to the transgressive reality of perversion. Perversion should therefore be part of a normative horizon that displaces decent theologies.

4. It is important to note that Althaus-Reid's work can also be read as Posthumanist theology and ethics. While I do not explore this at length, I do make a note that she is concerned with all living things.

sion of sexual and theological discourse whereby sex, desire, recognition, multiplicity, and differences are all indecent and central to her theo-ethical discourse. It is concerned with the materialization of sex, as well as with the bodies of the marginalized and displaced, particularly functionally and literally. Althaus-Reid's sexual theology gives theologians and ethicists a way to imagine the corporeal body as a centrality to the active reformulating ways of knowing and productions of knowledge (in other words, the body as an epistemic mode) for Liberation Theology, albeit a Radical Liberation Theology — a theology whose implication is praxis (materializing in a radical ethics) and rooted in the radical liberation of the marginalized, those who are living beings (people and things, queers, particularly).[5]

Althaus-Reid's sexual theology is not a liberal theology in any ordinary fashion, because it is concerned with many and multiple bodies; it is concerned and committed to the body radically displaced but situated firmly in community — the body displaced and nestled in the collective spaces of the border(land)s whose excess creates the proliferation of liberation. I consider this shape and form of theology and ethics to be a virtue and perversion to the normativity of Christian ethics relying on particular confessions serving the dominant structure of the church and cociety. Here I am referring to the excess of what the border(land)s produce. The excess is the queer feature of what *perversion ethics* offer.

Perversion, ethics, and creative disregard is a queer ethics. It locates the body as a vitally rich analytic tool that is primary for the task of critical moral reasoning and ethical analysis. Marcella Althaus-Reid's

---

5. I use the term "radical" in two ways in this essay: first, reaching back to the Latin, which refers to being 'rooted,' and second, reaching backwards and forwards to radical liberation movements, including radical feminist movements and radical liberation revolutionary movements. There is perhaps a third way that I can see this term being used: referencing 'radical' or different modes of being — queer, perverse, different, strange.

work disrupts patterns and ways of knowing; it is an epistemological rupture. Furthermore, her work creates tears in the epistemological web of normative ethics. These tears create openings for the excess to destabilize norms, which almost shape our value system. In this sense, perversion and the outcome of its ethics are uniquely tied to indecent ways of knowing and the ways in which bodies — indecent borderland bodies — produce knowledge and are always moral agents. Perversion, ethics, and creative disregard insofar that they are queer, is indecent in an Althaus-Reid(ian) manner.

My task is to use Althaus-Reid's method of Indecency queerly and constructively to create what I call Perversion Ethics. The indecent method is (in Anthony Pinn's words) creative disregard.[6] Pinn never ties these terms together, but reading these two thinkers side by side, indecency becomes a creative disregard to the norms that shape our values, and the epistemic function of indecency furthermore creates the matrix of epistemological tears for excess to take place. Perversion Ethics, as a method of indecency, is the critical reflection of morality that runs contrary, antithetically, and irreconcilably to the norms and sensibilities of society.[7] Likewise, it is the use of the margins of the margins to consider ethics. I will pair the spatial concept of borders and borderlands[8] with Althaus-Reid's work to accomplish this task, while also being inspired by the work of Gilles Deleuze and Rosi Braidotti concerning matter, reality, and a monist ontology. Us-

---

6. Anthony B. Pinn, *Embodiment and the New Shape of Black Theological Thought* (New York, NY: New York University Press, 2010). The entire book helps situate new contours of black religious thought and emobidment.

7. In the beginning of my research and preparing for an interview in 2011, I originally called this work "Indecent Social Ethics," and gave a lecture at Union Theological Seminary by the same title in December 2011. I have since started using "Perversion Ethics" to think about this work as I deploy Althaus-Reid's work and method of indecency.

8. Inspired by my reading of Gloria Anzaldúa and my own lived experience of being a mixed rooted nomad, or queerMestizaje.

ing postcolonial queer theory[9] in conversation with Althaus-Reid's Radical Liberation Theology, Indecencia becomes a virtue to ethical perversion.

This chapter is also rooted in a theory of new materialism that is uniquely queer. While I discuss and theorize bodies, I do so from a materialist perspective, but have not included stories of bodies or about bodies, nor do I include images of bodies. My resistance to including vignettes or stories or examples of bodies is another attempt to destabilize the ways in which we understand this work that is grounded in a theory of the body. In many ways, this book chapter is an attempt to further entangle continental theory that is particularly Deleuzian and queer, with the liberationist thought of Althaus-Reid and move past the stability of liberation thought that Althaus-Reid gives us. Because of these commitments, this book chapter reads much more philosophically than confessionally. It is my growing work in constructive philosophical theology that leverages continental thought as a theological and ethical tool that can be mobilized as uniquely queer and productive for sexual(ized) liberation in bodily ways.[10]

Ethical perversion cannot be understood outside of a matter-realist theory of becoming. As I understand it, matter is much more than a collection of things or objects; it signals a new and different way of organizing bodies and relationships as a result of material power

---

9. To my knowledge, I do not know of anyone using these terms together: postcolonial, queer, theory, except for the book by John C. Hawley. I look to postcolonial studies and decolonial theories and read queer theory from this perspective. It is a particular standpoint. While queer theory is dominated by Anglo American and European scholars, a helpful new intervention is a postcolonial queer theory. I see the work that I am doing part of this new intervention.

10. I should note that I am deeply moved by narrative and our stories selves. The Rev. Alba Onofrio (AO) continues to push me into an expression of thought and theory that is vibrant with narrative, lived experiences, and the stuff of our lives that really matters. I am aware that this book chapter stays in a purely theoretical mode, but the stories of queers and nomads have encouraged this work, including the very real queer nomadism of my own life.

structures. Using the philosophical and theoretical frameworks of Deleuze and Braidotti and the philosophy-physics of Karen Barad, I come to a *new settlement*[11] of theology and ethics whose driving feature is entirely a matter of indecency. I consider this new settlement of thinking theologically and ethically to be at the intersection of ethics, epistemology, and ontology. Following Karen Barad's[12] method at working in and across these disciplines, diffractively so, I read Althaus-Reid work as it cuts across these three philosophical domains.

In many ways, ethical perversion is the signal to betray normative disciplinary boundaries and is also an intentional move in creating new and different ways of deploying knowledge and patterns of thinking.[13] I think Althaus-Reid accomplishes this in her published work, and I simply look to other thinkers to help support my own creative and constructive gesture of ethical perversion in the perverting of norms and normativities. In the end, ethical perversion is not void of real materiality; it is matter becoming different, perverting norms and values at all corners of turnings.

Situating Perversion as an indecent tool for theology and ethics

The definition of perversion will not be a surprise to anyone. A quick search through an online search engine tells me that perversion is "the alteration of something from its original course, meaning, or state to a distortion or corruption of what was first intended." The second entry is: "sexual behavior or desire that is considered

---

11. This phrase is inspired by Bruno Latour.

12. Here I am referring to Barad's diffractive methodology that is found in *Meeting the Universe Halfway: Quantum Physics and the Enanglement of Matter and Meaning* (Durham, NC: Duke University Press, 2007).

13. Indecent Theology and ethics, then, is, in Rosi Braidotti's language "patterns of dissonance." What this encourages is new and different knowing practices and knowledge producing systems. They converge with one another in the borderlands of displacement, and the bodies enfleshing these knowing practices encounter *patterns of dissonance.*

abnormal or unacceptable." Another quick look at the thesaurus tells me that perversion relates chiefly to "distortion, misrepresentation, falsification, travesty, misinterpretation, misconstruction, twisting, corruption, subversion, misuse, misapplication, debasement." Secondly, and perhaps more interesting, the thesaurus suggests that perversion is related to sexuality in that: "sexual perversion is deviance, abnormality; depravity, degeneracy, debauchery, corruption, vice, wickedness, immorality." How could this be a source and tool for theology and ethics? Why is this important to even consider tools outside the dominant structure of theology and ethics, namely tradition as the normative source for theology and ethics? And third, when a definition of perversion entails a value statement, how can perversion not be related to ethics?

I can answer this in one sentence: The dominant strand of theology and ethics perpetuates a normativity that perpetually eclipses the possibility for the margins of the margins to access new and generative forms of theology and ethics that might aid in their flourishing; the experience of being in and on the margins of the margins is eclipsed and displaced. Because of this, I suggest that perversion becomes an *indecent* tool for theology and ethics precisely because perversion is rooted in a particular type of experience that aligns with the intentionality of one's character acting in community. In order to utilize the concept of perversion as an *indecent* tool for theology and ethics, let me first demonstrate the methodological brilliance of Marcella Althaus-Reid's work of *Indecent Theology*. From there, I will transition to the concept of perversion that is also uniquely tied to Marcella Althaus-Reid's work.

In a full-length text, Althaus-Reid deploys a new and creative theological framework, flanked by new methods emerging as a result of cross-disciplinary study. In her *Indecent Theology*, Althaus-Reid examines the theological framework of Liberation Theology. The content of this Indecent Theology is a particular critique that she leverages by way of re-introducing a liberative theological feminism, an intervention, seen in Feminist Liberation Theology, that she uses to bridge together queer theories and postcolonial theories to imagine a new methodological tool; she calls this an *indecent* method. The theological framing of this method is one way to deconstruct the dominant paradigm and normative demands of traditional productions of systematic theology, especially Latin American Liberation Theology. Althaus-Reid's method is a creative opening for queer theology and postcolonial theology that seeks to destabilize the existing theological and ethical discourse as a way to invite the voices, bodies, and subjects that are otherwise obscured and blotted out by dominant narratives. Bringing together the bodies, voices, and subjects that are eclipsed by normative and dominant theologies, Althaus-Reid says: "Lemon vendors who do not use underwear are indecent. The Argentinian theologian without underwear writes Indecent Theology."[14]

Indecent Theology emerges in opposition to Decent Theology — theology that is acceptable and ordered. Latin American Liberation Theology is one such theology that remains a decent order, despite its critique of class. It is because of this critique of class and the adherence to traditional forms of theology that Latin American Liberation Theology remains concretely heterosexually informed. For Althaus-Reid, this Decent Theology is a de-sexualized theology where the poverty of sexuality is clear. Theology, though, is a discourse that reminds us of the indecent features of life, historically and in the

---

14. Marcella Althaus-Reid, *Indecent Theology: Theological Perversions in Sex, Gender and Politics* (London, UK: Routledge, 2000), 12. I am aware that some Latin American theologians question the story of the lemon vendors. While I am aware of this, I am not making a statement regarding the veracity of Althaus-Reid's story. I am rather sharing this story as a means to highlight the indecent method. Lemon vendors betray what is decent!

future. In Decent Theology, what fails to happen is a commitment to the sexuality of this discourse; hence, theology emerges out of a hetersexual/heterocentric and heteronomrative framework that displaces the sexuality inherent in theology. I have often theorized this as the failure of the normative. The normative will always fail us; we cannot trust it to provide us a liberatory pathway that is rooted in productive sexualities. Indecency has a better chance in creating this opening. Althaus-Reid's method of Indecent Theology seeks to reorder and disrupt this outcome, thereby producing a new shape and form for Liberation Theology; she calls this *indecencia* and the body who enfleshes this method of doing theology — not only does not put on underwear, but — actively betrays the normative demands that are in place for producing theology; she perverts these normativities as a manner of virtue. This act and virtue of perversion is in the spirit of *torcer* (twisting) and twisting in deviant ways. It is in this way that perversion becomes a tool for theology and ethics. Advocating for a theology of radical movement, seen in the spirit of *torcer*, is precisely how the virtue of perversion can irrupt the stable and normative categories that eliminate the excess of life, the margins. Recognizing that ethical perversion privileges a theology of radical movement helps not only re-imagine perversion as a tool for theology and ethics, but also destabilizes perversion as a singular reality. *Torcer* disrupts this normative and singular reality and allows for the proliferation of multiplicity in perversion, a particular expression of ethics that privileges a framework of plurality and difference, rooted in *torcer*.

Perversion is active and intentional; it does not emerge as a surprise. Deviance is always an act stemming from thought and meditation, a material engagement that engages the excess of our experiences. When a person engages in the sexual practices of bondage — domination — sado-masochism, this is an intentional act. This results from how the "play" in "BDSM" emerges from the thoughtfulness; without the "play," it resembles fascism "(or perhaps fascism resembles an all too serious Bondage Domination Sado Masochism)."[15] Because material perverse engagements are engagements that transgress the stable categories of relationality, this creates moments of open excess to then explore a new contour of perversion. There is thought to these sexual practices that effectively pervert normative sexual practices for the sake of liberation; I suggest that this same thoughtfulness and play regarding perversion become part of one's deviant pattern for producing theology and ethics. In this sense, perversion as a tool for theology and ethics makes the naturalized — heterocentricism, heteronormativity, dominance, and normativities — explicit, so that what *is* can be not only be transcended, but destructed. But, not only what is ontologically the case for what can be transcended, but for what is distorted and the irruption of what becomes something different — perverted. That, if we engage in the thoughtfulness of deviant practices and imagine the practices of perverted differences, then our theologies and ethics become much more robust and envelop a much broader community; that thoughtfulness also puts flesh on our theologies and ethics, and our theologies and ethics materialize in indecent ways. Perversion as a tool for theology and ethics does not minimize its capacity to speak to the masses. Perversion is not a micro or molecular act; it is molar and has a global effect and flair, for when we create little moves against destructiveness in perverting dominant structures, we affect it globally. The same is true in the popular slogan for sustainable communities: "act local; think

---

15. I'm grateful for Jason McDaniel's teasing this out for me. He and I shared a conversation one Saturday night in March 2013, and he gave me the language to make sense of BDSM as play and thoughtfulness; and, play as part of contemplative / meditative actions / practices.

global." When we make a deviant act out of our thoughtfulness and intention — out of our thoughtful play, we affect larger structures that undoubtedly create new modes of liberation.

And so, the act of situating perversion as an indecent tool for theology and ethics requires the intentional and active departure from normative and decent theologies and ethics, which points to a horizon full of deviance, informed by indecent questions, that effectively perverts the normative structures.[16] This is neither a move of counter-normativity, not a counter move in order to "displace one normativity only to be replaced by another (for example, heteronormativity displaced so that homonormativity can take power), but a perversion in order to melt away the validity of a single normativity as both false and absurd."[17] It is creating space for multiplicity; it is using perversion to deviate from the normativities that structure theology and ethics, and is, perhaps, a post-normative move.[18] Perversion displaces the binary of normative and counter-normative. When deviance and inquiry become the mode of reflection and an ongoing pursuit of propelling action, perversion is a result. Perversion, then, becomes the centerpiece that supports one's analysis. It becomes a

---

16. This is a "little move against destruction." Thoughtfulness and imagination become modes of deviance.

17. My compañer@ (AO) offered this phrasing in an email exchange on Nov. 29, 2015, that helps elucidate my use of perversion and counter normativity.

18. This term, "post-normative," is an attempt to talk about what is outside the norm, but not beyond the norm. My compañer@ (AO) has very intentionally helped me see that we cannot inhabit a position of "beyond gender," implying a positionality in which we are not in any way bound up in or impacted by a binary system of gender, which is currently impossible (though access to various forms of systemic privilege can mitigate its effects). So, while I am not specifically talking about gender, this has been an important moment of learning. Post-normative is not beyond the norm, but what is outside the norm, the place of excess and where deviance is materialized, and a positionality that also signals the possibility of great impact on the marginalized.

methodological tool in re(con)figuring or recomposing theologies and ethics whose goal is to disrupt[19] traditional theologies and ethics.

Indecency as a tool for theology and ethics requires the intentional move beyond the "fantastic" and "phantasmagorical," as articulated by Althaus-Reid in *Indecent Theology* when speaking about trends of Marion theologies.[20] This move beyond the "fantastic" and "phantasmagorical"[21] is the indecent move; it is the rearticulation of a material theology whose roots are indecent, stemming from a radical deviation from the normative structures that keep theologies immaterial and in the realm of the "fantastic" and "phantasmagorical." This "material" refers to actual matter that makes up bodies as composite structures in today's world.[22] Material bodies, which are always becoming as a result of their multiplicity and differences (and reality of being radically material), become the axis on which the indecent tool is promulgated. Bodies serve as the centrality of indecency, a transgressive move that destabilizes desire and action into an entanglement of excess. Indecency as a tool for theology and ethics ruptures our reality and emerges from material bodies and in relationship with radical difference. It is in this way that theology and

---

19. I think here of Traci West's work on *Disruptive Christian Ethics: When Racism and Women's Lives Matter* (Louisville, KY: Westminster John Knox Press, (2006) and how this model of disruption points to a type of perverting normativities that invites new and different subjects and subjectivities to enflesh a liberative orientation.

20. Althaus-Reid, 39.

21. I encountered these words in the work of Emilie M. Townes. I have come to appreciate the ways that these two words help shape our moral imagination. The fantastic and the phantasmagorical is having a fantastic or deceptive appearance, as something in a dream or created by the imagination. It also relates to changing or shifting, as a scene made up of many elements.

22. Using the language of materiality is a departure from Althaus-Reid's use of material, which is a reference to Marxist analysis that serves to critique issues of class relative to gender and sexuality. While of course I appreciate the Marxist analysis, I much prefer the recent trends of materiality studies seen in the work of Rosi Braidotti and the New Materialisms movement. Dealing with the 'matter' of the world moves us to something that is beyond the 'fantastic' and 'phatasmagorical.'

ethics is able to move beyond the "fantastic" and "phantasmagorical." When material bodies become the perverted source for an indecent tool, the phenomenon that irrupts one's reality is a material phenomenon, a bodily and enfleshed phenomenon. Theology and ethics, enacted with the indecent tool and method of perversion, irrupts the stasis of normativities and immaterialities by being mediated in and through material bodies. It is in this way, then, that material bodies become the source for theology and ethics that one can situate perversion as an indecent tool for theology and ethics. Bodies are not decent, unless they conform to the dominant structures.[23] The bodies that I reference in this essay are the bodies residing at the margins of the margins — borderland bodies nestled in the interstices of multiple borders or constellations of interconnections, of differences becoming different. These bodies are indecent bodies and are an important source for an indecent theology and ethics.[24]

"OF DISOBEDIENT BODIES": SITUATING CREATIVE DISREGARD RELATIVE TO PERVERSION

Using perversion as a tool for theology and ethics, and suggesting there is a notion of materiality of bodies in deploying this tool, results in disobedient bodies — bodies who enflesh a type of indecency and deploy perversion in their material becoming. Disobedient bodies run contrary to the normative structures and discourses of power, and the normative sstructures and discourses of power which

---

23. Even bodies that are oppressed by multiple systems are not decent.

24. It is important to note that my use of difference and becoming (along with materiality) stems from my own interest and work with New Materialisms and feminist New Materialisms, Deleuze & Guattari's work, and feminist Deleuzians. It should also be noted that my work is a type of queer materialism that is rooted in a new contour of liberation theology.

result in regulating bodies into docility. Disobedient bodies enflesh "creative disregard." The phrase "creative disregard" comes from the black religious scholar Anthony B. Pinn, and I discovered this phrase in *Embodiment and the New Shape of Black Theological Thought*. In the context of Pinn's book, creative disregard means "those attitudes and sensibilities that run contrary to the normative workings of societal arrangements/regulations and are therefore considered problematic because they question what discourses of power and restrictions on life practices are meant to enforce."[25] This is a specific reference to the ways in which material bodies betray societal norms by enfleshing text and other forms of art and media. This perversion of the material and discursive body yields a new and different social body — one that is marked (or textured) with an aesthetic of difference. In Pinn's book, these bodies are deviant bodies and disobedient bodies, because they betray the normative structures that are used to regulate them and force them into particular normative actions. In Pinn's analysis, these bodies are black bodies who highlight the ways in which different bodies are only intelligible as deviant and perverted bodies.

This act of enfleshing "creative disregard" not only becomes a new and different aesthetic, but also becomes a new and different ethic relative to bodies of difference (black bodies for Pinn and *mestizaje* bodies for my own work). This new ethic considers the ways in which different media are marked, embedded, and enfleshed on bodies, yielding a new frame in understanding these bodies and the potential for relationality to which these bodies are oriented. In many ways, this is a discursive reality that marks material bodies in particular ways. *Mestizaje* bodies are the result of not only a radical mixing of colonized bodies and the colonizer, but also a radical mixing of culture,

---

25. Pinn, 21. Pinn seems to borrow this phrase from another scholar.

language, and imagination. In this sense, then, "creative disregard," the active hostility,[26] towards normativities that regulate bodies into docility is a type of ethical perversion, and these bodies whose axis is indecency chart a new path for ethical perversion to emerge. Because indecency is the centrality of ethical perversion, or axis point, it is important to note that this centrality is not a singularity. This centrality is an axis of becoming, an orientation of movement that grips both theory and action in a framework of difference. This centrality of indecency and prioritization of perversion is a material becoming.

Inserting 'creative disregard' relative to perversion means that indecency is at the core of material bodies — it is already part of the material that is helping the body become different in the world. These bodies have betrayed the internal structures that have organized them in society and have outwardly produced new and different forms of knowledge and knowing practices.[27] Their betrayal of these normative structures that not only socialize them but micro-manage their bodies into docility creates little moves against destructiveness, perverting the imposed docility. Thus, "creative disregard" is the indecenting of bodies, perverting the materiality in ways that not only create modes of counter-normativity but true perversion and indecency. "Creative disregard" is both an orientation and an active enfleshment, as is perversion. Pinn speaks of the ways in which black bodies mark themselves — either by tattooing or other texts, scarification, or otherwise — and this act of marking or texturing the body is part of the orientation and enfleshment. These bodies are disobedient bodies, perverting their very materiality so as to assume the indecency that points to liberation. And, by liberation, I am re-

---

26. Carmen Nanko-Fernandez uses a phrase "pastoral hostility" and Orlando Espin introduced me to this idea. Nanko-Fernandez uses this phrase in *Theologizing En Espanglish: Context, Community, and Ministry* (Maryknoll, NY: Orbis Books, 2010).

27. I call this "epistemological ruptures" in my work.

ferring to the radical displacement of normativities and dominance that yields a radical inclusionary politics that is often referenced by notions of "spiritual activism."[28]

INSERTION: BODIES AND ETHICS AT THE INDECENT INTERSECTION OF PERVERSION AND CREATIVE DISREGARD

Given that both perversion and "creative disregard" demand the material body, and that this body is not a docile body, it is important to note that this body not only enfleshes but also acts. The body that becomes indecent enfleshes a perverse morality whose axis is rooted in "creative disregard." The intersection of perversion and "creative disregard" creates a sustainable ethical framework predicated on ongoing betrayals of normative ethical action and theories that deliberately do not activate or incite radical inclusionary politics. As such, *engaging* bodies and ethics at the indecent intersection of perversion and "creative disregard" points to new figuration of bodies transcending the speciated divide. Our materiality as human animal bodies correlates with other material existing in today's world: trees, non-human animals, plants, and so forth. We cannot deny this. Ethics, then, must point toward a larger, more robust idea of being and becoming in the world where morality and ethics is framed by the ethics of perversion — an indecent model that organizes a perverse morality.

---

28. Spiritual Activism is a term coined by Gloria Anzaldúa in one of her last published essays. This idea refers to the radical inclusionary politics that Anzaldúa theorizes and enfleshes. The term "spiritual" points to the recognition that what is spiritual is part of the everyday life — there is no separation of divine and human. You can find this phrase in Gloria Anzaldúa and AnaLouise Keating "now let us shift: the path to conocimiento," in *This bridge we call home: radical visions for transformation* (New York, NY: Routledge, 2002).

INDECENCY IS THE (UN)VIRTUOUS ACT OF
RECOGNIZING DIFFERENCE(S)

If what is decent helps to fortify normative features of reality, including maintaining a status quo, which results in dominant theologies and ethics, then what is indecent helps to not only deconstruct and destruct normative features of reality but also decenter dominant theologies and ethics; what results, then, are indecencies and differences. This is accomplished by enfleshing an indecent orientation toward differences allowing for recognition of differences to help shape and shift relationality. This is the (un)virtuous act that stems from recognizing differences.

When Christian theology speaks of virtues, these are often understood as norms and values that characterize a person's behavior; it is an orientation that is paralleled with a divine relationality. As such, virtues are "infused" in a human by the act of divine grace. Virtues cannot be achieved by human persistence alone; humanity is dependent upon divine grace. I want to suggest that indecency provides an (un)virtuous act in recognizing difference. One's orientation and enfleshed relationality with the margins of margins displaces traditional characteristics and practices (including one's character) concerning theological virtues, and in fact produces or ignites new and generative ways of being marginalized. It is not only faith, hope, and charity that indecency disrupts, but it is the virtues of incredulity, despair and cynicism, and indifference to dominant norms and values, that help unmask the creative opening of recognizing differences. By this I mean that indecency is productive for destabilizing traditional values and virtues.

When bodies take shape in their creative disregard and extol the indecency of (un)virtuous acts, recognition begins to open up ways of being and becoming in the world. Recognition depends on the relationship that is shared, and is not dependent always on an otherness. There is a shared value of relationality that emerges, and recognition is a key feature of this shared value. What becomes normative, then, in this style of relating, is the way indecency privileges difference(s). While I neither stabilize ideas of a norm nor do I use this term as I do in my critique of the (hetero)norm, though I do mention the new creative norm as a norm of indecency. Furthermore, this new creative norm of indecency is dynamic and destabilized by the present-future queerness, which is embodied in materiality and becoming different.

The recognition of differences is key to indecency, and recognition is always in a dialectic with desire. It marks a new creative opening for bodies to materialize on a plane of becoming, and the norms, values, and limits of decent theologies and ethics prevent creative openings. Indecency creates moments of closure that initiate creative openings; they are part of enfleshing an orientation of creative disregard. An entanglement, while having both intersections of closedness and openings, creates a web of interconnection that serves as a metaphor for this orientation of creative disregard. While these necessary closures initiate creative and generative openings, it is on all accounts an indecent and (un)virtuous act to recognize difference(s). One cannot forget the impulse that perversion gives to these necessary closures and creative openings. Perversion of normativities is what ignites the closures and stimulates the generative and perverted openings. Perversion in this sense is, in many ways, an emergence of an axis of becoming different. This becoming different materializes in many and multiple ways along the plane of immanence, correlating to (un) virtuous acts of recognizing difference(s). What emerges in these creative and generative openings is the feature of multiplicity that helps point to the act of recognition as an ethical virtue.

MULTIPLICITY AS THE CENTRAL ORGANIZING
FEATURE FOR AN INDECENT METHOD

Normative — decent — theologies and ethics rely on the singularity of theory and method to expedite their thinking framework, which have in turn fortified decent, dominant, and diligent contributions. These frameworks of singularity privilege the center over and against the periphery; marginalia are not included in the singularity of these theories and the production of these theories is designed to impact the dominant sector only. When the margins of the margins become the point of departure for theological and ethical methods, what is noted is how multiplicity and difference become an important feature that is imbued in the method itself. One feature that stems from this is the occurrence of liberation theologies and their critiques of the ways that dominant theologies and ethics repeatedly erase and silence those existing in and on the margins — those who enflesh a particular material poverty.

Methodological attributes or components are important for theology and ethics, and indecency privileges the reality of multiplicity. I argue that multiplicity and difference are central organizing features of an indecent method. What this means is that when recognizing the starting point as the margins of the margins, one is already affirming multiplicity and difference, because the margins of the margins cannot exist as any singular mode or univocal being.[29] Deleuze is important at this juncture, as his theories of difference and multiplicity help give shape and form to my own understanding of an indecent

---

29. It is important to note here that Ontology comes into play when thinking about multiplicity and difference. I am inspired by Gilles Deleuze's work and his univocal ontology. While he accentuates difference and multiplicity, he also ties these individuating differences and ideas of multiplicity to modes of singularity and the same being. Deleuze argues that "Being is the same for all these modalities, but these modalties are not the same." Gilles Deleuze, *Difference and Repetition* (New York, NY: Columbia University Press, 1995), 36.

method. Deleuze, both in his own work and in the work of Rosi Braidotti, posits monism as a fundamental ontology. Ontology might seem like a strange feature to understanding indecency, but I argue that the question of being (particularly its univocity) is important when considering the ways in which power functions over against the margins of the margins. Attuning ourselves to the univocity of being or single matter positions difference and multiplicity as a value and process of becoming that resides at the heart of *that* matter. Indecency is a thing — it is matter becoming — that assumes the margins, arresting the enfleshed bodies in a series of becoming different and indecent.

Furthermore, when validating the margins of the margins, the sexuality of poverty, as Althaus-Reid does, new, different, and multiple epistemological frameworks take shape and shift. Material bodies are unmasked as ones who deeply suffer because of (the matter/material of) decent theologies and ethics. Recognizing this is the initial moment where one experiences epistemological ruptures.[30] This is part of the recognition process that disrupts the normative horizon when bodies enfleshing creative disregard emerge, especially when these bodies are recognized as raced, classed, gendered, sexed, and sexual bodies — difference and multiplicity are central. No single axis of the intersection can invalidate the multiple and different constellations (or differences) of the margins of the margins. The results are the creative and repetitious closings and openings, signaled by the matter of becomings, that perpetuate multiplicity and difference; which, during these closing and opening cycles, perpetuate the univocity of being at and on the margins of the margins.[31]

---

30. Nancy Bedford first introduced me to this phrase, while I was a student of hers at Garrett-Evangelical Theological Seminary. She mentioned that she borrowed it from Jon Sobrino. I'm grateful for this phrase and the ways that this phrase has particular utility is unmasking the mobility of knowledge, and its becoming.

31. I borrow the language of opening and closing from Heidegger. When talking with Jared Vasquez, he reminded me of the hourglass metaphor, where the shape of

When multiplicity becomes an organizing feature of an indecent method, indecency lingers in the interstices of what is multiple and different — the collective becoming of matter itself. There is no longer a singular starting point, since the starting point is the margins of the margins, in Althaus-Reid's language. These margins are complexly braided together, similar to borderlands, intersecting with many and multiple realities that become pieces of the foundation and framework of the indecent method. What emerges is a constellation of differences pointing to multiplicity (and difference) as the organizing feature of indecency. This organizing feature of indecency is a network of differences, and propelled and organized by multiplicity. Likewise, material bodies that are enfleshed with markings of the borderlands, and destabilized in these places also bind it.

RECOGNITION AS ETHICAL VIRTUE; OR, WHEN DESIRE CANNOT BE AVOIDED

Recognition is often considered both a colonizing feature of the dominant sector that both rest and rely (always) on the process of othering — a colonial tactic that seeks to normalize bodies into an existing dominant framework in order for these "others" to be controlled and surveyed. While this postcolonial critique is important and absolutely necessary when considering the work of Marcella Althaus-Reid, what must also be noted is the way desire can never be avoided during the process of recognition. Recognition, I argue, when practiced well, can be heralded as an ethical virtue.

I understand the process of recognition as the invitation of one offered to another, inviting this particular other into relationship largely due because all parties desire recognition; it cannot be avoid-

---

the hourglass's closing creates an opening. In many ways, this is part of the cycle of difference and repetition in the method of indecency.

ed.[32] What prompts this invitation is the excess of conscious desire, noting that desire does not stem from only one material body or one material thing. Desire stems from the excess (not lack) that we experience as ourselves in relationship with others as we desire ongoing recognition. It is excess and our own becoming different that causes both recognition and desire to take shape. What results is the ethical virtue of recognition.

What signals this importance in the thought and theory of Indecency and Althaus-Reid is the way the margins of the margins do not enflesh a poverty of desire or recognition. While Althaus-Reid has theorized the sexuality of poverty, what is missed is the overwhelming reality of desire at play with the process of recognition that is part of the material reality of the margins of the margins. Sexuality of poverty notes which material bodies are displaced, materially, by normative structures of power and capitalism. This is an exclamation of the class of bodies residing at the margins of the margins. These material realties, despite their poverty and ongoing displacement, continue to enflesh the desire to be recognized by their own communities and the desire for others to recognize them. Desire, then, can never be avoided, and is always in a dialectic with recognition. It emerges as an ethical virtue when the dialectic of desire and recognition stems from the many and multiple realities that the margins of the margins enflesh. An indecent relationality emerges as something entirely different than the way decent and normative theologies and ethics have constructed the norms and values of relating. Indecency overwhelms the dialectic of desire and recognition, thereby pervert-

---

32. Here I'm thinking through Hegel's *Phenomenology of Spirit* (Oxford, UK: Oxford University Press, 1997), Braidotti's Sexual Difference, and Deleuze and Guattari's feature of the "Third Person" that Roberto Esposito develops in *The Third Person* (Cambridge, UK: Polity Press, 2012). At these intersections lies the complex relationship of desire and recognition that is inherent in all relating practices that also complicate personhood.

ing this dialectic and allowing creative openings for recognition to emerge or become an ethical virtue. This is very much part of the process of becoming that is triggered by the recognition and validation of multiplicity as an organizing feature of indecency.

Indecent recognition as an ethical virtue (and by default, its indecent partner: desire) stems from the materiality of the body, the ongoing and deviant fragmented memory of otherness. Constant resistance to colonization and hegemonic standards points toward a radical invitation to relate with difference(s). This dialectic of indecent recognition and indecent desire disrupts normative roles that ethics demands — those of duty, value, and norms of relationality and relationships, helping the margins of the margins restore a new and creative form, framework, and shape to their induced perversion. Recognition, then, when highlighted as part of the process of desire, becomes an ethical virtue of perversion. Indecency prevails in all forms of relating that emerge at the margins of the margins — the place of displacement and the territorial spaces beyond colonial power. These margins of the margins are braided together like borderlands, networked spaces where the interstices provide a place that is outside colonial possession. These borderlands and their interstices create a more robust reality of multiplicity that becomes an organizing strand for both an indecent recognition and indecent desire. Multiplicity organizes these modes of indecency and points toward the reality that indecency is (the) virtue to ethical perversion.

INDECENCY AS VIRTUE TO ETHICAL PERVERSION

Traditional norms and values, rights, wrongs, and duties have long stabilized ethics.[33] Indecency radically disrupts this process by cre-

---

33. Here I am thinking of Consequentialist Ethics that is often characterized by Utilitarianism and Kantian Philosophies.

atively bringing new forms of value to bear on traditional ways of formulating and organizing norms and values. Considering inde- cency as a virtue to ethical perversion suggests that the stories we tell, the indecent, fleshly, bodily stories we narrate that emerge as little moves against destruction, are, in fact, moments when we per- vert ethical norms and perhaps create new models for ethics. It is neither confessions nor creeds recited during a traditional liturgical moment that frame ethical practice. Those are moments of decency, dominated by tradition and power that incessantly displace the mar- gins of the margins, and these creeds create the hegemonic standard that traditional theologies and ethics have followed and continue to follow. What *does* frame ethical perversion are the bodily confessions and exhortations that are part of relationality, liturgical moments of sexual ecstasy that are often called orgasm, menstrual cycles, pain, erections, and other bodily knowledge and knowing practices, all of which disrupt normative standards of ethical practice. When ethics has its starting place in the matter or material of the body, as a site for an indecent ethical discourse, both knowledge and action are part of an indecent creative disregard. Creative disregard, then, as the ac- tive enfleshment of indecency creates a new shape and form for ethi- cal frameworks. If indecency is taken as the primary methodological impulse to reframe (and essentially replace) normative structures that name, regulate, and filter bodies, then one result is a type of perversion. These moments of methodological impulses create new trends for virtues in that indecency becomes the virtue to ethical perversion — an enfleshed character trait that one lives.

Indecency as a methodological importance is also a shift in con- tent. What normally drives ethics and virtues are normative and hegemonic standards, beliefs, and metaphysical realities. In this sense, the content is decent, and what is shaped and formed results in decency that then flourishes during stabilized, normative, and decent 'liturgical' moments. When indecency becomes the shape and form of the content enfleshed by disobedient bodies, the styles of displacement irrupt[34] at the margins of the margins and the interstices of the borderlands become the very irruption of indecency where new and different (and also multiple) "liturgical" moments materialize, which is the place of excess. Decent theologies and ethics become alien to what is irrupting in the borderlands, and the ways that places of displacement enflesh indecency as a critical feature to the content that envelops it, creates models for decolonizing epistemic norms. These perverted epistemic features become part of the way that indecency becomes a virtue to ethical perversion. Epistemic realities emerge as a result of an attunement to a new character style of knowledge and knowing practices. The body produces the epistemological ruptures that emerge as one's different and multiple characters.

CONCLUSION

Analysis and knowledge has long been heralded as the apex, the pinnacle, of what fortifies rights and duties. Decent theologies and ethics depend on epistemological frameworks to secure rights and duties and implement traditional, nineteenth century, epistemological frameworks.[35] These epistemological frameworks do not take bodily positionalities or enfleshed standpoints as something central (nor do they consider material standpoints to be an organizing feature)

---

34. I borrow this language from María Pilar Aquino. She uses this in reference to the 'irruption of the poor' in *Our Cry for Life: Feminist Theology from Latin America* (Eugene, OR: Wipf and Stock, 2002).

35. Epistemology has flourished, since feminist and queer theories have intervened. New ways of evaluating knowledge and the production of epistemic practices have resulted. I look to these 'newer' ways of constructing knowledge as perverted and necessary.

to knowledge production and the framing of a new perverted ethical practice. Therefore, decent theologies and ethics do not start from the material body when evaluating the epistemological frameworks that support knowledge or knowing practices. Indecent theologies and ethics, however, prioritize the enfleshed and bodily epistemological frameworks, bodily positionalities, and enfleshed standpoints; this is a fundamental perversion of decent and normative theologies and ethics, including their stabilized epistemological framework. Because perversion is a first-order commitment to indecent theologies and ethics, I situate it as a virtue of ethical perversion. It is the perverted epistemological framework, the fleshly knowledge that the material body produces, that takes materially becoming bodies seriously. This virtue to ethical perversion also celebrates disobedient bodies — bodies existing in borderlands of perversion and the interstices of otherness, often characterized as "misunderstood bodies" — jot@ or raro. The dialectic of recognition and desire perverts the ways in which normative and hegemonic ethical frameworks exist. What emerges are knowledge practices stemming from real material bodies, pointing toward a normative horizon of perversion. This reality becomes, through material bodies, displaced by colonial struggles, the apex of indecency as a virtue to ethical perversion.

References

Althaus-Reid, Marcella. *Indecent Theology: Theological Perversions in Sex, Gender and Politics*. London, UK: Routledge, 2000.

Anzaldúa, Gloria and Ana, Keating Louise. *This bridge we call home: radical visions for transformation*. New York, NY: Routledge, 2002.

Aquino, María Pilar. *Our Cry for Life: Feminist Theology from Latin America*. Eugene, OR: Wipf and Stock, 2002.

Deleuze, Gilles. *Difference and Repetition*. New York, NY: Columbia University Press, 1995.

Esposito, Roberto. *The Third Person*. Cambridge, UK: Polity Press, 2012.

Hegel, G.W.F. *Phenomenology of Spirit*. Oxford, UK: Oxford University Press, 1997.

Pinn, Anthony B. *Embodiment and the New Shape of Black Theological Thought*. New York, NY: New York University Press, 2010.

Nanko-Fernandez, Carmen. *Theologizing En Espanglish: Context, Community, and Ministry*. Maryknoll, NY: Orbis Books, 2010.

A POSTCOLONIAL READING
OF BARTIMAEUS' STORY

Contributions towards the Construction of
Another Hermeneutic Model

OSCAR CABRERA

INTRODUCTION

Postcolonial reading in the Guatemalan context is framed by the ongoing US interventions in Guatemala. The US government has repeatedly made ideological and cultural intrusions that range from interference in labor law, experiments with the population, the overthrow of democratic governments, and religious and philanthropic actions that induced indigenous groups to accept state control and market economy.

From the early twentieth century until today, Guatemala has been affected by displacement, land theft, and exploitation on banana and coffee plantations. The oppression of indigenous people had its socio-religious event:

The emerging class differences in indigenous municipalities were expressed in the only way permitted among the Maya: the religion. Social conflict rose to the world of the gods, and returned to Earth in the form of wars between the Bible, saints and speakers. After 1944, these conflicts took an open political form, showing that Mayan Protestantism had become a politic and religious exercise, a protest against vice, superstition and also social order.[1]

Both European and US imperialism have been accompanied by a hermeneutic that, while pretending to liberate the souls of the afflicted, was enslaving minds and bodies. The sacred texts were interpreted for indoctrination, submission and obedience to a power structure and economy that to this today persists in Guatemala.

SOME ASPECTS OF THE GUATEMALAN SOCIO-POLITICAL CONTEXT[2]

There are anti-imperialist traces in the work of Miguel Angel Asturias. However, we "should make a current assessment of Asturias and the significance of the indigenous and African in his work,"[3] which for reasons of length and purpose we will not consider here. However, it is an important reference in understanding and recording North-American influence in Guatemala.

At the height of postcolonial criticism, I believe in the validity of Asturias, and his literary legacy can clarify the power relations created by the American neo-colonial intervention; it can also offer clues to the strength of the Guatemalan people.

---

1. David Stoll, "¿Pescadores de hombres o fundadores de imperio?,"n.p. [cited October 30 2014]. Online: http://www.nodulo.org/bib/stoll/ilv.htm.

2. Notes taken at the forum "El difícil camino hacia la justicia: el genocidio de Guatemala", School of Philosophy and Letters, University of Buenos Aires, 2013.

3. Interview with Walter Mignolo, January 6, 2014.

On the other hand, following the dictatorships of Estrada Cabrera and Jorge Ubico, there was a democratic spring (1944–1954) where the governments of Juan José Arévalo and Jacobo Arbenz removed indigenous forced labor, provided the Labor Code, and conducted a land reform (1952) in favor of peasant families.[4] By that time the religious landscape saw the arrival of large numbers of missionaries who had a previous network of political alliances with the previous governments. As Jesus Garcia-Ruiz states, that process was "an acceleration of the arrival of foreign personnel which coincides with the opening of the State regulations regarding religion. The period 1944–1954 encouraged the churches, many of which were involved in the 'War against communism.'"[5]

In this period the country was comprised primarily of peasants, and much of the land was in the hands of landlords and companies like United Fruit (La Chiquita) which was established in 1901. This company was the owner of large tracts of land, roads, and communications.

When Jacobo Arbenz aimed to expel United Fruit from Guatemala, representatives from the US government and the CIA got involved on behalf of the company, a fact that guided the organization of the invasion by Carlos Castillo Armas, who lead an army of opposition to overthrow a democratic government under the guise of being a communist power.[6]

Unfortunately for the government of Arbenz, Protestants interpreted the Mayan land reform as a time of liberation. The US govern-

---

4. Comisión para el Esclarecimiento Histórico (CEH), "Guatemala, Memoria del silencio II", (1999), 101–102.

5. Jesús García-Ruiz, "El protestantismo en Guatemala II", *Revista Análisis de la Realidad Nacional* 19 (2012): 39.

6. Hugo Murillo Jiménez, "La intervención norteamericana en Guatemala en 1954. Dos interpretaciones recientes", *Anuarios de Estudios Centroamericanos* 11, no. 2 (1985): 149–155.

ment used the eviction of the United Fruit Company to intervene inthe matters of the country and to accuse the democratic government of being a pawn of Moscow.[7]

The Guatemalan conflict is actually a social, economic, and ideological contention where methods and forms of repression similar to those used in Vietnam were used. Guatemala saw the dawn of disappearances, arbitrary executions, internal displacements, killing of children, public and mass rape of women, and cannibalism,[8] and the world was silent, while the vast majority of churches remained silent.

Behind the social upheaval the number of evangelicals increased, earning political spaces; and yet, their prophetic voice to denounce the atrocities that were happening was not pronounced. Rather some groups were accomplices in a discourse — a social and religious reading — which marginalized, discriminated and excluded.

One of the pastors of evangelical churches discussed that "unfortunately the evangelical church did not rule on the matter [conflict] and still remains silent, because it runs many risks; especially since I am in an area where violence is our daily bread." With this it is understood that some who wanted to talk were not allowed, and others who could do so were silent.

We cannot ignore that in shaping nations, religion is essential for the social, political, and cultural dignity of people. The lack of social and political participation of evangelical churches in Guatemala raises the question of the role played by the interpretation of sacred texts made during periods of social upheaval, and how that interpretation supported an attitude indifferent to abuses.

---

7. Stoll, "¿Pescadores de hombres o fundadores de imperio?," n.p. [cited October 30 2014] Online: http://www.nodulo.org/bib/stoll/ilv.htm.

8. Enrique Dussel, *Resistencia y esperanza: Historia del pueblo cristiano en América Latina y el Caribe* (San José, Costa Rica: DEI, 1995), 268.

An example of religious discourse[9] and interpretation can be found in the Sunday speeches of General Efrain Rios Montt[10], a member of the Word Churches, which I transcribe at length:

> Subversion has roots at home itself, subversion begins in one's family ... consists of costumed saviors of society, they are murderers, many massacres that have made ... really subversive goes on at home. ... Amnesty cannot be for Marxists, but to those who by necessity or threats have been involved in some anti-government activities. ... This position of authority ... was neither given to me by votes nor by bullets; neither votes nor bullets, God put me here.... The army does not kill indigenous, but massacres demons, because indigenous are possessed, they are communists.[11]

So far we can glimpse what was taught to the evangelical church related to the model of biblical interpretation and imperial intentions. The connection with US military training received at the time of dictatorships is also clear.[12]

NEOCOLONIAL MARKS AND RELIGION

The invasion and intervention of empires in Guatemala have left differential marks supported by religion. Initially conquerors performed a segmentation of human groups who served this or that master;

---

9. There are no media files because the television channels recorded over the tape.

10. Alejandra Gutiérrez Valdizán, "El Castigo al hombre que no tuvo el terror", n.p. [cited June 19 2015]. Online: http://www.plazapublica.com.gt/content/el-castigo-al-hombre-que-no-detuvo-el-terror.

11. Notes taken at the forum "El difícil camino hacia la justicia: el genocidio de Guatemala", School of Philosophy and Letters, University of Buenos Aires, 2013.

12. Documento Santa Fe IV, "América Latina frente a los planes anexionistas de los Estado Unidos", n.p. [cited December 29 2014]. Online: http://www.offnews.info/downloads/santafe4.PDF.

then the political, economic and religious intervention of the United States served their expansionist purposes.

Particularly in the religious aspect I want to highlight the presence of an evangelical hermeneutics that favored the elite groups, the authorities (government, missionaries, and politicians) which must be obeyed, "because that is what the Bible said."

In the 70s, when some Indians defied their governments, evangelical organizations like Wycliffe and the Summer Institute of Linguistics considered that "indigenous were to obey to its official sponsors that was acting on divine command."[13] These ideas were in other parts of the continent. Two fragments can provide insight on the interpretation imposed by missionaries in Guatemala and Colombia respectively:

> As you know, those same authorities, obedience to his government position by divine mandate report included subversive activities. [...] The shepherds reported that they were "terrorists caught between right and left." In fact, follow the instructions missionary to preach obedience to the government, it was assumed that they were monitoring the networks 'ears,' whose accusations were instructions for the death squads.[14]

In the area of Paez and guambianos a similar interpretation to the Guatemalan case is

> The Christian and Missionary Alliance is the leading evangelical mission. When I visited his station near Silvia in 1975, teachers Paez and Guambiano said they were reluctant to support the CRIC [Regional Indigenous Council

---

13. Stoll, "¿Pescadores de hombres o fundadores de imperio?," 19.
14. Ibid., 97.

of Cauca] because it refused to believe in God and did not respect the government. The government gives us evil but God has commanded us to obey, one cited Romans 13:1.[15]

There was no critical hermeneutics that would help to reflect the new faith (evangelical) adopted. Rather, in this new faith and new hermeneutics some evangelical groups distanced themselves from society and others allied with the country's structural power and the empire.

"We need to invigorate the soul of my people and straighten their body."[16] In Guatemala what separates are the social, economic, cultural, and religious aspects. This has been our reality from ancient times; each religious group wants to have the absolute truth, always with the suspicion of the falsity of the other.

Guatemala had a war of conspiracy theories, where both left and right tried to influence native people by silencing their strength. Perhaps new critical readings of the memories will allow other ways of thinking, being, living, and acting.

The majority of the evangelical beliefs in Guatemala obey ideas that are introduced from the United States. But the theological reflection of Latin American countries was never lived up Reflections of United States, parishioners of the time were seen as people incapable of producing new forms criticism of his faith, because who dared to question the authority of the leaders and the Bible was considered a rebel.

---

15. Ibid., 255.

16. Miguel Ángel Asturias, "Sociología Guatemalteca: El problema del indio", n.p. [cited December 14 2014]. Online: http://biblioteca.usac.edu.gt/tesis/04/04_0940.pdf, Guatemala, 1923, 7.

THE ARRIVAL OF NORTH AMERICAN
EVANGELICALISM IN CENTRAL AMERICA

In his book *Protestantism and Social Crisis in Central America*, Schäfer Heinrich states that in the early 1900s, the movement of Sanctification had organized its own churches (in the United States) combining religious perfectionism and social commitment. After the Civil War, millenarian eschatology was replaced by a pre-millennial eschatology which opted for retiring from politics and returning to the charitable help and the theology of individual sanctification.[17]

Behind the evangelizing ideal there were arguments, separations, exclusions, and alliances amidst a massive presence of North American missionaries and the feature of the slow rise of national actors. The social hostility "resulted in processes ostracism and exclusion, which gave rise to instincts of withdrawal, of 'social victimization' and the configuration of forms of internal self-legitimation"[18] as well as disputes over possession of the truth.

The history of United States fundamentalism is what, at the end, has been the construction of one of the largest representations of Protestantism in Guatemala. The Guatemalan evangelical church, although it has adopted liturgical and/or doctrinal forms during its own adaptation to the environment, has continued be, at its core, a reproduction of the evangelical model of that North American country.[19]

In my experience with evangelical churches I can retrospectively identify some elements that match fundamentalist ideas: (a) verbal

---

17. Heinrich Schäfer, *Protestantismo y crisis social en América Central* (San José, Costa Rica: DEI, 1992), 23–29.

18. Jesús García-Ruiz, "El protestantismo en Guatemala I", *Revista Análisis de la Realidad Nacional*, 18 (2012): 33.

19. Interview with Dr. David Suazo, Director of Theological Doctorial Education Program in SETECA, Guatemala, April 2013.

inspiration of God; (b) everyone [only] those who believe in Christ are justified by the blood that he shed; (c) everyone is a sinner; (d) everyone [some] of the redeemed are kept forever by the power of God, and (e) bodily resurrection for the righteous and the unrighteous, eternal happiness for some and eternal damnation for others.

As seen some aspects of biblical interpretation and its impact on social, cultural and political spaces in Guatemala, I desire to present to the reader an alternative reading that helps us to consider other views, other theological places from where we can be also a community of faith. Then I share with you some material investigated in Guatemala in 2013. From the examined documents, I focus on the pericope in Mark 10:46–52 and its interpretation.

EVANGELICAL READING OF THE MATERIALS IN MARK 10:46–52

The observations come from reading materials found in libraries of the two evangelical seminaries represented in Guatemala: the Central American Theological Seminary and the Guatemalan Bible Seminary. The first institution shows that (a) most of its material is produced abroad; (b) there is an emphasis on miracles; (c) they make a historical timeline based on the comparison of the Gospels' accounts; (d) the material of some faculty is an exact reproduction of foreign materials; there would be no original contributions from the exegesis.

The second seminary (a) has a higher quantity of books, but also mostly of foreign production, from such places as the United States, Spain, England, and Argentina; (b) the materials are more academic and of scientific analysis; (c) there are some materials which are more critical, more recent but retain much of the traditional reading; (d) there are links to other topics such as ethics, Latin America or the parallels with the Old Testament (Isaiah); (e) it has its own material production, but not about Mark.

Below, I log excerpts from materials that allow us an idea of interpretative looks to which the authors resort:

> Here, he just said the word and healed the blind. With or without resources, the Lord can heal.[20]

> The story of Bartimaeus is well known and as an illustration of salvation of the sinners, it contains lessons that coincide with many other similar works.

> "Let all those who wish to be saved to well mark the conduct of Bartimaeus, and diligently follow his footsteps ... Then when Bartimaeus contemplates the deplorable the condition where he is and perseveres, ... and he is finally cured." "The effect of the grace of Christ ought to turn him into a sectarian of Christ and introduce him into firmness and stability on the path of holiness."[21]

To expose some results of the hermeneutics used in these documents, I want to share some personal notes on Mark 10:46–52 and a brief investigation of the sociopolitical context.

EXEGETICAL NOTES ON THE STORY OF BARTIMAEUS

The story of Bartimaeus lets us see a man sitting, invisible, silenced and censored by others. However, Bartimaeus shows us a life in resistance, breaking the silence. It is the same text that encourages us to

---

20. Arturo Collins, Estudio Bíblico ELA, *Jesucristo en Acción: Marcos* (México: Ediciones Las Américas, 1996): 44–49.

21. John Charles Ryle, "*The Gospel of Mark*," n.p. [cited July 14 2016]. Online: http://gracegems.org/Ryle/Mark.htm.

perceive the breaks and ruptures that occur in the life of Bartimaeus, a man who contrasts the lack of vision with the possibility of using the word that comes from his need.

Another also burst in to break the dismal scenario of silence, of necessity, of social status and ritual: Jesus. It is Jesus who burst into the scene with concrete actions (stop, talk, call), breaking the social, cultural and religious construction of the moment, breaking with the dominant reading of the time.

Who gets the story — in this case, Mark — does it in a real context for a community with social actors that are reflected in the actors of the story: 1. Bartimaeus, who, despite his status as excluded and silenced, has a will in resistance; 2. the crowd, dominated by misunderstanding and insensitivity, tries to silence the voice of the excluded, and 3. Jesus, who hears the voicing of the need, and restores the dignity that was snatched from Bartimaeus.

SOCIOPOLITICAL BACKGROUND OF THE MARCAN TEXT

According to Richard Horsley[22] Roman conquest resulted in taxes and economic and cultural disintegration practices; in the case of the "Mediterranean society dominated by Rome … the exploitation of bonded labor was the major source of economic surplus."[23] The empire was hierarchical,[24] as there was a small ruling elite represented by officials and owners; moreover it was aristocratic, since that small

---

22. Richard A. Horsley, *Jesús y el Imperio: El reino de Dios y el nuevo desorden mundial* (Estella Navarra: Verbo Divino, 2003), 135.

23. Néstor Míguez, course notes of "New Testament World", ISEDET, Buenos Aires, 2014, 3–4.

24. Warren Carter, *El Imperio Romano y el Nuevo Testamento*, (Estella, Navarra: Verbo Divino, 2011), 14.

elite passed on the power and "determined the 'quality' of life,... controlled the wealth and enjoyed an elevated position."[25]

In this context, the socio-economic configuration of a character like Bartimaeus would indicate no chance of a worthy positioning; Bartimaeus was from a small town called Jericho; although this is a tradition inserted to instruct a later community, he should be placed in the imperial system of the first century. These small communities were crossed by an imperial ideology so pervasive, that the control exercised over these same subjected people was seen as legitimate; in addition, the actions of the state "become part of the ways to control civil society to regulate and guide the religious life as an ideological articulation."[26]

Bartimaeus is not only part of an imperial system that excludes him economically; he is part of a local Jewish system that excludes him ritually and socially. This character is left with no possibility of change in personal, social, or ritual status, he "is the other," which is not welcome or blessed in its context. Because of his illness, he is cursed, unclean; because of his impurity, he is discriminated against and excluded, is a beggar,"[27] and therefore, has no chance of getting some kind of value in the social, religious and economic circle of his time.

The system is indifferent to him and "the difference makes him excluded from a socio-religious system organized by the membership of those [who] are the same, pure and in good health and wealth."[28] Bartimaeus is part of a social map, where "human groups confer to

---

25. Ibid., 14.

26. Míguez, notes, 42.

27. Ivoni Richter Reimer, *El milagro de las manos: Sanaciones y exorcismos de Jesús en su contexto histórico-cultural* (Estella, Navarra: Verbo Divino, 2011), 74.

28. Ibid., 75.

places [people or things] their social meaning,"[29] and cultural and religious values, for example: the "honor and shame, the opposition of domestic and the political world, the dyadic personality and value of purity and impurity."[30]

Mark 10:46–52 may be located in a community permeated by its own inherited forms of exclusion and an imperial system that dominated ideologically, culturally and economically. By the purposeful nature, resistant and irruptive of the pericope, I think it moves stereotypical references, which means, it changes the traditional view of social and cultural aspects of the period.

As we can see in the preceding paragraphs, it is not difficult to link the socio-political reality of Guatemalan history with the text incarnated in its people silenced, with a will in resistance through exclusionary practices, need, pain, imposition, and domination. Like the blind Bartimaeus, the Guatemalan people have the need to be heard without labels, prejudice or condemnation; blind, excluded, indigenous, or poor have the freedom to choose, to abandon their stigmatized condition and to straighten and set free their body.

Finally, I have included two interpretative views from two Latin American theologians that allow us to understand other reading suggestions in the biblical text.

---

29. Reed, J. L. *El Jesús de Galilea: Aportaciones desde la arqueología,* (Salamanca: Ediciones Sígueme, 2006), 217.

30. Rafael Aguirre, Carmen Bernabé, Carlos Gil, *Qué se sabe de … Jesús de Nazaret* (Estela, Navarra: Verbo Divino, 2009), 48.

A COMPARISON AMONG THE GUATEMALAN EVANGELICAL READING AND THE HERMENUTIC READINGS OF NÉSTOR MÍGUEZ AND MARCELLA ALTHAUS-REID

a. Néstor Míguez in his book *Jesús del Pueblo* [Jesus of the People][31] shows a kind look towards the weak, who are rendered in need of begging amidst his poverty imposed by the ambition and the prejudice of others. Míguez sees in Bartimaeus a human being with dreams, "dreams without images" and desires without fulfilling, but with the ability to raise his voice in the face of those who wanted to silence him.

Míguez' book stresses the importance of the question: "What do you want me to do to you?" This is the focal point, because for Míguez, that question holds the whole secret of human freedom. Jesus did not think on behalf of Bartimaeus; rather he allowed Bartimaeus to express his own desire and longing. When others had commanded Bartimaeus to keep silence, Jesus asked him to speak. When others placed him aside, Jesus brought Bartimaeus into the center. When others depreciated him, Jesus showed Bartimaeus appreciation and listened to him. Bartimaeus is the human being who can say what he wants from his own dignity. In fact, before giving him sight, Jesus restored his ability to speak and, therefore, reinstated his dignity.

b. Marcella Althaus-Reid in her book *Indecent Theology*[32] encourages us to rethink theological loci. Departing from a critique of feminist hermeneutics and its stagnation, Althaus-Reid encourages us to think of a "theology with women's gender, within women's fragmented body, not just with women's eyes." Those eyes are both

---

31. Néstor O. Míguez, *Jesús del pueblo: para una cristología narrativa* (Buenos Aires, Argentina: Ediciones Kairos, 2011), 93–96.

32. Althaus-Reid, *La teología indecente: perversiones teológicas en sexo, género y política* (Barcelona, Spain: Ediciones Bellaterra, 2000), 59–61.

seduction and subjection, subjection to males, whose gaze never holds unless the woman in question is easy or indecent.

To think about new theological loci and new positions for Guatemalan women within the realms of the home, the society, and the church, implies to think indecently, undisciplined, and rebellious ways. Althaus-Reid reminds us that the metaphor of the "women's eyes" in Latin America marks the limits and regulates sexual transgressions. To think theologically with "women's eyes" entails idealistic illusions regarding things that can change just by looking at them. Guatemalan women need to re-read Bible texts with dignity, equality, self-respect, and a return of their memory in the country.

HERMENEUTICAL NOTES

Moreover, it is clear that the process of conquest has been around for a long time and has been manifested in the emergence of a territory over another in military, political, cultural, and economic forms. This is the case with Rome over a vast territory that included Jerusalem, Judea, and Samaria.

The imperial domain has a link with racism and underdevelopment that can be seen in the dependent regions "who have denounced the consequences of alienation and disintegration that inhibit their ability to progress and integration, as well as the tendency of the dominant powers to support authoritarian regimes reproducing the repressive models."[33] In the story of Bartimaeus, the bottom framework lets us see the exploiting religious domes were allied with the Roman authority and its forms of repression of the masses.

In the story of Mark, subordination is used to "identify the untreatable emerging within an X dominant system, and that means that

---

33. Torcuato S. Di Tella et al., *Diccionario de Ciencias Sociales y Políticas* (Buenos Aires, Argentina: EMECE, 2001), 363.

the dominant discourse cannot completely appropriate an otherness that resists being contained."[34] The story would point a discourse of resistance, anti-imperial and counter-hegemonic, which gives voice to the marginalized, mobilizes bodies contrary to social practices, allows a proposal for individuality, decision-making, and otherness where "the non-hegemonic announces the limits of hegemonic thinking."[35]

The subordination can be read in the text through the voices evoking the discourse and seek a mediated release through the creative reconstruction of a tradition of a subject that is silenced by a crowd but also by economic, cultural, and political systems. Representations (codes, symbols) in the narration of Mark contain an ideological load that provokes the receiver/reader a perception that places in the present what is not there anymore; that is, Mark uses certain images as a complaint and evokes the memory of marginalization to talk about their own context and time.

Mark encouraged resisting through raise our voice, or taking up the pen to denounce the imperial actions and the complicity of local authorities. Mark opposes both imperial rule and the collaboration of the aristocracy, so that the images used urge resistance of an imperial order and incarnation of an alternative order.

FINAL OBSERVATIONS

Mark 10: 46-52 is an invitation to the churches to discover that behind the crowd there is a warning not to reproduce exclusionary practices. The crowd is initially not empathic and inclusive with Bartimaeus subsequently confronted with the teaching and example of Jesus,

---

34. Mónica Szurmuk Y. Robert McKee Irwin, eds., *Diccionario de estudios culturales latinoamericanos* (México: Siglo XXI, 2009), 256.

35. Ibid., 256.

confirming once again that Mark is pointing to a flaw in the community of faith and invites to new practices of inclusion and dignifying.

From the biblical text there is an invitation to the Guatemalan churches to rethink stereotypes of being church, of the slanderous representation of the other in contrast to the new forms of inclusion that Jesus proposes, who approaches various social groups, whom Mark has carefully selected to demonstrate the shortcomings of their community, and in the context of the story, Jesus encourages faith communities to establish a respect for the dignity of others and the freedom to take their own decisions.

Although evangelical groups probably came to Guatemala with ideals of change by people committed to the Gospel (ecclesial, educational, health), I must say that the hermeneutics used took them away from the social reality. Evangelical eschatology forgot historic commitment to the people, as the eternal made the earthly irrelevant.

Although Guatemala currently is not under the physical form of imperial power, this power imperial did act in establishing an ideological presence that has been part of the socio-political configuration in Guatemala and influence on of the representation of the other as one who does not understand the divinity more than from the perspective of reading foreign.

The Guatemalan subalternity compels us to question whether the theological thought of the United States can enter into open and equal dialogue with the Guatemalan theological thought and its various local nuances. In this respect, the category of subaltern evokes the memory of the coming of the gospel, in what position we assume and whether it is time to make new criticism of our evangelical origins.

References

Aguirre, Rafael, Bernabé, Carmen, Gil, Carlos. *Qué se sabe de … Jesús de Nazaret*. Estela, Navarra: Verbo Divino, 2009.

Althaus-Reid, Marcella. *La teología indecente: perversiones teológicas en sexo, género y política*. Barcelona, Spain: Ediciones Bellaterra, 2000.

Asturias, Miguel Ángel. "Sociología Guatemalteca: El problema del indio." No pages, Cited December 14 2014. Online: http://biblioteca.usac.edu. gt/tesis/04/04_0940.pdf.

Collins, Arturo. *Jesucristo en Acción: Marcos*. México: Ediciones Las Américas, 1996.

Comisión para el Esclarecimiento Histórico (CEH), "Guatemala, Memoria del silencio II" (1999).

Di Tella, Torcuato. *Diccionario de Ciencias Sociales y Políticas*. Buenos Aires, Argentina: EMECE, 2001.

Documento Santa Fe IV, "América Latina frente a los planes anexionistas de los Estado Unidos." No pages. Cited December 29 2014. Online: http:// www.offnews.info/downloads/santafe4.PDF.

Dussel, Enrique. *Resistencia y esperanza: Historia del pueblo cristiano en América Latina y el Caribe*. San José, Costa Rica: DEI, 1995.

García-Ruiz, Jesús. "El protestantismo en Guatemala I." *Revista Análisis de la Realidad Nacional*. 18 (2012): 33.

García-Ruiz, Jesús. "El protestantismo en Guatemala II." *Revista Análisis de la Realidad Nacional* 19 (2012): 39.

Horsley, Richard A. *Jesús y el Imperio: El reino de Dios y el nuevo desorden mundial* — Estella Navarra: Verbo Divino, 2003.

Jiménez, Hugo Murillo. "La intervención norteamericana en Guatemala en 1954. Dos interpretaciones recientes." *Anuarios de Estudios Centroamericanos* 11:2 (1985): 149–155.

Míguez, Néstor O. *Jesús del pueblo: para una cristología narrativa*. Buenos Aires, Argentina: Ediciones Kairos, 2011.

Reed, Jonathan. *El Jesús de Galilea: Aportaciones desde la arqueología*. Salamanca: Ediciones Sígueme, 2006.

Reimer, Ivoni Richter. *El milagro de las manos: Sanaciones y exorcismos de Jesús en su contexto histórico-cultural*. Estella, Navarra: Verbo Divino, 2011.

Ryle, John Charles. "*The Gospel of Mark*." No pages. Cited July 14 2016. Online: http://gracegems.org/Ryle/Mark.htm.

Schäfer, Heinrich. *Protestantismo y crisis social en América Central*. San José, Costa Rica: DEI, 1992.

Stoll, David. "¿Pescadores de hombres o fundadores de imperio?." No pages. Cited October 30 2014. Online: http://www.nodulo.org/bib/stoll/ilv.htm.

Szurmuk, Mónica and Irwin, Robert McKee, eds. *Diccionario de estudios culturales latinoamericanos*. México: Siglo XXI, 2009.

Warren, Carter. *El Imperio Romano y el Nuevo Testamento*. Estella, Navarra: Verbo Divino, 2011.

Valdizán, Alejandra Gutiérrez. "El Castigo al hombre que no tuvo el terror." No pages. Cited June 19 2015. Online: http://www.plazapublica.com.gt/content/el-castigo-al-hombre-que-no-detuvo-el-terror.

Made in the USA
Coppell, TX
07 June 2023

17818291R00173